ENEMY COAST AHEAD

ENEMY COAST AHEAD

Guy Gibson
VC DSO DFC

ISIS
LARGE PRINT
Oxford

Copyright © Royal Air Force Museum, Hendon, 1946

First published in Great Britain 1986
by Goodall

Published in Large Print 2002 by ISIS Publishing Ltd,
7 Centremead, Osney Mead, Oxford OX2 0ES
by arrangement with David Higham

940.544
1439108

British Library Cataloguing in Publication Data
Gibson, Guy, 1918-1944
Enemy coast ahead. – Large print ed. –
(ISIS reminiscence series)
1. Gibson, Guy, 1918-1944 2. Great Britain.
Royal Air Force. Bomber Command
3. World War, 1939-1945 – Personal narratives, British
4. World War, 1939-1945 – Aerial operations, British
5. Large type books
I. Title
940.5'44'941'092

ISBN 0–7531–9790–1 (hb)
ISBN 0–7531–9791–X (pb)

Printed and bound by Antony Rowe, Chippenham

Contents

Preface

By Air Marshal Sir Harold Martin
KCB DSO DFC AFC
(who flew on the Dams Raid
with Guy Gibson)

It is good to see again in print Guy Gibson's vivid account of his wartime flying covering over 170 operational sorties.

In his introduction Sir Arthur Harris makes clear the extraordinary courage, ability and leadership which put Gibson amongst the greatest airmen this country ever produced.

Here we have Guy Gibson's personal account of the attack on the Ruhr Dams which won him the Victoria Cross. There have been a number of other attempts to record this exploit, some good, others contrived. The German reports were confused and often inaccurate.

This is the way it was. Gibson worked early on with Sir Barnes Wallis, took part in the trials, chose and trained his squadron, and on 16th May 1943 he magnificently led us. Guy died on 19th September 1944 returning from acting as Master Bomber on a raid on Rheydt. He crashed in flames near Steenbergen in Holland where he is buried in a grave lovingly tended by the Dutch and unforgotten by all who knew him.

MICK MARTIN

Introduction

This is a magnificent story, well and simply told by as great a warrior as these Islands ever bred. It is also History.

Guy Gibson was not a professional airman; he joined the service in peacetime "because he wanted to learn to fly". War supervened and he remained an airman until his death in action.

His natural aptitude for Leadership, his outstanding skill and his extraordinary valour marked him early for command; for Great Attempts and Great Achievements. His personal contribution towards victory was beyond doubt unsurpassed.

In every facet of his character he was a thoroughbred. He was not only admired but loved by all who knew him.

In this book he tells of the Bomber's work as he saw it from the necessarily somewhat circumscribed viewpoint of an individual cog in a vast machine, as Commander of a Flight and later of a Squadron.

Guy Gibson fought from the first days of the "phoney" war (phoney because we had nothing to keep fighting with) until his death. He lived to see the dawn of certain victory; and no one man did more to bring it about. He would not stop fighting. He resisted or avoided all efforts to rest him from operations. For his first "rest" he asked to be transferred to night fighting, and as a highly skilled night pilot he was of great value to Fighter Command in raising and training the night-fighting force which eventually defeated the "blitz". To enforce a second "rest" on him I had to make a personal appeal to another warrior of similar calibre — Winston Spencer Churchill — who there and then ordered Gibson down to Chequers and took him with him to the United States. There he arranged for Gibson to be detained for a short period of travelling round air bases to talk to American airmen. In a third and final effort to force him to rest from operations, he was put on his Group's staff. A few days later he was found in his office with — literally — tears in his eyes at being separated from his beloved crews and unable to go on operations.

It was in fact breaking his heart.

He always had direct access to me, and on further pressure from him and his AOC I quite wrongly allowed him to return to operations.

He appointed himself "Master Bomber" — the most dangerous and most vital task of all — on his last operation, which was, of course, a complete success. He was heard to give his crews a pat on the back over the radio and start them homeward. He never returned.

Throughout the story something is indicated of the difficulties of obtaining the means and the equipment which during the last eighteen months of the war enabled us to find and hit ever smaller objectives, under more and more difficult conditions. That is another story, of the wonderful achievements of our scientists, which will some day I hope be written. The difficulties were immense, but they were overcome. No one did more than Guy Gibson to overcome them.

It may well be that the references to "parties" and "drunks" in this book will give rise to criticism, and even to outbursts of unctuous rectitude. I do not attempt to excuse them, if only because I entirely approve of them. In any case, the "drunks" were mainly on near-beer and high rather than potent spirits.

Remember that these crews, shining youth on the threshold of life, lived under circumstances of intolerable strain. They were in fact — and they knew it — faced with the virtual certainty of death, probably in one of its least pleasant forms. They knew, well enough, that they owed their circumstances to the stupidity, negligence and selfishness of the older generations who since 1918 had done little to avert another war and even less to prepare for it.

If, therefore, something of cynicism was occasionally manifest in their attitude to whatever might remain to them of life, and if on occasion the anticipation of an event, or the celebration of a success and an unexpected survival, called for a party, for the letting off of steam in an atmosphere of eat, drink and be merry, for next time we shall most certainly die — who amongst the older generations who sent them and tens of thousands like them to their deaths, will dare criticize?

If there is a Valhalla, Guy Gibson and his band of brothers will be found there at all the parties, seated far above the salt.

ARTHUR HARRIS

Foreword and Dedication

In writing this book on the past four years of war, I have had to work without notes, and without help from diaries. I have never kept a diary because I never even dreamt that the lot would fall to me, in 1944, to try to describe the work of aircrews in Bomber and Fighter Squadrons.

The fact that I have been extremely lucky to have survived must go without saying. Only a few will disagree, and they don't know. But I hope that living people who have served with me will forgive me if I have left them out, or worse, put words into their mouths which they never said. A memory is a short thing, and flak never does it much good. However, the aim of this book is to illustrate the growth of a small baby in 1939 to the awesome colossus that it has become today — the growth of Bomber Command.

Not only in size and bomb capacity, but also in accuracy it has achieved immense proportions, and has now reached the stage, perhaps the ultimate state, when whole industrial areas or single factories can be wiped off the face of the earth in a single night, despite weather conditions and despite opposition over the target itself.

In admiring the air crews who are now engaged in completing the destruction of the Third Reich, we must remember that their lot, side by side with the American daylight crews, is to wage the toughest war of all. The losses in percentage in any one air raid are not unduly high — rarely above 10 per cent — but remember this used to go on for some sixty missions, and the bare fact remains that out of a squadron of twenty-five crews, not many are left at the end of three months. Well, these boys know all this, and yet not in the slightest degree does it deter them from pressing home their attack with the highest possible sense of duty; in fact, they are proud to be members of the only offensive team bringing the war home to the Germans, inside Germany itself. These boys have got guts; and they must have or they never would be able to do the job.

Nor must we forget the ground crews, who make these raids possible by their untiring efforts under very trying conditions. Nor the Squadrons and the Groups, and the WAAF and the clerks, the Ministry of Economic Warfare, the Directors of Bombing Operations in the Air Ministry, and Air Chief Marshal Harris himself and his staff. And perhaps, above all, the scientists and MAP backroom boys who have made such progress.

It will happen that by the time this book is published new events will be taking place in Europe. New place-names may be appearing in the headlines of our daily papers, and the role of the heavy bombers may even be changed to that of tactical necessity rather than strategical. If that is the case, then let no one forget the work done by home-based bombers during the dark years of 1940, 1941, 1942 and 1943, who alone fought the enemy on his own ground, and alone stand as one of the mighty factors that have brought about the changed war situation. All-powerful in war, let the bombing forces be all-powerful in peace over Europe . . . Then, when one task has been done, the yellow skies of Japan will hear the same dreaded hum of thousands of aircraft, American and British, the same crump of bigger and better block-busters and the rattle of cannons. And the Japs won't like it.

To dedicate a book of this nature is not easy. Many different people are involved. Above all, I should like to mention the wives, the sweethearts and the mothers of all crews operating from this country against Germany.

Peace and war are vastly different. But the atmosphere our crews live in is shared by their next of kin. One moment they are together living their own lives and happy; a man and wife walking hand in hand down a country lane may in a few hours be separated, perhaps forever. True, sailors leave home for the countless dangers of the Seven Seas, but their people have not got a television set which can see them every few days dive-bombed, torpedoed, undergoing the hardships of war on the sea. Those at home worry, but they don't know, and they don't want to know. A soldier in the front line, it is true, lives in the turmoil of battle; but his girlfriend does not see him every week grimy, unshaven, stepping over the dead bodies of his comrades to advance another few yards. His people cannot see him doing his job.

But picture peaceful England on a cool spring evening; the flowers are blooming, the hum of serenity is in the air. Suddenly there is a snarl of four motors, and a few hours later your airman is fighting the hell of flak and destruction over the target.

At home they wait, brave and patient, asking the same questions, again and again: I hope he gets back all right; when are they due? It is grim for them, grim and terrible. For this reason I should like to dedicate this book to "Those at Home": my wife — your sister — his brother — the girlfriends — and the mothers. But I know they would say no. They are brave people, and like all brave people they would have it no other way but to turn their heads aside and say: Give this book to Them.

I therefore dedicate this book to the boys who have not been so lucky; who have given all they can give to their country for Freedom's sake. Let us never, never forget Them.

To the following Pilots and their Crews who fought with me against our enemy:

83 Squadron

P/O Keith Brooke-Taylor	Killed	April 7, 1940
P/O Wilfred Roberts	Killed	April 7, 1940
F/O Kenneth Sylvester	Missing - Presumed killed	April 15, 1940
F/O Neville Johnson	Killed	May 15, 1940
P/O Alan Vagg	Killed	May 15, 1940
Sgt Stanley Jenkins	Killed	May 23, 1940
Sgt Peter Josse	Killed	May 23, 1940
P/O Charles Greenwell	Missing - Presumed killed	June 4, 1940
F/O Ian Haydon	Missing - Presumed killed	June 4, 1940
S/Ldr Denys Field	Missing - Presumed killed	June 6, 1940
Sgt George Little	Missing - Presumed killed	July 2, 1940
P/O Douglas Redmayne	Missing - Presumed killed	July 2, 1940
Sgt Cyril Hallett	Killed	July 8, 1940
Sgt Leonard Howard	Killed	July 8, 1940
P/O Oliver Launders	Killed	July 8, 1940
F/Lt John Bowman	Missing - Prisoner of war	July 21, 1940
Sgt Geoffrey Jones	Missing - Presumed killed	July 26, 1940
P/O Bill Tweddell, DFC	Missing - Presumed killed	July 26, 1940
T/W/O Walter Barber	Missing - Prisoner of war	Aug. 9, 1940
P/O Ian Muir	Missing - Prisoner of war	Aug. 9, 1940
F/O Ellis Ross DFC	Missing - Presumed killed	Aug. 13, 1940
F/Lt Allen Mulligan	Missing - Prisoner of war	Aug. 13, 1940
Sgt Douglas Hayhurst	Missing - Prisoner of war	Sept. 16, 1940
A/S/Ldr James Pitcairn-Hill, DSO, DFC	Missing - Presumed killed	Sept. 19, 1940
S/Ldr Anthony Bridgman, DFC	Missing - Prisoner of war	Sept. 24, 1940
Sgt James Loveluck	Missing - Presumed killed	Oct. 26, 1940

29 Squadron

P/O L. G. H. Kells	Missing from "Battle Climb" in Blenheim	Mar. 1941
Sgt Skillen	Missing	1943
P/O Graham-Little	On leaving 29 Squadron joined one of the first Mosquito NF Squadrons. Killed in an air accident	May, 1942
Sgt Freer	Killed at West Malling on the night of London's last Blitz	May 10, 1941
P/O D. Parker	Killed in action	Jan. 1943
P/O D. Humphreys	Killed while on an intruder flight in a Hurricane; was S/Ldr DFC	
Sgt J. French	Posted to a Havoc Squadron, afterwards killed in a Hudson	
P/O D.I. Buchanan	Killed at Digby in a Beaufighter	Feb. 1941
P/O R. Miles	Killed at Bluebell Hill, Wrotham	July 1941
P/O A. Grout	Destroyed 2 E/As. on his 1st Op. Killed at Staplehurst	July 1941

106 Squadron

F/Sgt Appleyard, DFM	Killed on operational flight	July 26, 1942
P/O Worswick, DFC	Missing - Reported killed	June 2, 1942
W/O Young, R.F.H.	Missing - Reported killed	Aug. 25, 1942
F/O Loftus	Posted	May 4, 1942
F/Sgt Bussell, H.C.	Missing - Presumed killed	Mar. 30, 1942
W/O Merrals, DFC	Missing - Reported killed	Aug. 1, 1942
F/Sgt Picken, W.J., DFC	Missing - Reported killed	Mar. 5, 1943

P/O. Dunlop-Mackenzie	Missing - Presumed killed	Mar. 26, 1942
P/O Cann	Missing - Reported killed	Mar. 26, 1942
P/O Duff, DFC	Posted	June 9, 1942
P/O Stoffer	Missing - Reported killed	April 24, 1942
P/O Prescot-Decie	Missing - Prisoner of war	April 24, 1942.
F/Sgt Dimond	Missing - Presumed killed	Mar. 30, 1942
Sgt Fixter	Missing - Prisoner of war	May 3, 1942
Sgt Power	Missing - Reported killed	April 17, 1942
F/Sgt Hard	Missing - Prisoner of war	May 3, 1942
S/Ldr Robertson, DFC	Missing - Reported killed	July 27, 1942
P/O Scratchard	Missing - Reported killed	April 17, 1942
P/O Grein	Missing - Reported killed	Aug. 12, 1942
Sgt Wale	Missing - Reported killed	May 19, 1942
Sgt McHardy	Missing - Presumed killed	May 19, 1942
Sgt Brinkhurst	Missing - Reported killed	Dec. 22, 1942
P/O Williams	Missing - Reported killed	Sept. 14, 1942
P/O Coates	Missing - Reported killed	Aug. 16, 1942
P/O Butterworth	Missing - Reported killed	Oct. 3, 1942
P/O Crowfoot, DFC	Missing - Reported killed	Oct. 16, 1942
P/O Broderick	Missing - Presumed killed	July 9, 1942
F/Lt Healey, DFM, DFC	Missing - Reported killed	Jan. 13, 1943
Sgt Gaskell	Missing - Reported killed	Aug. 1, 1942
Sgt Hart	Missing - Reported killed	June 2, 1942
P/O Carlile	Killed	July 21, 1942
Sgt Stamp	Missing - Prisoner of war	Sept. 19, 1942
Sgt Butler	Missing - Reported killed	July 26, 1942
Sgt Marshman	Killed	July 21, 1942
P/O Downer	Missing - Presumed killed	Sept. 14, 1942
S/Ldr Howell	Missing - Reported killed	Sept. 14, 1942

Sgt Smith	Missing - Reported killed	Sept. 8, 1942
Sgt Anderson	Missing - Reported killed	Dec. 14, 1942
Sgt Abel	Missing - Reported killed	April 27, 1943
F/Lt Broderick, L.C.J.	Missing - Prisoner of war	April 13, 1943
F/Lt Curtin, Bar to DFC	Missing - Reported killed	Feb. 21, 1943
F/Sgt Cronk	Missing - Reported killed	Jan. 11, 1943
F/Sgt Hayward, VC	Missing - Reported killed	Feb. 11, 1943
S/Ldr Hill	Missing - Reported killed	Oct. 15, 1943
S/Ldr Hayward, E. L., DFC	Missing - Reported killed	Mar. 29, 1943
Sgt Irvine	Missing - Presumed killed	April 8, 1943
F/Sgt McDonald	Missing - Reported killed	Mar. 12, 1943
Sgt Markland	Missing - Reported killed	Feb. 18, 1943
P/O McGregor	Posted	July 24, 1943
F/Sgt Phair	Missing - Reported killed	Jan. 13, 1943
Sgt Piercy	Missing - Prisoner of war	Oct. 15, 1942
P/O Page	Missing - Reported killed	June 24, 1943
Sgt Reed	Missing - Reported killed	Feb. 3, 1943
Sgt Thompson	Missing - Prisoner of war	Feb. 4, 1943
P/O White	Missing - Prisoner of war	Oct. 13, 1942
F/O Wesley	Missing - Presumed killed	Feb. 23, 1943
F/O Windsor	Missing - Reported killed	Feb. 25, 1943

617 Squadron

S/Ldr Melvyn Young	Missing - Believed killed	May 17, 1943
S/Ldr Henry Maudslay	Missing - Believed killed	May 17, 1943
F/Lt David Astell	Missing - Believed killed	May 17, 1943
F/Lt John Hopgood	Missing - Believed killed	May 17, 1943
P/O Burpee (Canada)	Missing - Believed killed	May 17, 1943

P/O Byers (Australia)	Missing - Believed killed	May 17, 1943
F/Lt Barlow (Australia)	Missing - Believed killed	May 17, 1943
P/O Ottley	Missing - Believed killed	May 17, 1943
F/Lt H. S. Wilson	Missing - Believed killed	Sept. 14, 1943
S/Ldr David Maltby	Missing - Believed killed	Sept. 14, 1943
F/Lt Ralph Allsebrook	Missing - Believed killed	Sept. 15, 1943
F/Lt L. E. S. Knight (Australia)	Missing - Believed killed	Sept. 15, 1943
P/O Dival	Missing - Believed killed	Sept. 15, 1943
S/Ldr George Holden	Missing - Believed killed	Sept. 15, 1943
F/O Allan Rice	Missing - Believed killed	Dec. 20, 1943
F/Lt Youseman	Missing - Believed killed	Nov. 18, 1943

AND MY CREW

Missing, night September 15, 1943

F/O Spafford	"Spam"
F/O Taerum	"Terry"
F/Lt Hutchison	"Hutch"
P/O Deering	"Tony"
F/Lt Trevor-Roper	"Trev"

CHAPTER
ONE

Flight Out

The moon was full; everywhere its pleasant, watery haze spread over the peaceful English countryside, rendering it colourless. But there is not much colour in Lincolnshire, anyway. The city of Lincoln was silent — that city which so many bomber boys know so well, a city full of homely people — people who have got so used to the Air Force that they have begun almost to forget them. Lincoln with its great cathedral sticking up on a hill, a landmark for miles around. Little villages in the flat Fenland slept peacefully. Here nice simple folk live in their bastions on the East Anglian coast. The last farmer had long since gone to bed; the fire in the village pub had died down to an ember; the bar, which a few hours ago was full of noisy chattering people, was silent. There were no enemy aircraft about and the scene was peaceful. In fact, this sort of scene might not have changed for a hundred years or so. But this night was different — at least different for 133 men: 133 young fliers, and I was one of those men. This was the big thing. This was it.

We were flying not very high, about 100ft, and not very far apart. I suppose to a layman it was a wonderful sight, these great powerful Lancasters in formation, flown by boys who knew their job. Below us, and also practically beside us, at 200mph flashed past trees, fields, church spires and England.

We were off on a journey for which we had long waited, a journey that had been carefully planned, carefully trained for, a mission which was going to do a lot of good if it succeeded; and everything had been worked out so that it should succeed. We were off to the Dams.

Those who have seen a Lancaster cockpit in the light of the moon, flying just above the earth, will know what I mean when I say it is very hard to describe. The pilot sits on the left of a raised, comfortably padded seat fitted with arm-rests. He usually flies the thing with his left hand, resetting the gyro and other instruments with his right, but most pilots use both hands when over enemy territory or when the going is tough. You have to be quite strong to fly a Lancaster.

In front of him the instruments sit winking. On the sperry panel, or the blind-flying panel as bomber pilots call it, now and then a red light, indicating that some mechanism needs adjusting, will suddenly flash on. The pilot of a bomber must know everything. He must know the duties of the rest of the crew inside out, and should be able to take any one of them over should the occasion arise. The flight-engineer is the pilot's mate and sits beside him watching the engine instruments. Most flight-engineers were ground mechanics of Bomber Command who have volunteered to fly on operations, and a grand job of work they do too.

It is warm inside and both pilot and flight-engineer are very lightly clad, their oxygen masks hanging on one strap from the corner of the face. These masks are necessary evils. When over enemy territory they are worn continuously, not only because oxygen is required but because the pilot has no time to take his hand off the wheel and put the microphone up to his face. The result is that one gets quite chapped after six hours with the thing on. Many times the question is asked, "Why can't we have throat microphones like the Americans?"

Between the two front windows is a large instrument, perhaps the most important of all: the repeating compass, worked by a master unit at the back. The pilot's eyes constantly perform a non-stop circle from the repeater to the ASI,[1] from the ASI to the horizon, from the horizon to the moon, from the moon to what he can see on the ground and then back to the repeater. No wonder they are red-rimmed when he returns.

Such is the scene. The glass house. Soft moonlight. Two silent figures, young, unbearded, new to the world yet full of skill, full of pride in their squadron, determined to do a good job and bring the ship home. A silent scene, whose only

---

[1] Airspeed Indicator.

incidental music is provided by the background hiss of air and the hearty roar of four Merlin engines.

In my Lancaster it was pretty warm even though Hutch had turned off the heat. I was in my shirt sleeves and my Mae West. Incidentally, my Mae West was a German one, pinched off some fellow shot down back in 1940, and the envy of the whole squadron. The windows were open and a jet of cool air was blowing in, making a tremendous screeching noise. I yelled to Pulford, the flight-engineer, at the top of my voice, "Close that window, for Christ's sake."

Pulford, a Londoner, and a sincere and plodding type, was pushing and struggling and at last got the thing closed; like the silence at the end of a crash the noise snapped off and we were in comparative silence. Then I spoke to Terry. "Where are we now, Nav.?"

"I think we are about a mile to port. I'll just check. What do you think, Spam?"

Spam was the bomb-aimer, and it was some time before he answered because he had been taking off his parachute harness and was now picking up his position from a roller map. It looked like a roll of lavatory paper. But no matter what it looked like, it had to do a pretty important job: the job of that roll and Spam and Terry was to get us to the target. "Yeah, you're right, Terry, we are a little over a mile to port; there's the railway going to King's Lynn."

Spam, the Australian, was the best bomb-aimer there is, but he was not too hot at map-reading, and

Terry looked over my shoulder to check him up. Later he popped back into his cabin to make a quick calculation. Then I was told to alter course 3 degrees to starboard, and by the slightest pressure of the rudder the great Lancaster almost imperceptibly pointed her grim blunt nose a little farther south, and the boys on either side did the same.

After a while Terry spoke again:

"Ten minutes to the coast. We will be able to get a pretty good check there — we go slap over Yarmouth."

Good boys these, Terry and Spam. F/O Taerum came from Calgary, Canada. He had a soft Canadian accent, was well educated and in love with a very nice girl, a WAAF from Ireland called Pat. Probably the most efficient navigator in the squadron, he had done about thirty-five trips and knew what he was doing. I never knew Terry to lose his temper over anything, but sometimes he and Spam would argue the point over where they were. Spam, or F/O Spafford, DFM, as his real name was, came from Melbourne, Australia. He was a grand guy and many were the parties we had together; in his bombing he held the squadron record. Just before, he had asked me if he could take off his parachute harness because we were flying so low, anyway, that we would not have been able to bale out even if we had the chance. But that just illustrates what he thought of flying. It was just one big gamble and he had put his counter on the right mark. Spam had done a little more than Terry, about forty trips, and used to fly with one of the crack pilots in 50 Squadron. When he came to our squadron I think he was a bit nervous of my flying, but he seemed to recover after his first few trips. Both had pretty good accents deriving from their respective Dominions. I have, if anything, a southern English accent which in the air sounds rather a drawl, with the result that when we, as the offensive team in the bomber, got annoyed with one another, no one, particularly ourselves, knew what the hell we were talking about, which was a pretty good thing anyway.

In the back sat Trev — in the rear-turret in Air Force parlance — and of all places in the bomber I think it is the most uncomfortable. He was in his shirtsleeves, too, but later on pulled on his old teddy-bear flying-suit, not because it kept him warm but because of its smell. All clothes which have been on a lot of raids have a smell, a peculiar but not unpleasant smell which shouts aloud to all bomber crews who are in the know that the wearer, or owner, whichever the case may be, is pretty experienced; a Gen-man. A wife or loving mother would send the thing to the laundry if she had her way, but you try to do that with the boys. As far as I can see, the stronger the smell the better it is liked!

F/Lt Algernon Trevor-Roper, DFM, rear gunner, came of a pretty good family, and all that sort of thing, was twenty-eight, English, Eton, Oxford, and sixty-five trips. He was one of the real Squadron characters. At night he might go out with the boys, get completely plastered, but would be always up dead on time in the morning to do his job. He got his DFM for shooting down two fighters which tried to down him one night last year. Now his wife was living in Skegness and was about to produce a baby within the next few days. I guessed he was thinking of this. Anyway, he was pretty silent, because he hadn't said a word up to now. He was probably thinking exactly what I was thinking: was this the last time we would see England?

Farther forward Hutch was in his place at the wireless. He had flown with me on about forty raids and had never turned a hair. He was one of those grand little Englishmen who have the guts of a horse. On most trips he invariably got air-sick, but after he had done his stuff just carried on as if nothing had happened. He was in love, too, with a girl in Boston. In the front turret was Jim Deering of Toronto, Canada, and he was on his first bombing raid. He was pretty green, but one of our crack gunners had suddenly gone ill and there was nobody else for me to take.

As I sat back in my comfortable seat I could not help thinking that there were seven men in a bomber bound for somewhere in Germany. Seven men with wives and sweethearts, for all we knew sleeping in one of the houses we had just roared over. England virtually was at peace, but we were at war, the toughest, hardest war there is — the bomber war. I had been in the racket for some time and it had become practically part of me, but when

I thought of all the friends I knew who had come and gone, to be mere memories, a name on the casualty sheets in the Air Ministry, or the scroll of honour in a Squadron Mess, then I shuddered. After a while I just sat back in my comfortable seat and relaxed and dismissed these thoughts from my mind and concentrated on steering my course. Suddenly in the distance, like a great arc drawn across the land by silver paper, came the North Sea — the sea which now seemed unfriendly because we were going the wrong way. I hoped it would look different a few hours later.

And then Terry was saying, "Yes, there's Yarmouth coming up in front."

"That's right."

"Yeah, there's the harbour."

"Sure it's Yarmouth?"

"That's it all right."

"OK, alter course 110."

"110 OK."

"OK."

And our noses were then going straight for the point at which we had to cross the Dutch coast. The sea was as flat as a mill-pond, there was hardly a ripple. Once we were over we dropped lower and lower down to about 50ft, so as to avoid radio detection.

I tried to put in George the automatic pilot, but unfortunately it was U.S. and as I engaged it the nose plunged forward and I just disengaged it in time. One of the aircraft on my left flashed me a red

light, as if to say, "What the hell are you doing?"
Then I settled down again, but after a time tried to
light a cigarette. In doing so we again nearly hit the
drink, and the boys must have thought I was mad.
In the end I handed the thing to Pulford to light for
me. The night was so bright that it was possible to
see the boys flying on each side quite clearly. On the
right was John Hopgood, in M Mother, that grand
Englishman whom we called "Hoppy"; one of the
greatest guys in the world. He was devoted to his
mother and devoted to flying; used to go out with us
a lot, get drunk — used to go out a lot to Germany
and do a wonderful job. He had no nerves, he loved
flying, which he looked upon rather as a highly
skilled art in which one can only become proficient
after a lot of experience. He was one of the boys
who firmly refused to be given a rest and had done
about fifty raids with me in my last squadron.
Perfect at formation was Hoppy, too. There he was,
his great Lancaster only a few feet from mine, flying
perfectly steady, never varying position. Once when
training for this raid we had gone down to Manston
in Kent and shot up the field with wings inside
tail-planes, and even the fighter boys had to admit it
was the best they had ever seen. I should say Hoppy
was probably the best pilot in the squadron.

On my other side, flashing him a message with his
Aldis lamp, rather as ships do in a convoy at sea,
was Micky Martin. Micky Martin came from
Australia and he too had done a lot of flying. He
was slightly more split-arse than Hoppy, and flying

to him was nothing unless it was dangerous. In fact, many times after a raid on Berlin or Hamburg, instead of coming back with the boys at 22,000ft, he would scream down to the deck and fly home via Holland, Belgium and France, shooting up anything he could see. That, to him, was a bit of fun and something that he and his crew liked. However, to-night he had to be good and stick to the plan because if he didn't things would go wrong, and so there he was flying dead level with Hoppy on the other side. Now and again he would drop down even lower than I was, and I was a bit frightened in case he hit the drink. But apparently he knew what he was doing because he never came closer than 30ft to the water. Farther back were the rest of them — Melvyn Young from America, leading Bill Astell and David Maltby — followed by Henry Maudslay leading Dave Shannon and Les Knight, who were both Australian. This was my formation, and a great team they were.

The sea was calm as I had never seen it before, and as Micky got lower and lower on the water I could see his reflection quite clearly coming up to meet him. In the north there is that bomber boys' bad dream — the glow. Some scientists call it the Aurora Borealis, but you ought to hear what we call it when there are fighters about! That glow never disappears in the summer; and this was summer. The hours of darkness were limited; we had to go fast to get there and back in time.

There were no other aircraft operating in the whole of the home-based Air Forces. No one even knew that we were operating except for a few, and even they did not know where we were going.

But deep down in the ground two hundred-odd miles away were the Germans. In their plotting-rooms they sat watching their cathode-ray tubes, waiting for some indication that would set all their defences alert. The lower we flew the closer we could get before they picked us up, but I knew that at a range of about 30 miles they would get us even if our bomb-doors clove a furrow through the water. Then their guns would be ready. Then the fighters would take the air. Then there would be a chattering and a babbling in the Observer Corps plotting-rooms. And so, Huns and Quislings would sit up late at night in sandbagged emplacements waiting for the roar of the Lancasters.

Hutch was reading the message.

"What is it, Hutch?"

"He says we are going to get damn drunk tomorrow night."

"Send him back this: You're darn right we are. It's going to be the biggest binge of all time." And then Hutch was busy flashing this message.

Soon we passed over a little convoy who engaged us with the challenge signal. We quickly fired the correct Very light before they opened up on us, and as usual they flashed us "Good Hunting." Hutch, who was as good with his Aldis lamp as he was with

33

his key, and who did not drink, replied: "We are going to get damn drunk tomorrow night."

The skipper of the ship, whoever he was, did not reply because he must have been wondering whether this was a code message, or else we — the boys on board — were nuts.

As England receded far behind our tails, Terry, who had been quiet, had been working out our ground speed on the G Box, a special navigation instrument which shows the aircraft's position relative to the ground. He suddenly said: "There's no wind tonight, Skip, so we shouldn't have any drift — but we'll just check, so I'll throw out a flame-float."

Then he yelled to Trev behind: "Will you get a drift, Trev?"

A little later Trev's voice was heard from the back. "OK. There's no drift, the flame-float is about 10 miles behind; it's still straight behind my guns."

So Terry was very pleased and was able to get down to his calculations. Later he came up again and said unemotionally: "Our ground speed is 203½ miles an hour; we will be there in exactly one hour and ten minutes, thirty seconds. We ought to cross the coast dead on track, so everything's fine. Incidentally, you're 1 degree off your course."

Navigators are funny chaps. They always think a fellow can steer a course to an absolute degree, and I smiled to myself as I swung myself back. Navigators have a union called "The Navigators' Union", which is about the most powerful thing there is. Now they are even taking over squadrons, let alone being captains of aeroplanes, and, anyway, I think they deserve it. Navigation is a tricky job, and after four years of war they really know what they are doing. Probably for sheer precision the night navigators of Bomber Command are the best in the world, because they have to be for their very own sakes, for the laws of survival.

One hour to go, and one hour left before Germany, one hour of peace before flak. I thought to myself: here are 133 boys who have got an hour to live before going through hell. Some of them won't get back. It won't be me — you never think you are not coming back. We won't all get back, but who is it will be unlucky out of these 133 men? What are they thinking about?

Are they just thinking about their job, or steering their course? What is the rear-gunner in Melvyn Young's ship thinking? Because he won't be coming back. What's the bomb-aimer in Henry Maude's ship thinking? Because he won't be coming back. What is the rear-gunner in Hoppy's plane thinking? What are his ideas on life? Because he is going to bale out at about 80ft, survive by a miracle and be put in a prison camp. He and the bomb-aimer are going to be the only boys in this raid to be taken prisoner. The rest are going to be killed — those who don't get back. One hour to go, one hour to think of these things, one hour to fly on a straight course and then it will be weaving and sinking to escape the light flak and the fury of the enemy defence. And as I thought of these things, and many other things, of my wife, who thought I was instructing; my dog, who was killed last night; of the scientists who made this raid possible. I wondered, what am I doing here, anyway? How am I here? Why have I been so lucky? And I began to think of those first few days when the war became a reality, and we became changed from peacetime Air Force play-boy's to fellows faced with death many days in a year, every year, for four years.

CHAPTER
TWO

Peace and War

August 31 1939, a pretty hot day. I was sitting on the centreboard of a little sailing dinghy, clad in swimming-trunks, trying to get a tan from the early autumn sun. At the same time I was trying to splice a broken sheet, a job which I found very difficult even though I had been a Scout some years back. The sun was terrific. The sea had taken on a deep hazy blue colour.

In the back of the boat, surrounded by cushions, sat Ann, blonde and pretty. She was asleep. Windy, my all-swimming and all-flying cat, who had put in more flying hours than most cats, lay purring on her lap. I gazed at her reflectively, thinking, of many things. A few hundred yards off lay the shore. I could faintly hear the murmur of the surf, but it was not rough today, and so we, anchored a little way out, were only slightly moving. This suited Ann, who, though glamorous, was apt to get seasick.

From Monkstone Beach came the noisy chatter of children building castles, playing leap-frog and generally making the beach one vast happy playground. One group, I remember, were hurriedly building a small seawall to protect their elaborate sandcastle. As the tide came in, wave after wave would lap against the wall, crumbling it. Now and then a larger wave would cause a small breach and some water would go into the moat. This would quickly become a weak spot in the defences, but instantly willing spades dug in sand, fast and furiously, to repair the breach; but at last it was all over and an extra big wave washed the whole lot away, amidst shrieks and yells, and also amidst the wetting of many small pairs of pants! Then they packed up for lunch.

I could not help thinking that the little scene was significant. Although war seemed very distant, I was fully up with the news, and there was no doubt that this was pretty grim. Germany had delivered an ultimatum to Poland; this had been rejected. Berlin had said "Unless . . ." and then there was that Russo-German pact.

I never thought that Poland would fight for her Corridor. She had cavalry, Germany had tanks. She had only a few ancient aircraft, Goering had long been telling the world the strength of his pet baby, the Luftwaffe. And if Germany invaded Poland we would be in it too. Then what?

We were unprepared; only last week I had been flying in our summer home defence exercises. Twice we had "raided" London from the direction of Holland. On neither occasion had we seen any "enemy" fighters, and had flown on another 150 miles to "flatten" the English Air Force Headquarters at Abingdon. When we landed we had boasted about this to all and sundry, but later on the Army told us that we had been "shot down" by anti-aircraft fire when we crossed the English coast on the way in. This tickled us a lot because, although this was just sheer wishful thinking on the part of the ack-ack boys, we had, in fact, been fired at by the Hook of Holland. The formation leader of our wing had swung rather wide when making his turn there, with the result that the squadron on the left infringed neutral territory. This was my baptism of fire, and it looked to me very cissy, just a few black puffs in the sky; but how lovely it was to be ignorant, and anyway, they were shells fired by friendly guns and were some way away, although accurate for height.

But bad though the situation was today, it had been much worse last year. Then we did not even possess Hampden bombers, but operated in Hawker Hinds, top speed 185, load 500lb, range 200 miles. Yes, this crisis was better than the last. It was a standing joke in Lincolnshire last year that we bomber boys did everything in the way of preparation for war, while Chamberlain and Hitler were conceiving a world safe for Democracy. We had loaded our guns, we had filled our tanks, we had even camouflaged our aeroplanes in warpaint. The only snag was there had been no bombs on the station. These turned up three weeks later!

Anyway, it was no use thinking of these things; it would not do any good. Besides, this was my holiday, and I began to go to sleep, conscious only of the hot sun on my back and the ripple of the waves on the free-board of the boat. War for me just did not exist.

Suddenly a boat slipped by and a voice woke me up. "Hey, Guy, there is a telegram for you on the beach."

This was the son of the local doctor, a keen sailing enthusiast himself. So what? A month or two back I had taken a long navigation course. Maybe the telegram came from the Adj. to say that I had failed, or passed. "Thanks, John — you woke me up," I yelled after him, but John was already some distance away trying to get the best out of a calm day.

On the beach there was a boy, the apple of the eye of his proud parents, whom I knew slightly. For good or for bad, this boy could swim a few strokes, and here was his opportunity to show his young girlfriend that he was much better than Bill, his ten-year-old rival. And so, telegram in mouth, he had jumped into the warm water and was approaching. I watched him with indifferent interest with Ann, who had by now come to. He was swimming rather like a crab, a mixture of side and breast stroke, and making a noise like a hyena, and my telegram was getting wet. As he got closer I could see that it was not a greetings telegram. At last he reached the side, but we could not get him aboard because before I could grab his hand he had turned and begun his struggling journey back to the beach.

I looked at the telegram. The ink had run, but I could see it had been addressed to the village post-office. This was because I had not known my address when I came away and actually I was staying at Mrs. Thompson's for the modest sum of 4s 6d a day — a price which suited my flying-officer's pay very well. The telegram was marked "Urgent". The daughter of the village postman, who knew me slightly (I think I met her at a village hop), had seen this and had jumped on her bike and brought it down to the beach. Ann's voice broke the silence.

"Hadn't you better open it?"

Still thinking of Exams I read it aloud. It was pretty straightforward. All it said was, "Return to Unit immediately".

Two hours later I had packed. I had given Windy to Mrs. Thompson to look after for the duration, but I knew that she would never recognize me again. Then came a lot of goodbyes. Goodbyes to the Crawfords, at whose house I had stayed last summer; there were a few tears, and I felt like a film war hero about to return to the front. Goodbye to Ann. Goodbye to Ruth Windsor Bowen, with whom I had quarrelled earlier in the season and had just made it up. I'd had a date with her the night before, but she had gone off with another chap. There was Desmond, who had just joined the Army. There were many others, but I cannot remember their names.

Then Freddy Bilbey drove up in his Alvis. Freddy had just come down from Oxford, where he had been reading biology. He was twenty-three, fair-haired, good-looking and a great friend of mine. His Alvis was 1928 vintage, and as we set off down the village, receiving a friendly wave from odd fishermen and yokels whom we knew so well, that raucous exhaust blared out its tune for the last time.

As we snorted down the road, overtaking anything going our way in a most alarming manner, we kept silent. At Carmarthen we stopped for an early supper and mine host of the "Boar's Head" gave us two most beautiful steaks and some good beer to wash them down. Then, on our way again, past Brecon through the valley to Hereford. Then on the broad highway to Stratford-on-Avon. Several times we lost our way.

Already signs of coming war were apparent, particularly in the great queues for petrol outside filling-up stations; I suppose everyone thought that petrol would be rationed on the first day of war. Many times we passed cars packed with luggage and families on the way back to their own homes, probably to find when they got there that most of the children, anyway, would have to be evacuated back to the country again.

As we whirled along, my thoughts were mixed. I had a feeling of dull, pent-up excitement, a funny empty feeling, because this time it might be the real thing. It was Freddy who broke the silence.

"You know, Guy, it is a queer feeling, this — we don't know, either of us, what we are going to do in the next few days, do we? Yesterday we were looking forward to a cocktail party. Now what are we going to do? I don't suppose you have any idea."

"I certainly don't. If there is a war — and I'm afraid it looks mighty like it — my squadron will be used for close support in France, and I don't suppose we will live long enough to know much about it, or care." I was convinced of this; that is why I said it. "But, surely, you'll have to use your medical experience in some way?"

"Yes, I'm OK. I have finished with Oxford and passed my MD. I think I'm going down to Kent to an advance dressing-station which will move into France as soon as things get hot. I think it's going to be pretty bloody."

I smiled to myself. Freddy, the idealist, the doctor. He was going to save lives, and I, a realist, was going to take them. Two jobs of war both very different, both very necessary, and as I watched the countryside roll by I wondered what would happen, what this time next year would hold for me.

How I loathed the Nazis. How could the common people of Germany allow such a world-conquering crowd of gangsters to get into power and stay in power? Ruthlessness and swaggering, domineering brutality, that was their creed. The Rhineland, Austria, Czechoslovakia, Abyssinia and Albania, the beginning of a long list. I thought of the children playing on the beach with the sand-wall and their magnificent sandcastle. How that little scene was like the world situation. The oncoming tide was Nazism. The sandcastle was freedom and the children were the Democracies. Their own weak wall was no protection against the massing, encircling rush of the water. But if only they had built it in time, before the tide had begun to come in, with sand and stone and cement and with the aid of all the other children who were sitting idly on the beach. Then the tide could have been held until it had receded again. If only nations would stick together when international freedom was in danger, whatever their ideals, whatever their language, then they could muster such armed forces that the aggressor would be unable to break the vital barrier.

America was saying this was a European war. "Let's stay out." Russia had made her pact. The rest of the friendly neutrals were strictly non-belligerent, and it looked as if France and England would have to carry the baby.

I was no serviceman; I joined the Air Force in 1936 purely to learn to fly. Last April I was due to leave the RAF to become a test-pilot — a good job with plenty of money in it — but Mussolini had put paid to that when he invaded Albania. Now Hitler had ruined my summer leave and was likely to do the same thing for many more summers to come.

That England was unprepared there was no doubt. Although the Navy talked about the big blockade which would bring Germany to her knees in six months, although the lion had its wings, what were the facts? We had very few bombers, mostly Wellingtons, Hampdens and, perhaps best of all, the good old Whitleys. None of these could carry many bombs and only a few could even find their targets. Navigation was at a very low ebb. Our fighters were mostly Gladiators and Mark I Hurricanes and a squadron of Spitfires. Typhoons and Lancasters were but twinkles in their designers' eyes.

Of flying training-schools there were few and those were in easy range of German bombers. The Empire Air Training Plan had not even been put into operation. What would happen after the initial wastage? Would we go on fighting, getting smaller and smaller until there was nothing left? The last few war pilots serving in the RAF today told us that the life of the average bomber boy was only about ten hours in the air. There's no future in that. What would happen to the towns and factories when the Germans started bombing them on the first day? We had no anti-aircraft defence of any strength. Only this summer I had been invited by a Brigadier to attend the standard Army summer game of shooting at a pilotless aeroplane, the "Queen Bee", down at Manorbier. I went, and for two hours watched the Army gunners fire hundreds of shells at the little biplane as it flew forwards and backwards over their heads at 5,000ft. It was pretty poor shooting and it wasn't even touched. However, when it glided down to make its pilotless landing

"George" held off too high and it crashed on one wing into the sea. I remember an Army officer saying, "Well, we got it in the end, didn't we?" and the look on the face of the RAF officer who had to repair it for the shoot next day!

Look at the state of the Army — few tanks, few modern weapons, few trained personnel, although it certainly wasn't their fault. Look at our own civilians; they even complained that we were keeping them awake when we flew over London trying to find out how to intercept the night bomber. They called us the playboys of Mayfair! Dull apathy and smug complacency seemed to be about to bring the British Empire tottering to its knees, if it didn't knock it out altogether.

In 1936 the Air Force had begun to expand, but the process had been painfully slow and even now we were not much bigger than we were in 1938.

Munich. What a show! But perhaps Chamberlain had done the right thing, who knows? All I knew was that, thank God, we did not make war in 1938.

As for France, our ally, what of her? In July we had flown down to Marseilles and back, over Paris and Lyons, to show the flag. On the way we passed over many airfields, but not once did we see a single French aircraft. Where were they all? Where was her Air Force? No one seemed to know. She, too, had had her fair share of "finger trouble" in her Governments.

Why had two great nations come so low? Perhaps it was the old story. The cream of their youth had fought the last war, and were either killed or too brassed off to try to pull their countries together afterwards. This left those other people to carry on. If, by any chance, we had a hope of winning this war — and it seemed very remote — then in order to protect our children let the young men who have done the fighting have a say in the affairs of State.

I had read books on the last war and knew that apart from the many lives lost and the chaos, misery and devastation it caused, new, evil and unknown things blighted the country, such as inflation, racketeers and industrial money-grabbers. I hoped that this would not happen in this war and, if it did, that there would be the severest punishment for such criminals.

My thoughts were interrupted as we rumbled down Woodstock Road, past my old school, St Edward's, into Oxford. Freddy drew the old Alvis up in front of a pub and we went in to have a quick one. After a couple of beers, in walked some boys he knew. They were all in the same boat. Some were going to the Oxford University Squadron, others were going back to their army units, others were waiting for the Navy to call them up. We left after the twelfth can, feeling much better, and went to have dinner. It was fairly late and we were pretty hungry, and fed like kings with some excellent 1928 burgundy.

Then, after a few more drinks, I was almost literally poured into the train.

"Goodbye, Freddy; good luck."

"Goodbye, Guy. God knows when I will see you again. All the best."

And the train started north.

What a journey! The train had been blacked out. It was completely packed with soldiers and civilians, all going somewhere. After many stops, during which there was shouting and yelling and clinking of milk-cans, and with my hangover getting steadily worse, we arrived at Lincoln at 4am. After much trouble and the signing of a couple of forms, I was taken by transport to Scampton. Sunny Scampton we call it because it is in Lincolnshire and one doesn't see much sun up there. It's a fine old Bomber Base dating from the last war, but as we drove in through the gates I saw that the windows had been blacked out and that the street-lighting had been switched off.

In the Officers' Mess there was a dim sinister blue light. You couldn't possibly see to read, but then there were not enough blackout curtains for every building. As I was having my breakfast and about to go to bed, all the boys came in. Normally there is no one about in an RAF Officers' Mess at 6 o'clock in the morning, but this was different. They had been standing by since dawn. They had not changed; they were cheerful in their greetings.

"Wotcha, Gibbo!"

"Good leave, old boy?"

"Hullo, you old so-and-so; so you've come back for the war, have you?"

But a little later there was a silence when we heard that at dawn that morning Germany had invaded Poland, and I went to bed.

The next two days moved very quickly with tremendous activity on all sides. Complete bedlam reigned all over bomber stations in the north and ours was typical. There were tractors driving round the perimeter roads in the sweltering heat, some with long bomb trailers bouncing behind; others pulling our Hampdens along cinder tracks far into the country to dispersal points fairly safe from enemy bombs. All round the airfield sand-banked gun emplacements were being put up by aerodrome defence squads, but there were not many guns. Gas officers were running round placing yellow detectors in the right places. These detectors were of two kinds and always amused me. The yellow ones were supposed to turn red in the presence of gas, but they failed to do so on many an occasion. Then there was another which resembled a piece of cheese hanging on a hook. What these were meant to do I never found out, but the cheese was always disappearing — perhaps the birds in the district liked the stuff!

All the station transport was spread out over the whole area of the camp, so it was nothing out of the ordinary for the CO to find a petrol bowzer in his back garden. No one was allowed to leave the camp.

Deep down in the ground below station headquarters lived the denizens of the operations

49

room. This was strictly out of bounds to everyone. At the door, a great half-inch steel structure, sat a couple of airmen armed with rifles. Many an identity card was examined here, and the two lads had the time of their lives turning away such ogres as the station warrant officer. Inside, in the gloom of the blue lights, moved WAAFs and clerks, preparing maps in many shapes, cutting them, clipping them, rolling them, folding them. There were maps of Holland, maps of France, the Siegfried Line; there was even a map of Berlin.

In another corner two officers were sorting out target maps. I noticed as I passed by that there was a photograph of Wilhelmshaven clipped to each. In the middle, surrounded by a huge desk, was the Station-Commander, looking very harassed. He had cause to be, for in front of him was a great pile of files marked "War Plan: phase 1, phase 2", etc. All these were directives to be used only in time of war, or in case of mobilization. His round face was a puzzle, frowning at all this extraordinary activity. The frown would develop into a very black look now and then, especially when some WAAF giggled at something whispered to her by the pimply, young airman who spent most of his time standing on a ladder pushing pins into a map on the wall.

In the hangars there was the ringing of metal against metal as cowlings were being beaten out and dents knocked in. There was that empty noise all hangars have, drowned occasionally by the raucous voice of some fitter singing his weary love-song. And then the Flight-Sergeant or "Chiefy", would come rushing in and the song would stop.

Taking things all round there was, as the saying is, a tremendous flap going on.

Not so the air crews. We were sitting or lying on the grass in front of the Squadron Mess most of the day. The sun was beating down and most of us had taken off our flying kit, which was lying strewn around untidily and scattered in all directions. We were officially "standing by". For what, we did not know, but we thought it was sure to be a bombing raid somewhere, sometime. Conversation was carefree — of girls, of parties, but strictly limited about the war. He had all heard that our ambassador in Berlin had presented Hitler with an ultimatum asking for the withdrawal of German troops from Poland. There was still some hope. I was holding forth to my crew that we had been recalled from leave too early; and that it was a damn shame because Hitler would never bomb Great Britain until after the Nuremberg Rally on September 13th.

As no one had been allowed to leave the camp, there had been some pretty heavy drinking going on at nights. As usual on these occasions, the squadrons concerned — our own and 49th, our deadly rivals in the camp — had had a pretty good beat up, and all the boys were quite content to sleep off their hangovers. At such a time as this I can only remember kaleidoscopic scenes: the CO roaring someone up for not having his parachute handy;

anxious faces crowding round the radio for their hourly news bulletins, snatching hurried meals, then back to the hangar in an overcrowded truck. One poor chap fell off when the back dropped and broke his leg — he was our first war casualty. Those gramophone records, the heat. Extra large headlines in the newspapers every day, including a memorable "No war this year". My old batman, Crosby, coming in to wake me every morning at 4 o'clock saying in his doleful bass voice: "Here's your cup of tea, Sir. The news is much worse today, Sir. Shall I run you a bath, Sir?"

A world about to go mad. For us a funny feeling that the next day we might not be in this world.

And so September 3rd found the boys of A Flight sitting in the Flight-Commander's office. We had just finished our morning tea, which a Naafi girl had brought in, and the room was full of smoke. Oscar Bridgman, the Flight-Commander, sat with his hat at the back of his head, his feet on the table and his chair liable to fall over backwards at any minute. He was a tremendous character, was Oscar. He had a quick temper, but could fly as well as any man. I could never wish for a better Flight-Commander and we were all right behind him. Then there were the rest of them. Jack Kynoch, tall, swimming champion, not too much sense of humour. There were Mulligan and Ross (we used to call them Mull and Rossy), two Australian boys who joined us back in 1937. They did nearly everything together.

Sometimes they would have long heated arguments which were the amusement of the whole Flight. There was Ian Haydon, English, married to a very pretty girl called Dell. Very wrapped up in Dell, Ian always shot off to Lincoln, where they lived, as quickly as possible every night. He was a bit morose because he hadn't been able to get home for a few nights. There was Silvo. What a chap! A tall fellow, who got into most amazing scrapes. There was Pitcairn-Hill, a permanent, and in fact the only permanent, commissioned officer in our Flight. He had been a boy at Halton. A strait-laced and true Scot. An excellent sportsman, Pit used to play rugger for the RAF. Then there were others whose names I need not mention but who were just as much a part of A Flight as any. We were proud of ourselves, we boys of A Flight, because we were always putting it across B both in flying and drunken parties.

Suddenly the door opened and in came Chiefy. "All kites ready for testing." "OK, Flight," said Oscar, as he took his feet off the desk, and F/Sgt Langford went out again. Great fellow was F/Sgt Langford. He was the NCO in charge of maintenance in our Flight. For years he had been coming in saying that all aircraft were ready for testing, and no doubt he is still doing it to this very day.

I could write a lot about the ground crews. They are wonderful men and do a really hard job of work for very little pay; only their pride in their squadrons keeping them going.

Oscar had just been reciting a limerick about the Bishop of Belgrave when suddenly the door burst open and Crappy came in. Crappy Kitson looked as though he was about to have a baby. There was something wrong. He did not say much but just went over to the window and turned on the radio. In silence we listened to Chamberlain's solemn words telling the world that a state of war existed between Britain and Germany. So the balloon had gone up. This was war. No one knew quite what to say. Oscar inhaled slowly, then blew the smoke out through his nose. Then he said quietly and rather strangely: "Well, boys, this is it. You had better all pop out and test your aeroplanes. Be back in half-an-hour's time. There will probably be a job for you to do."

I went off out to look over C Charlie and found her sitting on her usual dispersal point. She was my own aeroplane, and a lousy one at that. On take-off she swung like hell to the right and flew in the air with her left wing low. Sometimes an engine died out, but that was nothing. We loved her because she was ours. At that time I did not have a full crew, but my second pilot was a Somersetshire man called Jack Warner, and there was old MacCormick, Mac for short, who was my scruffy radio operator. It did not take long to check the old faithful over. The ground crew had done a good job of work and she was quite all right.

When we came to the Mess those terrible gramophone records pushed out by the BBC were grating on. We had a quick lunch, which was interrupted by the Tannoy: "All crews to the lecture room immediately. That is all."

We expected to be told to take off immediately for Germany, or to be told that the Germans were taking off immediately for us, but instead Group Captain Emmett, the Station-Commander, was there to give us an address. He did not say much. He was a big, kind-hearted South African, with fingers like a bunch of bananas, fond of food and drink. He said nothing much, just a few words that we were now in the war, that he expected the full support of all officers and men on the Station to back him up and to back Bomber Command up in whatever operations we had to carry out. He told us that we would probably be operating according to the standard plan; that is, two weeks of maximum effort (which means raiding, as often as possible), one week of sustained effort (which is approximately half the maximum), then one week of rest. He told us that the German Air Force was not very good, anyway, and was pretty sure to have suffered losses in Poland. Then we went back to finish our lunch. We waited all day but the dreaded order never came. That night the bar was empty. The boys were writing letters.

Next day Rossy and I went down to A Flight Office alone. I do not know where the other boys were — I think they were playing cricket out on the tarmac. Suddenly Leonard Snaith, walked in. He was the Squadron-Commander; well known in the Air Force. One of the high-speed Schneider trophy pilots and a great fellow, he was a small man with a sad, mousy face. He, too, used to play rugger for the RAF and also held the quarter-mile record. In fact, he was an excellent type all round. But he had a slow temper and it was best not to get on the wrong side of Leonard. But he was not there to talk of rugger today.

He said in a strange voice, "We are off on a raid."

Rossy and I said nothing.

"We have got to provide six aircraft — three from A Flight and three from B Flight. I don't know where the target is. I think it is against shipping — probably German battleships. We are carrying four 500 pounders each; they have all got a delay of 11_seconds, so we can go in pretty low. F/Lt Collier is leading the three from B Flight. You two had better come with me. Take-off will be at 1530."

As I saw him write my name on a small scrap of paper my feelings were completely indescribable. A few days ago I was sunbathing, having the time of my life, carefree, looking forward to simple things, and now I was going to war, probably never to come back. Rossy felt the same. Although he didn't say anything, his face was as good as a loudspeaker.

Soon everything was fixed. The crews had all been got together, the bombs had been put on our aeroplane, and we went to the briefing. Actually, to call it a briefing would be absurd. We all gathered round a table while the Station-Commander told us where we were going. "You are going to attack the German pocket battleships which are lying in the Schillig Roads at the entrance to the Kiel Canal. If by any chance there are no warships there, you may bomb the ammunition depot at Marienhof, but on no account, and I must warn you that serious repercussions will follow, must you bomb civilian establishments, either houses or dockyards. The weather will be bad. You will have to attack very low. There have been some reports of balloons in this area, but you will not see them; they will be flying in the clouds. Do not stay in the area long. Return if you think that an attack cannot be carried through according to plan."

After these words of wisdom, Snaith quickly outlined his plan. We were to take off in formation. I was to be on the right, Rossy on the left. When we approached the *Von Scheer* we were to spread out to about 500 yards on either side and attack from three directions. Someone asked what would happen if the bombs bounced off the armoured decks. The reply came from the Station Armament Officer, who said that the idea was to lodge the bomb in the superstructure, where it would go off after the aircraft had passed safely over it. Then spoke Pitt, a Flight-Lieutenant, who used to be a schoolmaster. He was now Station Intelligence Officer. He told us that ships of the pocket-battleship class were armed with machine-guns, and read us a long paragraph from Air Publication 3,000, in which it is stated that the best height to attack in order to avoid flak is about 3,000ft — that is, above the machine-gun fire and below the heavy flak fire. He again repeated that on no account were we to bomb Germany.

After that another man got up and told us how to take off with a bomb load on. None of us had ever done it before and we did not even know whether our Hampdens would unstick with 2,000lbs of bombs. The advice we got was to ease them off by working the tail trimming tabs after the tail had come up. If we were still on the ground when the hedge came along we were to yank back the stick as hard as we could and pull the emergency boost control. All this sounded good gen to us because nobody knew anything about it, but on looking back I sometimes think how absurdly little we did know at that time, bearing in mind that since then thousands of Hampdens have taken off with heavier bomb loads.

There was not much time to waste as we dashed down to the crew room, our plan of action ready. As we went out to the bus little Willie gave us one final word of advice. On no account were we to break formation unless he gave the signal. We were to stick together and act as an element, not as individuals. This was about 2.30.

Just as we were climbing aboard the lorries to take us out to our aircraft a message came from Ops: "Take-off delayed to 1600." This was a bit tough on the boys because they were now all fairly het up and most of them would have preferred to get into the air rather than hang around for another hour. So we lay in the sun, smoking, saying very little but thinking what an extraordinary thing it was that in a few hours' time we would know what aerial warfare was like.

At 1530 another message came through to say that the take-off was delayed until 1700. This time a roar of four-letter words went up to greet the messenger. By now we were very nervous; in fact, my hands were shaking so much that I could not hold them still. All the time we wanted to rush off to the lavatory; most of us went about four times an hour.

At last the time came to climb aboard the lorry and we moved off to our aircraft. The boys who were to be left behind stood round self-consciously; they did not know quite what to say because no one knew anything about this sort of thing. In the end they gave a quick wave of good-bye and someone said, "Have a good time. See you tonight."

As I climbed up into my pilot seat, Taffy, one of the ground crews, bent over my ear and said, "Good luck, Sir; give those bastards a real hiding." I don't think I replied, but smiled up at him with that sort of sickly smile which one gives when one does not quite hear what another fellow says. But Taffy, the rigger, was one of the old school. He knew what was wrong, and as he put my safety harness over my shoulders he made a funny remark. "Now don't you worry," he said. "You will be OK. You will always come back." Up to now he has been right.

At about five minutes to five we ran up our engines and then taxied out one after another, waiting for 49 boys to take off led by George Lerwill. It is still George's doubtful boast that he was the first aircraft in 5 Group to take-off for Germany.

One after another we watched them go. Some swung very badly, but apart from that did not seem to have much trouble for the take-off. And then off went Willie, followed by Rossy, a stream of dust blowing back making them completely disappear from view for a few minutes.

By now I was calm and quite ready for what was to come. I grasped the brake lever firmly and pushed both throttles to full, then I let off the brakes and the old Hampden slowly got its tail up, and after about thirty seconds lumbered into the air and we were off to Germany.

The aeroplane felt very heavy, there was no doubt about that. It was some time before we picked up any speed at all, her turns were sluggish and she tended to slip inwards. After a while I managed to catch Willie Snaith up and we set course over Lincoln Cathedral. Dimly I heard Jack Warner say, "OK. Course 080° magnetic speed 160," but my thoughts were far away as I saw the fields pass underneath.

I could not believe that I was leaving England to go to Germany to carry out an act of war. It was unbelievable. Many times we had flown off like this on mock raids, but there was always a certainty of coming back; we could always be sure of that first can of beer in the Mess afterwards. Now it was different. The fields looked very beautiful — even Lincolnshire looked beautiful. I didn't want to leave, I wanted to turn back. I even wished that old C Charlie would develop some trouble so that we'd have to return, but no such luck. She hummed along like a sewing-machine, blast her. Then, far ahead, the coast came up and soon we were over Butlin's holiday camp near Skegness. Only two months ago I had spent two days there with a crowd of other boys in the Flight, and what fun we had had. But the camp disappeared far behind and Germany was two hours ahead.

Slowly the time passed. We were flying low, about 1,000ft, and the waves down below looked grimmer than I had ever seen them before, but maybe this was my imagination.

Little Willie was looking straight ahead. I think he was concentrating on the course he was steering. My own head was on a swivel because I had heard from one or two chaps who had fought in the last war that this was the only way to survive. Perhaps this looking straight ahead business was why Willie missed seeing a German flying-boat which passed about 500ft below us. It was a Dornier 18 and was merely doing a steady rate 1, turning to the left. Quite clearly I could see the two German pilots with their white, anxious faces looking up at me through their windscreen. Probably they thought we would attack them. The thought crossed my mind to go and have a bang myself, but it is written way back in the code of bomber rules that the bomber's job is to get to the target and get back again, not to go doing any fancy stuff, and so we kept straight on, watching Willie's straight head.

About 40 miles from Wilhelmshaven the cloud suddenly descended to about 300ft in rain and we closed formation. I had to open the window, getting very wet, in order to see Willie at all. The sea was now very rough down below, and to put it mildly the weather was stinking. About 10 miles from our objective we could see gun-fire ahead; that must have been the first boys doing their stuff. The cloud was now about 100ft from the deck. To my mind this was fine for bombing warships because we would have been able to attack in bad visibility and climb up into the cloud to avoid the flak. But to my astonishment Snaith suddenly began to turn to the left. Not quite knowing what he was doing, I followed. I saw poor old Rossy on the other side looking left and right, watching his wing-tip, which seemed to be about to go into the drink at any minute. Then the leader straightened up, and I suddenly realized that he had turned back. Of course, he was dead right, there was no doubt about that. For all we knew we were miles off our course: the gun-flashes ahead might have been the Dutch islands or they might have been Heligoland, and he was not going to risk three aircraft in order to make an abortive attack; but now our blood was up, we were young and keen and we wanted to go on alone. The temptation was very great, but discipline held; we had been told not to break formation and that was what we must not do.

On the way back we saw the same flying-boat which we saw on the way out. I think it must have been put there to spot aircraft coming in. We had jettisoned our bombs in the sea and now we were not bombers, but fighters. I saw no reason why we should not shoot this thing down, and called up the leader and told him so, but there was no answer and so we missed a wonderful opportunity to shoot down the first aircraft of the war.

When we re-crossed the coast at Boston it was dark. All the beacons had been moved to code positions and Willie's navigator got hopelessly lost. We floated around Lincolnshire for about two hours finding our position. It was only when the moon came up that we were able to follow the canal right up to Lincoln and turned north to our base. And so at last we landed. It was my first landing in a Hampden at night, and I think that went for all. What an abortive show, what a complete mess up! In fact, for all the danger we went through it couldn't be called a raid, but, nevertheless, we went through all the feelings, even worse perhaps.

The first thing I saw when I went into the Mess was a look of surprise on the boys' faces as they drank their cans of beer. "We thought you had been shot down," they said. "A wireless operator in Z for Zebra saw you go down vertically towards the sea. What happened?" I told them I didn't know what the hell they were talking about and went to bed. Looking back it is funny to think that out of all those boys there, with one exception, I was the only one who never was to go vertically down towards the sea or land.

Such was the first raid. True, it was abortive. True, we did not press home our attack, but in those days we knew so little about the whole thing that it is a wonder that we flew through such weather and got back at all. We had seen flak fired by the enemy; only on the horizon, but it had been fired at us. There it was, and I thought that if they are all like that they won't be too bad.

But although we had not done so well, a few Blenheims of No. 2 Group had done some good work and managed to damage the *Von Scheer*. They had flown in low, about two hours earlier, had seen the "washing on the line", and one 500lb bomb had lodged in her superstructure, blowing the aircraft and catapult gear out of the ship when it went off. Next day the papers were full of it. Much was made of the crews who had managed to press home this attack, and S/L Doran, who is now a prisoner of war, was given the DFC, an award well deserved.

In America and other neutral countries this raid was good propaganda. It showed that no matter how decrepit the old lion had become, it was still capable of kicking off hard and on the right foot.

The Germans, too, were not slow in their propaganda to claim that we had bombed civilians and that reprisals would follow a hundred-fold. Goering and Hitler were said to be fuming; the fat Luft-Marshal wanted to send 100 bombers over London, but Hitler made him stay his hand. Goebbels, that nasty little man, was quick to introduce a brand-new method of enemy showmanship by making one of the airmen who was shot down broadcast to England on the Haw-Haw wavelength. The conversation, as far as I can remember, ran something like this:

Announcer: "Now tell me, Sergeant, are you well?"
Sgt-Pilot (hesitatingly): "Yes, very well."
Announcer: "Are you being treated well?"
Pause, then:
Sgt-Pilot: "Everyone is very kind to me."
Announcer: "How is the food you are getting?"
A longer pause.
Sgt-Pilot: "Wonderful, just like home."

What a ham effort! You could practically see the revolver sticking in the poor lad's back.

Next day I became the second war casualty. I had just been down to move my kit from C Charlie after the night before. When I entered the Mess I noticed a large black Labrador sitting in the hall. Being fond of dogs I went up to him and gave him a friendly pat to show that he was welcome to the Mess, but the dog did not agree. In a flash his great jaws had clamped down on my hand and then I was running into the washroom, hand streaming with blood and with half the seat of my pants missing. They were new ones, too. As the monster chased me, jaws dripping for another bite, Pitcairn happened to come out of the bar with his flying-boots on. A hefty man was Pit, and one kick lifted the brute into the air and it ran away howling. Then I was free, but the damage was already done. I could practically see daylight through the great holes in my hand, and even if I say it myself, it was extremely painful. The boys and I wanted the dog court-martialled on the spot, but it happened to belong to the Group-Captain, so he was given a free pardon and told not to do it again. The Group-Captain came to see me while I was having the fifth stitch put in. He was breathing heavily because he had just had his lunch. "I hear you had some trouble with Zimba," he said. "Pity. You want to watch him." Watch him! I nearly blew up on the spot. Of all the things to say. But then I wasn't feeling too good at the time. Poor old Zimba had to pay later for his crimes though. After running up the unenviable score of 2 certs., 4 probables and many damaged, he was finally posted elsewhere. Maybe his score is even greater today.

Wing-Commander Jordan, who had taken the squadron over, gave me thirty-six hours' sick leave for this incident. Jordan was a fine type, and in the few days he was in the squadron everyone got to know and like him very well. He spent most of his time shouting. I remember one day I went into his office and he had two telephones, one on either ear. To the Group-Commander he was explaining that he only had nineteen aeroplanes and the nineteenth would not be serviceable for some days. On the other 'phone he was speaking to the Mess about the bad condition of the roast potatoes he had had for lunch. After a while I think he got mixed up between the two 'phones and the Adjutant had to close the door before he burst his sides. He was never afraid of taking decisions, and the thirty-six hours' leave he gave me was entirely off his own bat, as at that time there was definitely no leave for anybody in the Services.

My brother was getting married on the 5th and I was to be his best man, so the thirty-six hours came in handy. The journey to Rugby was most eventful in a browning-off sort of way. It was still boiling hot and the blood from my hand had begun to soak through the bandage and on to the sling. As I stood waiting for my train at Nottingham station an old woman came up. "Bad luck, you poor young boy," she said. "Kiel, I suppose?"

Then a young man — "My brother was on your do. Simpson's his name. He wasn't wounded too, was he?"

At the wedding an old man put the cap on it. He sidled up with the air of a man about to give away a great secret. "I was in the last lot, my boy," he whispered. "I admire you for that."

I nearly shot a cat. Can't a chap walk around with a bloody arm in a sling (and I mean bloody) without everyone presupposing he had had it shot off or something? Dogs bite sometimes. One bit me. But it was no good, and I reached for the bottle.

I arrived back in Scampton with an aching arm and a bad hangover. All the boys had left and the aeroplanes had gone too. Someone had learned that in Poland the Hun was wiping out scores of aeroplanes on the ground, and so War Plan, Phase 10, was in action. They had flown all their aeroplanes over to Ringway, near Manchester, where they would be safe from enemy bombers. I had heard by jungle telegraph that the boys were having a very good time in Manchester, and it was not surprising, therefore, that as soon as the doc had pulled out my stitches I was on my way.

It was a dull, cloudy day when I arrived there and taxied up to the clubhouse. Then Rossy told me the news. The boys had certainly tucked themselves well in. Oscar had taken over a pub where there were bags of beer, a jukebox and some very pretty barmaids. One of the boys claimed already to have made the grade with one, but he was a bit of a line-shooter about these things.

This pub was in a pretty good strategical position, halfway between Manchester and the airport. Thus, service transport could be used to get to Manchester, which saved time and money, which in turn could be used for other things, such as drinking.

For a few days we lived rather primitively; about forty of us slept on palliasses on the floor of a large committee room upstairs. There were no washing facilities and the pub had only one bathroom. But whoever chose Ringway chose well, because this was the recruiting centre for the Manchester WAAFs. They were all in civilian clothes and some were extremely nice girls. These were the type who volunteered to come in right at the beginning when things looked bad, and not because they were forced to by the grim alternatives offered by Ernest Bevin.

There was little work at Ringway. Each day all we had to do was to test our aeroplanes. This usually took about half an hour and involved some pretty good beat-ups of the clubhouse. The rest of the day we spent having baths and shaving and making ourselves generally presentable until the bus took us to the pub at 5 o'clock. Now and again there were flaps. Once a German battleship was reported in the Irish Sea, but flaps were not alarming and generally we had a very easy time.

There were many parties. Needless to say, the sight of a boy in blue drew much attention in all the bars. For our part we were out to have a pretty good time. The war occupied our minds and we all thought that we would be fighting for our skins within a month. So why not make merry while the sun shone? And the sun did shine in Manchester. The hospitality was almost embarrassing. People just could not do enough. Houses were thrown open, girls were plentiful, theatre tickets were booked and we lived like kings.

At that time some poor long-suffering souls were nightly droning over the Third Reich for their sins but not dropping bombs. They were either on reconnaissance or dropping leaflets advising the Germans to surrender or to throw Hitler out or both. In Manchester the word got around that we were the boys doing this job, although it was the last thing that we would claim to do. And so, one Sunday when Oscar took off for Scampton with the sole purpose of getting some money and some clean clothes, I was rather shaken when one of the waitresses in the aerodrome café came up to me while I was watching him go. She spoke softly, as though she had something on her mind. "I hope he comes back all right," she whispered. "I hope he comes back, too," I answered, thinking of the five quid he owed me and which I should see the next day.

Gradually we began to know all the local people, and from then on our time was not our own. Every night there were parties and girls and everything else. We were fond of Manchester and it seemed that they were fond of us. One day when Bruce Harrison and I were having coffee in a café a couple of WAAFs under training came and sat at our table. That night we took them out. There wasn't much to do, but we sat in the Midland Hotel until midnight, drinking Haigs and listening to the salon orchestra. I had never really thought much about women up to now; they were things that just came and went in parties. Sometimes they were dumb, sometimes they were too intelligent, rarely had I been impressed by any one. I think it was the war or else those eyes, but to cut it fairly short I fell in love, that awful boyish love which hurts. From then on there was not a moment in the day when I did not think of her. She could fly, her handicap was 12 at golf, she had driven in the Monte Carlo Rally. She was pretty. She was wonderful, and so it went on. But although Barbara was very sweet, one day she told me quite firmly that her heart was with someone in the Fleet Air Arm. So that was that. I saw her quite a bit afterwards, but it wasn't the same. But it struck me as funny that it should take a war to make a chap even think of falling in love.

One misty day at Ringway, Sam Threapleton, the second in command of the squadron, rolled in from the east. He had come over to reorganize. He had heard that we were having too good a time. Someone had sent him to see what we were up to. In the afternoon he requisitioned a temperance hotel and de-requisitioned our pub. Naturally there were many downcast faces in the squadron, especially as some of the boys were beginning to have a pretty good time in that locality. The temperance hotel was miles away, and although I should not say this, we had one of the most drunken parties I have ever had in my life the only night we ever slept there.

By now some weeks had passed. There had been rumours that we were going to stay at Ringway for the duration. But someone in Bomber Command decided otherwise.

It looked as though the enemy was too preoccupied over in Poland to do any bombing in England for quite a while. But next day, when I was sitting in the crew room waiting for the fog to lift, Mac, my wireless operator, came to me suddenly. "There is a message coming from Group," he said. There was a pause, then we went to the wireless room. In order to defeat the remarkable delays of up to ten hours on the long-distance GPO line, we had rigged up a little wireless set in direct communication with Scampton. This was strictly against orders, but it served its purpose. When Mac had taken it all down he handed the slip of paper to Rossy, who was the code king. Of all things that take a long time to do, decoding a message is one of the worst, and so there was much impatience as we crowded round looking over his shoulder. The first sentence he wrote slowly. This cypher started off on a particularly difficult letter: "From Base to 83rd detachment, Ringway."

We waited.

We were going to France?

We were going to Iceland?

This was war. This was the real thing.

Maybe this was from Oscar to tell us that he was coming back tonight and to tell us to provide a girlfriend for him.

Then Rossy read the rest. "Return Base PM for concentrated night-flying training." As Rossy read the last sentence there were yells of disappointment.

"Night flying. What a bind!"

"Leaflets. O Christ!"

But Bruce was thinking of the party that night. Mull was thinking, I imagined, of a girl he was going to meet at the Café Royal. Silvo was probably thinking of nothing. I thought of Barbara and cursed.

When we got back to Scampton I found myself well behind the rest of the aircraft because I had not been able to catch up in my slow old C Charlie. Just to show them what was what, we beat up the place in no mean manner. When we whipped over the Control Tower in a split-arse turn, I thought I saw a little figure standing on top, waving. I was not sure who, but the very sight of that little figure sent a sinking feeling down my spine. I therefore pulled off a sneaky landing right on the far side of the field where I thought I could not be seen. When I got to the Flight Office I found I was right. It was little Willie. He was back. For three years I had known that if anyone didn't like beat-ups it was Snaith, and this time I had buzzed the field properly, as they say.

And this time I paid the price. The next few nights found me officer i/c night flying. But after Ringway I was pretty broke, anyway, so I didn't care.

The days passed slowly, September petered away and brought the fogs of October. Night-flying training had been cancelled. Why we did not know, but it had been. We were now standing by for shipping strikes. Every day they wanted nine aircraft from each squadron bombed up, ready to start at half-an-hour's notice. It was a question of being up at 7am, all day in the crew rooms, smoking, reading, sometimes listening to lectures. Then as soon as it got dark we were released. Not a happy life. Not a life good for a bomber-pilot's soul, and we soon began to get browned off. The only spot of enjoyment we had was our Ringway clipper, an old Anson which used to take us to Ringway on our twenty-four hours off, so that we could renew some old dates there. Even this got stopped when some brass hat got to know of it.

And so the days dragged on through October in the same dreary routine. It seemed that the whole war had begun to go through thick oil. It was moving at a snail's pace. Standing by. Standing to. Standing down. A dull procession. Gradually we began to realize that our parties of the month before were a waste of money, a waste of time, a waste of everything. We were not going to be flying in the front line in France; we were not going to die. This was a static war. It made me smile a bit because at last I could go to the dentist. In the early days of

September I had had an appointment with the dentist but didn't turn up. He had seen me in the Mess afterwards. "I did not come along," I explained, "because I didn't see any point in having my teeth fixed and going through agony in the process, when I was likely to die within the next few days." That was what I honestly thought at the time, and it was typical of the feelings of all the boys up there.

Now it was different. It seemed that Germany was now licking her wounds. What she would do next was one big question mark.

What we would do next was pretty easy to guess — nothing. Poland had been overrun. Two great armies were now facing each other across the Maginot Line, yelling through loud-speakers all sorts of threats, insults and invitations to the Frenchmen to turn against their British allies.

There was a story which got around that showed that even the Germans had a rather peculiar sense of humour. One day during the heat of battle a Messerschmitt 110, then brand new and secret, was forced to land on a flat space between the Maginot Line and the Siegfried Line. All day long both sides watched carefully for any move by the other. For their part the British and the French organized a very special patrol to creep out when it got dark and to try to tow the secret aeroplane into the French lines. Night came; it was cloudy and pitch dark. On their hands and knees, the patrol slunk out, hardly daring to breathe in case they were heard by the

Germans. At last they reached the Messerschmitt. After minutes of suspense they managed to get a rope round the tail, but they were greatly hampered by the fact that they could not use any light at all. But after an hour they had at last done their job and began to crawl back. Suddenly two German searchlights flashed straight on to them. There they were, silhouetted brightly, feeling like thieves caught in the act. Then one of those great loudspeakers roared out with a voice that could be heard 10 miles all round: "IF YOU WANT LIGHT WHY THE HELL DIDN'T YOU SAY SO?" Then they opened up with machine-guns.

Next day the French guns opened up a barrage on the Germans as a reprisal. And the world waited and said, as in a game of consequences, "What a funny war!"

Not so funny for some air crews though. We were lucky — we weren't the guinea-pigs — but one or two squadrons at Hemswell, up the road, had to pay the price. We did not know a thing about aerial warfare and it was up to us to learn. Someone had to be unlucky. One squadron of twelve aircraft was sent to attack three destroyers off Heligoland. Only six came back and they had the queerest story to tell. They had found that a destroyer does not possess machine-guns, as they had been told, but very strong AA fire in the shape of light flak guns which make a single low-level attack practically suicidal unless backed up by waves of aircraft. They found that a destroyer could manœuvre too quickly for single attacks, and they found that German fighters were up to meet them even though they were not within sight of land.

Another squadron went to attack shipping in the Bight; one Flight was separated from the other, but no shipping was found, anyway. On the way home it appears fighters were sighted and the Flight-Commander decided to jettison his bombs in order to gain a few more miles an hour. The bomb doors opened, the pilot pressed the button. It was the last thing he ever did; they were only 500ft and all were blown sky high. Nothing was ever found. Many stories like this can be told, probably from the German side as well. This was a new war in the air and this was ourselves learning it.

A raid on Wilhelmshaven by Wellingtons without fighter cover was a good example of not knowing, but I am not blaming the planners at that time. Then it may have seemed sound that a close formation of Wellington bombers could have protected themselves against repeated attacks of Me 109s, but the proof of the pudding lies in the fact that a raid of that nature was never repeated. Why? Because it was hell for the crews and uneconomical for the country. At the same time that raid gave a very good clue to the German claims. In all they claimed to have destroyed fifty-four aircraft, a figure well above the number of Wellingtons actually operating at the time.

The Germans, too, were having their fling. They began at Scapa Flow. This was unsuccessful because of extremely poor bombing. According to the BBC only a rabbit was killed, and I think this was true. But later a submarine, closely following the film script of a current motion picture, stealthily stole through the boom defences of the great naval base and sank the Royal Oak and slipped out again. "There appears to have been some laxity in the boom defences," said someone in the Admiralty. "This has now been remedied."

A few days later the Hun airmen made their next sortie. Across the misty waters of the Firth of Forth they came, about twelve of them, to attack shipping lying off Edinburgh. Our fighters, first Gladiators, then Spitfires, were up in a flash, and a few Heinkels failed to return. Remarkable though it may seem, some of the pilots who carried out this raid were of the better German types, men who used to fly for Luft-Hansa. There is a story that one of our more ardent auxiliary Squadron-Leaders had quite a party with one. He had already shot down a Heinkel, then chased another past Drem, on to the green fields of Berwick, where he saw it land safely. After having put up a good show, and anxious to be the first airman to capture his own personal victims, the Squadron-Leader made a plan. After circling the field twice, his only audience being the crew of the Heinkel, who sat outside their wrecked aircraft watching him with interest, he decided to land. In he came, motor well on, flaps right down. No sooner had the wheels touched muddy earth than crash! and over the Spit went on to its back. The

Squadron-Leader did his best to get out, but it was no use. He was trapped, and so he hung there upside down, listening to the unpleasant sound of dripping petrol and waiting for help from outside. The Germans, having watched all this with a certain amount of amazement, at last decided to do something about it. Running over, they had him free in a second. As he emerged from the wreck the Squadron-Leader quickly pulled out his pistol. "You are all under arrest," he said. "Do any of you speak English?" In a casual Oxford accent the Nazi Captain answered quietly, "I usually do, I was educated at Malvern and Trinity. By the way, Squadron-Leader, that was a pretty lousy landing of yours!"

Such tales got around. Whether they are true or not is unknown, but there must be some basis for such a story, and this was a stock one for many moons around the pubs in Lincoln.

Here I must say that the auxiliary boys at that time had not quite been able to get the full hang of operational flying. It was true that a year later they were to distinguish themselves in the most glorious fashion possible, but in the dark days of 1939 they were very light on the trigger. But more of this later.

November brought rain. The squadron began rapidly to fill up. New faces appeared from training units. One day we were sitting around in the Flight Office doing nothing in particular when five new types walked in — Jackie Withers, Tony Mills, Bill Tweddell, Dickie Bunker and Greenie Greenwell.

All were English except Greenie, who came from South Africa. They came in nervously, not quite knowing what to expect. Except for Jackie Withers they were all pretty young. Oscar looked them over. I do not think they expected to see such a young Flight-Commander, and I don't think they expected to see their Flight-Commander with his tunic undone and his hat on the back of his head, his feet on the table and behaving so casually.

"All you fellows have very good records," he said, taking out his pipe; "that is why you have come to my Flight. All the stooges go to B Flight! All I want from you while you are here is loyalty and good flying discipline. You may have been taught to fly Hampdens well, you may even think yourselves aces, but I am afraid you are in for a shock. You are going to be second pilots. This means that you have got to learn to navigate, and this means you will hardly ever fly as pilots except on night-flying tests."

Quickly he allocated each a pilot. Tony Mills went to Jack Kynoch, Greenie went to Ian. "You, Gibbo" — he looked at me with that funny smile of his — "because you've got the scruffiest wireless operator and worst aeroplane, and because you are just a little fellow yourself, you can have him." He pointed to Jackie Withers. I knew Oscar was joking, but I know Jackie didn't.

"OK, Oscar, thanks very much," I said, and then turned to Jackie. "You're a lucky devil; you have come to the best pilot in the squadron." I just got out of the door in time, followed by yells of "You bloody old line-shooter," "He's awful, he'll kill you," and a hail of flying-boots thudded on the door as I banged it behind me.

Then I had a look at Jackie. Jackie was an amusing character. His mother was an opera singer, he himself had been trained as a ballet dancer. He could play jazz on the piano as well as any man. He could even sing like Harry Roy. But the main thing about Jack was that he had a heart of gold and the guts of a lion, and some time later I was to find out that he could fly very well, too.

One day late in November someone said that someone had reported that three German destroyers were within 2 miles of Newcastle. We were detailed to carry out a recco. If this was true and if the destroyers were there, both squadrons were to take off as quickly as possible and carry out a medium-level attack. Needless to say there was nothing about, and we were about to return to base when we got another message which told us to sweep the North Sea within 20 miles of Sylt. Jackie, sitting in front, said, "Oh, hell, I haven't got any maps." But it didn't matter because we followed Oscar all the way and didn't see a thing, not even a fishing-boat. When we got to Sylt there was nothing about except a long layer of cloud, over the mainland. I suppose that was why there were no fighters about. When we got back we knocked back a few cans in the Mess on the strength of being the first crews in our Group to see Germany in daylight — another doubtful boast.

★ ★ ★

All this time the German pocket battleship *Deutschland* was making a nuisance of herself in the Atlantic. Her sister ship the *Graf Spee* had already been disposed of. And so the Bomber chief looked to the Air Force to dispose of her with equal skill. One day it was reported that the *Deutschland* had left Kiel and was on her way out to attack shipping in the North Atlantic. She had been reported steaming north up the Norwegian coast, south of Stavanger. At dawn there was a tremendous flap at Scampton. First of all, all crews were wanted. In the end only nine aircraft from each squadron.

The briefing did not take long; there was not time. Aircraft were to attack in Flights of three. The total number of aircraft in the formation was about fifty. In case of fighter attack we were to bunch together and get as much mutual protection as possible. At the last moment Joe Collier took my place and left me fuming on the ground. But he was to regret his keenness a few hours later.

And so they set off. The raid was led by W/Com. Sheen, who commanded 49th Squadron. In one aircraft was an observer, and his job was to look for the *Deutschland* through binoculars. If he recognized it as such he was to fire a coloured light so that all bomb-aimers in the formation would attack the ship with a clear conscience, knowing that they had not attacked a British cruiser hurrying to the battle.

Across the windy waters of the North Sea they went, flying at about 10,000ft, and at last they came to Norway. It had only taken them about two hours to get there because there had been a terrific tail wind behind them, so Sheen, in the leading aircraft, enthusiastically decided to fly further up the Norwegian coast than necessary. Keeping well outside the three-mile limit and in wonderfully clear weather, watching all the fjords and little towns pass by, the formation went up far north to a point where it was hopeless to go on any further. Then it turned west for England. By now the tail wind had developed into a head wind which had developed into a gale. Our Hampdens were not very fast, and by looking down on the sea you could soon see that the ground speed was very, very low. After about four hours on this course the observer on board developed the startling theory that the whole formation had overshot the north tip of Scotland and were now over the Atlantic. He therefore promptly advised that they should all turn south-east. This was done. There was no inter-aircraft radio communication in those days and if there had been the ether would have been very thick with rather unattractive words. After a while the resident navigator on board the leading aircraft managed to convince the observer that he was talking through his hat, and again the formation turned west.

By now they were beginning to get short of petrol. They had all been flying for ten hours and many eyes were glancing at the gauges, which were registering round the 100 gallons mark. Land was not in sight. It looked as though the whole formation would have to land in the sea.

Suddenly out of the mist ahead appeared a small fishing-smack. It was about 5 o'clock in the evening; it was just getting dark, and an old man with his hand on the tiller had done his day's work and was about to go home. He was somewhat surprised when about fifty Hampdens suddenly began circling his little boat flashing urgent secret messages; but as he had no wireless or lights on board all he could do was to wave at them, thinking they were merely having some fun. Another squadron, meanwhile, commanded by a Scot called Willie Watt, in gaining altitude during the turn happened to see land in the distance and broke off quickly, and another fifteen minutes found them safely landed at Montrose. One after another the other squadrons did the same thing. One Sergeant-Pilot was coming into land when one engine stopped for lack of petrol. He quickly opened the other to full power, but this also stopped within a few seconds. He crashed into a graveyard near the aerodrome, but managed to walk out of it.

December 1st was an uneventful day except for the fact that the Russians invaded Finland. Why they did this will not be known until after the war, but I myself have the greatest faith in the Russians, and I am sure that whatever the reason they planned this invasion, it was a pretty sound one. I didn't think this at the time, though.

December 1st was also the day I went on three days' leave — my first few days off since my dog-bite. We were not allowed to go very far because we had to be within twelve hours' recall, so I drove down to Coventry to stay with my brother. He was in the Warwickshires and his headquarters were in the centre of the town. The leave was uneventful except for the usual amount of beer and a game of rugger. But one night at a party I met a girl called Eve Moore, whom I liked very much the moment I met her. She was small and very fair and, above all, could talk. In those days of hectic parties and boring war news, it was nice to meet someone who could discuss books, music and places. Most people who discuss these things well don't look so good, but this girl was really attractive. Her parents were in shipping at Cardiff.

I was still smarting after my broken heart (so I thought) with Barbara, and as most of the boys in the squadron claimed to have regular girls, I saw no reason why I should not have one myself, and Eve looked all right to me. It was pleasant being able to live normally, going round with a nice girl for a couple of days, but it was soon over.

On the last night we had a party in the "King's Head" Hotel which packed up about three next morning. It was a pretty ordinary sort of party — the usual chattering sort with bags of hooch around. The only thing I can remember particularly outstanding about it was that I mixed rum with whisky; a thing a connoisseur or an old hand would

85

never do even in his worst moments. After saying goodbye to my brother and the rest of the boys and girls, I got into my car to drive the hundred-odd miles back to Scampton. One never feels very good at 3 o'clock in the morning and the rum and whisky didn't help: besides, the blackout was terrible. My head-lights were the standard mask type, which, as everyone knows, give no light whatsoever. After an hour of losing my way and nearly hitting hedges I gave up and went to sleep to wait for the dawn. An hour or two later I woke up with a splitting head and the vilest taste in my mouth. Rum, they say, always does that.

As soon as I got to Scampton I drove straight to the hangars and went to sleep in the pilots' rest room. I was a few hours overdue and I did not want Willie to catch me with my breath smelling of rum. It was quiet and peaceful in this warm room and I had a lot of sleep to catch up. Just as I was dozing off some of the boys came in. "Hello! Gibbo's back," I heard someone say, through a haze. Then another voice, "God, look at those bags under his eyes; he must have had a wizard time!"

There was a snigger of dirty laughter and that was enough for me.

I jumped to my feet. "Get out, you dirty-minded devils," I yelled at the two sprogs who had been doing the talking. "I have just driven 100 miles in the blackout with a hell of a hangover. Now scram." The two went out sympathetically. They knew exactly how I felt.

December brought dirty weather. Although we spent our time standing by, always waiting for the order to take off, although we even took off on two occasions to hunt for the elusive *Deutschland* and were recalled within an hour of being airborne, we couldn't claim to be earning our pay. Life was very boring. Every day fog clamped down on the aerodrome, and it was quite an event if we could see the farmhouse on the far side, about a mile away.

One day someone in the Air Ministry decided that Scampton's flying-field was too small. That farmhouse was in the way of the proposed expansion. It would have to be knocked down. Johnnie Chick, the Wing-Commander, who had taken over from Sheen in the other squadron, had a brainwave. Why not knock it down ourselves with 500lb bombs? We would get some low-level practice, and it would be interesting to see the behaviour of these bombs when dropped at low altitude. A competition between squadrons was quickly organized and everyone waited for the great day.

At last a suitable occasion arrived. And at the last moment the Air Ministry had stepped in and said that we could use only dummy bombs, but these could have a live smoke charge fitted to the tail to make the thing look realistic.

Off the boys went one by one. They were bombing at about 100ft, and although they tried hard, no one was much good; some over-shot, some dropped short and bounced clean over the building to explode about a quarter of a mile beyond. We learned a lot that day. We learned that low-level bombing was harder than we had thought; and most important of all, that bombs bounce for a long distance when fitted with the tail action fuse. Someone suggested that it would be better if these bombs were fitted with spikes so that they should stick in the ground, rather like a dart. Funnily enough, Johnnie Chick swept the field by placing his bomb into the top bedroom window — funny because he was lousy at darts.

And so December passed by. Once or twice we organized competitions. There were landing competitions; there were bombing competitions. All this to try to keep ourselves busy. But taking things all round, everybody was getting browned off. We ourselves began to think that this was a phoney war.

One day Oscar, Ian and I flew down to St. Athan in South Wales, to have some secret equipment fitted to our Hampdens. It was a dirty trip; low cloud all the way. Just when we were breaking cloud in the Bristol Channel at about 500ft a convoy opened up on us and we all missed being shot down, thanks to the inaccuracy of the gunners concerned. We must have been sitters. The weather closed in more and more, so we decided to stay the night and go back next day. This suited me down to the ground, as I was able to go to Eve's house and meet her parents. Then back to beat-up Cardiff with the boys.

On Christmas Day, the first wartime Christmas, we stood by from dawn onwards for a large enemy shipping strike. As we stood around at lunchtime, eating oranges and other rations to be used only for the flight, we thought of other more fortunate souls who were drinking and making merry. But later someone heard our prayer and the whole thing was cancelled. Then the party started. First, to the Airmen's Mess to serve them their dinners, accompanied by the howls of delight from our erks. Yells of "Up 49th," then a louder, deafening noise from the 83rd supports: "It's not 81, it's not 82; it's 83." Then an equal crack back from the 49th boys, until the dining-hall resembled a vast smoky, howling bedlam.

This is an old tradition of the RAF on Christmas Day all officers must serve the airmen with their Christmas fare and all airmen can call the officers whatever names they like, and so many rude words were flying around. As the beer flowed faster and faster, so the party got rougher and rougher and the words even more rude. In the end it is another age-old tradition that all officers must leave the dining-room when plates begin to sail through the air, otherwise they might get hurt.

Then to the Sergeants' Mess, where for twenty-five years the NCOs have had the privilege of slipping a gin into some unsuspecting officer's beer. I have had it done to me and I didn't remember getting home that night. This time no punches were pulled. This was a wartime

Christmas; there might not be another one, not in our lifetime.

After we had seen that all the other ranks on the Station were enjoying themselves and were fully stocked with beer, we all went up to the Officers' Mess to have our own dinner. This was a complete shambles. There were no women in the Mess, none were invited. This was a stag party, and what a party! I remember that as the evening drew on one squadron got to one side of the room and the other to the other, and suddenly someone shouted: "Come on, boys — free for all!" I remember being pulled out from underneath a mass of writhing bodies to be told I was wanted on the 'phone. It was Eve wishing me a happy Christmas. Then back into the fray. It was amazing that no one got hurt.

At last I thought I had better go to bed. I had had my fill and found it rather difficult to walk straight. As I was trundling along the corridor there happened to be four fire extinguishers in the way. These I did not see, partly for the obvious reason and partly because the corridor was dark. Anyway, I had the misfortune to trip over them and one by one they went off. I did not know what to do. First I tried to sit on them to keep the liquid foam from going on the corridors; that was no good. The stuff seeped through my trousers and then began to spray out again. There was no way for it. Nearby was a large and ornamental door covered with glass. One by one I threw the fire extinguishers out, making a most horrible noise of tinkling glass and squirting extinguishers. Then I went to bed, feeling that I had done my best in difficult circumstances.

Next day the Mess Secretary impolitely informed me that I had been taken off drinking for a month in the Mess because of the wilful damage I had caused the night before. I was furious and went to see Willie Snaith, but he put it another way which made me satisfied. "Look, Gibbo," he said, "they have done you a good turn. Think of the money you will save so that you can spend it on your girlfriend." That remark meant a lot to me and for the next month I didn't touch a drop.

And so 1939 ended. It ended on the wrong note — a note of a party and not a note of war, but if we had known what we were in for in the next three years that party would have been even bigger.

CHAPTER
THREE

Learn by Mistakes

Everyone will remember those early days of January 1940. Snow came in all its fury. There was snow everywhere; it blocked the runways, blocked the hangar doors, it got into the aeroplanes, it made life unbearable. The road to Lincoln was blocked for a week. The Mess ran out of beer. A long-range Wellesley bomber on the other side of England, in response to urgent requests, came over low one day and dropped us a few crates by parachute, but the boys soon drank it all up.

Mull and I decided one night to go to a cinema in Lincoln. We set off in my car down the road in the blinding snow. It was quite impossible to see through the windscreen, and he had to walk beside the car with a light, while I drove as slowly as possible. Suddenly we arrived back at the main gates again; somehow or other *en route* we had turned right round and had gone back the way we had come. We saw no cinema that night.

Meanwhile, a few officers on the camp who had seen service in the fast war told us that the thing to do when the weather was bad was to get round a piano and sing songs. We had no ideas of our own, we could only copy them. So there we were, Jackie Withers hammering away at the keys while the boys sat around with their beers and me with my orange juice, singing at the top of our voices. Many songs were sung — some good, some bad; mostly bad.

One night Oscar came howling with laughter into the Mess. It was unlike Oscar to howl with laughter, so we asked him what was wrong. He could hardly speak. "Go into the billiard-room," he said, "and see what I have seen." Quickly we went along, and there a sight met our eyes which made us almost collapse. Three padres were sitting solemnly around a piano, each with a glass of beer in his hand, each one looking very serious. They were singing: "Here's to the next one to die".

As is usual in any Service when operational air crews, or whatever they are, cannot risk their necks, out of the pigeon-holes and office crevices of Higher Authority comes red tape. So to us came the order to transform our squadron into a school. Every morning we had to attend three-hour lectures. We began to call ourselves the 83rd OTU.[1] There were lectures on navigation, lectures on armament, lectures on meteorology — all stuff we knew years ago. There was a parade every morning at 8.30 and a roll call taken so that Flight-Commanders could be sure that all were present. Life was miserable, broken only by quick 48-hour leaves in which I

---

[1] Operational Training Unit.

managed to get over to Sheffield to see Eve, who was appearing there in her show.

About the end of January, when the snow was beginning to thaw and the waters had run down the side of the aerodrome and had swamped the WAAF quarters, came a series of conflicting rumours. Both squadrons were to move north to Kinloss and Lossiemouth to hunt for submarines and to stand by in case of a chance to bomb German warships. At last the rumour became a fact and much preparation was made to go. I wangled with Willie Snaith to let Jackie Withers take the aeroplane up there, so that I could take a train to Glasgow and pay another quick visit to Eve, whose show had moved up there.

It was a rotten journey, and most people who have done a wartime night journey in a third-class compartment to Glasgow have nothing to boast about. The trains were not running to time by any means and I was forced on my way to Lossiemouth to stay the night in Perth.

At last I arrived at Lossiemouth. The boys met me in the golf club and told me that they had had a good trip up, but that all the aircraft were unserviceable because when they had taken off the slushy surface the ice had punctured all their flaps and they were now being repaired. It was a few days before we did anything.

Life at Lossiemouth was very pleasant. The Gulf Stream plays around the Moray Firth and it is warm and spring-like up there even in February. Day after day we would spend our time walking on the beaches, watching the fish come in the harbour and the queer gesticulations of the salesmen. Sometimes we would do a little flying. The Station-Commander and the Squadron-Leader Administrative Officer, whom we called the Brains Trust, had come up too, why I did not know, probably to do a bit of shooting.

As usual, rumours began to set in after we had been there a while, and the favourite one was that we were going to be there for the duration. Again the prospect seemed pleasant, for Scotland is certainly a very lovely place.

Day after day we practised formation flying and I am told that in the end the whole squadron got very good at it. But we nearly had some very serious accidents. One day we had to take off on the short run in a squadron take-off, and Willie Snaith told us to use full flap. This, of course, means full take-off flap, which is about 30 degrees. Old Pitcairn-Hill, my section leader, however, took Willie at his word and slammed his flaps right down. As it is the right thing to do to keep very close to the leader on take-off, Pit and I nearly came to grief. With his full flap he became airborne just over the hedge at about 60mph. As I was not airborne my wheels hit the hedge and we very nearly went for a burton. But the crowning achievement of all was our great antisubmarine patrol, led by Sam Threapleton. It was an unfortunate affair and was really no one's fault, but in the squadron records it is still written in as a black mark.

We were all standing by one day in the crew room when we were told to take off and fly to a point near Norway where a German ocean-going submarine was returning from an Atlantic cruise. We were told not to bomb any other submarines in the vicinity because they might be British submarines hunting the Nazi. Loaded up with special bombs, we were away. After a few hours a Very light shot up from Sam's aircraft and we knew that he had sighted something. Instantly Jackie Withers took up the cry. "Yes, there it is, there he is," he cried. "There's the submarine. It's a German all right." Instantly all aircraft with bomb doors wide open sailed into the attack. We were all bad shots and our bombs missed by a few feet and the submarine hurriedly crash-dived. Then we resumed our patrol. A little farther on we came across another submarine, but this time we gave it a wide berth; our orders had been not to bomb submarines in the vicinity because they might be British. Then we returned to base.

An Admiral was waiting for us when we landed and he was not in a good mood. In the operations room he told us in scathing terms that we had attacked His Majesty's submarine — and that it was only just our bad bomb aiming that had saved her crew. Then Sam began to go red in the face and we all realized that the second submarine which we had carefully avoided was the Atlantic raider. This sort of thing happens in all forms of aerial warfare and we all thanked God that we hadn't killed any of our own sailors.

There were many parties up at Lossiemouth and the local people were very kind in initiating us into such lovely Scotch drinks as Glen Grant Cream and Glenfiddich, but again we were getting bored. Often we would take off, go far into the North Sea to try to find something, but nothing was found. I have never seen so much sea in my life with so little in it. However, we were thankful for the good weather and at least we did get some hours in.

Fortunately an order came for us to return to Scampton just before we really got browned off, and it was a happy day for the whole crowd when our wheels finally touched good old Scampton mud on 19 March 1940.

When we went into the "Saracen's Head" that night none of the usual crowd was around. This was unusual, but we soon learned the reason. Next day the papers were full of the great raid made on Sylt by squadrons of Hampdens as a reprisal for the German raids on Scapa Flow and the Firth of Forth. This was not exactly a *débâcle*, but it was not a successful attack. The Germans said that no damage was done at all; they even took American journalists round to show them, but they did not show them the northern aeroplane base at Hornum, where most of the bombing took place. One fellow had the misfortune to drop two bombs on the

Danish island of Bornholm, but this was just sheer bad luck, as they were attacking from 2,000ft, and the searchlights from Hornum two miles away were blinding. Most of the pilots who took part in this raid, like ourselves, had never carried out an act of war, and their reports were highly illuminating. They found the flak very interesting and "pretty" and the searchlights very bright and everything very new. But they didn't hit the target . . .

The next weeks were spent in concentrated night-flying training. Off we would go over the snow-covered fields of England, map-reading our way from here to there at 2,000ft; sometimes we would lose our way, but with each practice we got better and better. It seemed now that Hampden squadrons were going to be used for night raiding only; they were too vulnerable in daylight.

At this time the Germans suddenly launched on England their new secret weapon, the magnetic mine. At first everyone was puzzled as to how this thing was laid so close into our channels and estuaries. The Navy was on guard well outside to prevent any high-speed motor launches carrying out their evil work, so it was presumed that the whole thing was done by sea-planes.

As most sea-planes took off from bases between Sylt and Borkum on the north-west coast of Germany, the Commander-in-Chief of Bomber Command instituted secret patrols whose job was to fly between these two islands all night long and drop a bomb on any flare-path light in the sea to keep these mine-laying sea-planes from taking off and landing. Strange as it may seem, these security patrols were very successful, and they did succeed in curtailing the work of sea-planes for the job. But by then the Hun had already modified his Heinkel 111 for the job and these aeroplanes were taking off from bases well inside Germany, and so nothing much could be done after the first few days.

When we had got fairly proficient at night flying we were despatched on a form of armed reconnaissance over Germany so that we could learn our way about over the Third Reich. I never carried out a leaflet raid myself, but many of our pilots were lucky enough to do so. I say lucky enough because I mean it. The first raid over enemy territory is always the worst, and a leaflet raid was a pretty good way of breaking the ice to show the type of procedure to be carried out on these raids. But everyone will always admit they were always a complete bind.

Meanwhile in the squadron Sam Threapleton had gone. We were sorry because he was a grand type; a good-living Yorkshireman who had a great sense of humour. But he was replaced by an even better type, S/L Dennis Field. Field was golf champion of the Air Force. He immediately got down to organizing his Flight in order to bring it into rivalry with our own. Spring was in the air, the squadron was fully trained, we had plenty of crews. It looked as though the war would soon get moving, and there was nothing for us to do but sit and wait. We were thankful for the respite we had had since September 3rd because then we were not ready, now in our limited way we were. We could fly at night; we could navigate fairly accurately; we could drop a bomb within half a mile from 12,000ft; we could even land on the beam. Yes, that respite had been very welcome and in a way we had made full use of it.

As the spring days passed we watched with pride the flowers we had planted in our garden grow up and bloom; we knew we had a few weeks to wait but we were ready.

CHAPTER
FOUR

The Fun Begins

April 9th dawned cold and clear. For some reason I was awake, and as I lay in bed, warm and comfortable, I listened to Bruce snoring in the next bed and pitied the girl he was to marry. I tried to look at my watch, but it was too dark and I cursed, remembering we had forgotten to pull up the anti-gas curtain the night before; that's the worst of having a late night. I had no idea of the time and settled myself down for a restful doze. Suddenly with a thump on the door and with a crash of tinkling teacups rattling in his shaky hand Crosby, my batman, came in to do his stuff.

"Good mornin', Sir; nice mornin'; but 'itler's on the move again. 'E's invaded Norway."

In a flash I was out of bed and shaking Bruce.

"They have done it, Bruce," I yelled. "Wake up, you old stooge."

Bruce was in a bad way and it took him some time to recover from his coma, but at last he came to. Then we got moving. In half an hour we had breakfasted and were saluting Oscar smartly in the Flight Office.

Much speculation went on to find out what we were going to do. Oscar as usual thought it was all a bluff.

"I can't see how he can get away with it." He seemed to be talking to himself, rather than to the other boys in the room. "The Navy have said they will sink every ship in the Skagerrak, both by submarine and surface craft. I cannot see Hitler's idea in provoking an action with far superior naval forces. After all, what have they got? At Kiel there's the *Scharnhorst* — that's in floating dock — and a few cruisers, then there's the *Gneisenau* and a pocket battleship at Hamburg. They haven't got a chance."

I am afraid I completely failed to see his point. I was thinking of his E-boats.

"I would have attacked France first," someone said.

"Me too."

We were all puzzled. Then the telephone rang. It was Willie. Impatiently we sat around listening to Oscar.

"Yes, Sir." "OK, Sir." "We are all ready, Sir." "How many, Sir?" "All right, I'll come up."

As he put down the 'phone there was a clamour of voices.

"Good show, chaps."

"Put me down, Oscar."

"You have got to include me."

"How many do they want?"

"Do you want a crack crew? If so, I'm all ready." This was Bruce shooting his line.

"Shut up, you crowd of beggars," cried Oscar. "If anyone's going, it's me. After that Gibbo and Rossy. Hang on the 'phone, Ian; I am going up to see the CO."

To say that we were all keen would be a masterpiece of understatement. For months we had hung around; for months we had waited for this. We had waited so long that we were all completely brassed off.

It was not unnatural, therefore, that the chance to fly on operations seemed, that day, to be the sweetest thing in the world. Quite a change from those bad nervous days in September.

For two days we waited, then we got the gen. Because we had done more night flying than other squadrons we were detailed, ours and 49, to carry out some very special missions. We were to drop our first magnetic mines in German coastal waters. While the winter months had dragged on, our scientists, the backroom boys, had not been idle. They developed a special weapon, weighing about 1,700lb, which was virtually sweep-proof. This weapon was to be known as a vegetable and was to be planted with great accuracy in special spots somewhere in the Skagerrak and Kattergat.

The plan was simple and at the time seemed good. Germany was trying to invade a country by sea. The ships and supplies she had collected together for the job were extremely hard to attack.

103

They moved at night, and our Navy was unable to operate in the Baltic waters. Although the port of Kiel was packed with ships laden with tanks, guns and troops, no bombing attack had yet been made which might harm civilian establishments. To get from Kiel to Oslo (which had already fallen) these ships had to pass through one of three well-marked channels. In the middle there was the Great Belt, over in the east there was a channel between Copenhagen and Malmö, and in the west there was the bottleneck channel at Middelfart. It was our job to mine these channels so thoroughly that we would, in the conventional tabled form:

(1) sink a large ship, thus blocking the channel;

(2) damage a great number, forcing them to return or go aground;

(3) drown a few thousand German troops (we hoped).

These mines, which contain a lot of explosives, could be dropped in fairly deep water, and even if the ship was some distance away the force of the explosive was such that it would always practically lift it out of the water.

The Norwegian Expeditionary Force was already in existence. By preventing German reinforcements from getting to southern Norway we hoped that our mines would play a large part in winning the Norwegian war.

Everyone was very optimistic. Many blatant articles appeared in newspapers, written by armchair warriors; bold statements were made by leading men, among them the famous "Hitler has missed the bus". And in America it was said that "the fox was now out of his lair and can now be caught". I do not blame anyone; we all thought the same. After all, we were a seafaring nation and our sea-power was being challenged. Someone had dared to put to sea under our Navy's nose — a blue nose, it is true — but a long one at that. Now we were going to show them who actually ruled the waves.

And so business did well in London bars and many a glass was raised to Hitler's great blunder. In the City stock prices were on the up and up.

On the 11th at about 7 o'clock off we went. Our orders were simple. We had to plant our mines in the middle channel at a dead reckoning position. After that we were to make a reconnaissance of Kiel Harbour to see how much shipping there was in that port, and also to check up at Middelfart and the amount of activity going on there at the railway sidings. Then we were to come home.

On no account were we to let our mines fall into the hands of the enemy. These were our secret weapons; we must not make Hitler a present of them, as he had to us. Special orders were issued to this effect. If we were unable to reach the right spot the mines were either to be brought back or jettisoned in deep water. If over land and something went wrong, we were to abandon ship so that it would crash in the right way and blow itself and its weapon to glory.

As we flew out I thought of these things. Pleased as Punch to be on ops., but hoping like hell that an engine wouldn't stop over land, as this meant abandoning ship, and that meant being a prisoner of war for the duration.

The trip itself was completely uneventful. We found the spot. We saw our mines gurgle into the black water. Then after we had made a quick reconnaissance at Kiel at a safe altitude (to find that low cloud blacked out all chance of a recco.) we went up to Middelfart, where we noted fiendish activity at the railway station and wished for a couple of bombs. While we were there we noticed that the best landmark for miles around was the bridge — a magnificent steel structure, rather like the Firth of Forth Bridge, but not so large. We noticed plenty of ice clinging to the banks in these April months and thought it must have been pretty cold down there on the ground. Then after eight hours we came home.

Now in a Hampden the pilot can't move out of his seat, so after eight hours I was feeling pretty cramped. Eight hours on your bottom is a long time, but worse was to come, nine, ten, even eleven hours at a stretch — an awful long time.

This prompts the obvious question, and to the curious I would say the answer is usually "No", but in an emergency, beer bottles or empty Very-light cases may be used. Sometimes a long rubber tube is utilized and this trails behind through a hole in the aircraft. However, ground crews who dislike their pilots have been known to tie a knot in this, with disastrous results, and most pilots usually avoid having anything to do with it. Anyway, I repeat to the curious that the answer is usually in the negative.

Two days later there was much excitement in the camp. Four ships full of troops were reported to have been sunk with all hands near where we had been gardening, i.e. planting vegetables. This was very satisfactory. Everyone was pleased. Our weapon was working.

On the 14th we were ordered to lay mines at Middelfart. It was a big effort, consisting of about forty bombers all told. The weather was going to be bad, so the Met man said. He explained that a warm front was moving westwards towards England at 15mph, bring with it cloud and rain. When we took off it was about 100 miles out to sea, and this meant that we would have to land elsewhere on return. It was instrument-flying all the way there, then came a patch of clear and we saw Denmark ahead. It did not take Jackie Withers long to pinpoint on the southern point of Sylt. Then we set course for the Bottle. As we buzzed along about 2,000ft above Denmark we ran into more low cloud. Although we were skimming the tops, its base must have been pretty well on the deck.

"You're sure we pin-pointed at Sylt?" I yelled at Jackie.

"That was Sylt all right; I saw the sea-planes."

"OK. I'll come down on ETA. Let me know when we start or about three minutes before if possible."

A little later Jack told me to start easing down. Gradually at about 300ft a minute the old Hampden slid into the murk. All the time came Jack's voice reading the altimeter.

"900ft; 500ft."

There was a silence for awhile, still we were going down; outside the swirling cloud, inside the soft glow of the instrument. It was getting darker and darker. I saw my altimeter and it was reading nearly zero. "Come on, Jack, what's the height?" I said, pressing the emergency intercom button. With a click his voice burst in,

"Sorry, my intercom plug came out. Christ, if my altimeter's reading right we're ruddy submarine!"

Quickly we levelled out. Then I saw the bridge. It was Middelfart Bridge all right, straight in front of us. There was nothing for it, no question of recklessness. If we went up we would be back in the clouds and completely lost, we could only stay low down. And so Mac, in the mid-upper position, was very surprised when he saw a bridge whistle over him.

Then:

"Bomb doors open. We're here."

"OK. Hold it."

"Steady, steady, not too soon."

"OK. Mines . . . GONE."

There was a slap and a clonk as the mines shot out, then a flakship opened out on us. We were only about 100ft, but soon we had pulled up into the cloud with A/C Tointon in the bottom rear position firing his guns like a man possessed at the invisible flakship. I didn't blame him; he had only come along as a passenger and he was getting his money's worth. These were the days when no air crews were NCOs. The jeeps[1] were AC1s and the gunners were AC2s. Both got the grand sum of sixpence extra a day flying pay. Most of the gunners, such as Tointon, had never even been to a gunnery school, but had picked up what they could in the squadron in their spare time.

Soon we were on our way home. I shall never forget that journey. It rained all the way and was pitch black. Now and again the aeroplane became charged with static electricity and resembled a poor edition of Piccadilly Circus in peacetime. We had been diverted to Manston and a south-westerly gale was glowing into our nose, making our ground speed a little under 100mph. After two hours we passed over the lights of Holland. Then another two hours were in front of us before we could see Manston. Most pilots when flying on instruments sometimes get the funny feeling that their instruments are giving false readings and they are quite certain that they are about to turn upside down any moment. After a while I was no exception

---

[1] Wireless Operator.

and I had repeatedly to shake my head, rather like a ballet-dancer does when coming out of a pirouette, in order to keep myself upright.

Then we were getting QDMs from Manston. Soon out of the low cloud and rain there suddenly came a green light, then another. It was Manston telling us to land, and we did not waste any time.

This trip took nine hours, mostly on instruments. No wonder I didn't wake up till four in the afternoon next day.

Sylvo did not come back. He had got his QDMs but had gone floating down the Channel into the Atlantic; they never found him.

In 49 Squadron two crews failed to return: both were married. I pitied the poor Adjutant, who had to break the news to their wives. Low, one of the Squadron-Leaders, had lost his way and crashed on the beaches near Newcastle, killing the rear-gunner. Taking things all round it had been a terrible night, and of all the aircraft despatched, Jack and I were the only ones to lay mines in the right spot. Naturally, we were pretty pleased with ourselves and the next night we sat up late patting ourselves on the back — ignorant idiots that we were.

While we were fighting our way around at night, other squadrons were doing their stuff by day. Hampdens from No. 5 Group flew long sorties up to Norway to seek out German ships; usually cruisers lying in fjords.

On one occasion two squadrons had stood by all day to take off and carry out a medium attack on the cruiser *Leipzig*, which was lying off Hilversund. Three times they were ordered off, three times they had been cancelled. Whoever were giving the orders, and they thought it was the Admiralty, were behaving like schoolboys.

Next day they were ordered off at 10 o'clock. Just as they were getting airborne a red Very light shot up from the watch office and those who were airborne had to land again overloaded with bombs as they were. This time it was, in fact, the Admiralty who had caused the delay. If some of the Admirals could have heard what the boys were saying, they would have scuttled themselves.

At last they all got away at about three in the afternoon. By the time they reached Norway it was dark in the fjords, the fog had come up, visibility was bad. After a fruitless search during which nothing was seen, they turned back.

Their Lordships were furious. Said A.V.M. (Bert) Harris, the Group Commander: "Order, counter-order, disorder . . ."

When, however, these Hampden squadrons were given their chance and did get to Norway in daylight it was pretty fierce slaughter. Their orders were to fly in a very tight box so as to bring as much defensive armament as possible to bear on oncoming fighters, but the Germans were no fools; they had found a weak spot in the Hampdens, for at that time there was a blind area on either side, and the Huns made the best of their knowledge.

One squadron, led by S/L Watts from Edinburgh, was "bounced" near Stavanger. Far out to sea was some cloud cover, but it was a long way away. He immediately did his best to get the whole squadron into a tight fighting formation by diving towards the deck. If he had been foolish enough to try to climb for the cloud he knew the whole squadron would have straggled and would have been picked off one by one. But the Germans were flying in Messerschmitt 110 fighters, which have one gun which can fire sideways. Their mode of attack was to fly in formation with the Hampdens perhaps 50 yards out and slightly to the front, and pick off the outside men with their one gun aiming with a no-deflection shot at the pilot. The bomber boys could do nothing about it; they just had to sit there and wait to be shot down. If they broke away they were immediately pounced on by three Messerschmitt 109s waiting in the background. If they stayed, the pilot received a machine-gun serenade in his face. One by one they were hacked down from the wing man inwards. Watts said it was a terrible sight to see them burst into flames at about 20ft, then cartwheel one wing into the cold sea. First B Beer went; that was poor old Peter.

Who was next? There was H Harry on the outside. The German gunner carefully took aim, then a few minutes later H Harry had disappeared beneath the flaming waves. That was poor old Charles.

One pilot made the hopeless gesture of pulling back his hood and firing his revolver at the enemy gunner, but it was no good, and his brave act was the last thing he did on this earth.

At last low cloud was reached and four out of the twelve managed to scrape home.

Poor old Watts. A few weeks later when returning from a raid on Hamburg he hit a balloon cable at Harwich and crashed into a grain elevator. His funeral pyre burnt for two days and two nights.

But despite their bad luck and despite the odds against them some squadrons met with success off Norway. For instance, Bud Malloy managed to hit a cruiser from about 10,000ft with a 500lb bomb. It burst into flames and reconnaissance later established that it had been sunk. I think this was the first time in its history the Royal Air Force had sunk a warship from 10,000ft.

I could write much about the bravery of these pioneers, many of them fine, experienced pilots who met their end so prematurely off the grim coast of Norway. The lessons they learned, despite the price they paid, proved very useful to the lucky ones who survived.

Meanwhile, the battle of Norway was not doing so well. Our troops up in the north were having to contend with nearly non-stop dive bombing. This made the landing of supplies almost impossible.

True, we had a few Gladiators out there on a frozen lake operating against the enemy, but they had to face the most awful series of setbacks which were nearly impossible to overcome.

They were just a group of keen pilots, fighting to the end, to the last aeroplane, and even when Hurricanes were flown off the *Glorious* to join battle with the Hun, it was no use; the Germans had complete and utter air superiority and there was no way out of it. Of these men also in the north I could write a lot, but it is not my job; my story must deal with the bombers of that time.

By the 19th it was obvious that Hitler had not missed anything. He may have missed the sea bus; he was certainly buying up return tickets on the airborne bus. All day long Junkers 52 transports were ferrying men and materials into southern Norway from aerodromes in northern Denmark. Sometimes as many as 200 transports were seen at any time on any one field.

Aalborg was one of these aerodromes.

Oscar, Rossy and I were detailed to carry out the first bombing attack of the war on this vulnerable target. It was the first time, in fact, that British aircraft had been detailed to attack an aerodrome. There was some doubt about our load. Some said all incendiaries; others plumped for 500-pounders. In the end we carried 30 by 40lb fragmentation bombs and one 250-pounder (for the hangar) and a few incendiaries (for luck). We were to attack from 1,000ft at dawn on the 20th, aiming at the aircraft on the ground and destroying as many as possible. I asked myself at the time why so few aircraft were detailed. Why not the whole squadron? There were plenty available. Then we could have done the thing properly, but I suppose the idea was to conserve losses and this bogey was to dog the Air Force for a couple of years to come. We were always to nibble at targets and never destroy them. No one knew exactly why, no one asked. Certainly not the boys; it was merely our job to carry out orders.

There was a Mess party on the night of the 19th, and I remember sitting with Rossy drinking lemonades, watching the other boys getting tight. I was glad when Oscar walked over to us and lit his pipe. "Let's go and get a meal," he said. "We will take off in two-minute intervals at 1 o'clock onwards."

It was about ten minutes to one when I climbed into C Charlie. It was a lousy night, rain pouring down and cloud about 300ft. When we turned on the intercom, only a high-pitched buzz came to our ears. The rain had leaked into it and had made it completely unserviceable. While I was swearing at Mac, who was trying to get it working, Oscar went off with a roar, followed by Rossy.

Mac did his best, but the water had done its worst, and we had to change to Jack Kynoch's aeroplane, which was the spare.

At about 2.15 we at last got airborne, all soaking wet; all browned off. We knew we were going to be late; we knew that the defences would be very hot when we got there, having been roused by the two

115

other boys. And to crown it all, Jack's aircraft was so stiff on the ailerons that I could hardly move them.

When we reached the Danish coast we set course for Aalborg. After a while we passed over a convoy. This was wrong; we should have been over land. Where the hell were we? Jackie didn't know — I certainly didn't.

"When's the ETA up, Jackie?"

"About another five minutes."

"OK, we will look around then."

Then we found we were over water. I do not know how it had happened; we had somewhere mistaken our pin-point, or perhaps there was another gale-head-wind which had slowed down our ground speed. We pushed on, hoping, not knowing quite what to do. Suddenly in the north, heralded by a bright fan-light glow of many colours, the sun came up in all its glory. We could now see we were over land, and, in fact, we could see everything — villages, farmhouses. We could see all we wanted — and more. Then Jackie's voice, slowly and carefully:

"I say, Guy, don't look now, but I think that's Copenhagen on the left."

"You're damn right, it's Copenhagen," I shouted.

Then we dived for the deck in a steep turn for home.

"We're miles off our course. How long will it be before we are over the sea?"

Jackie made a quick calculation.

"About an hour if you go flat out," he said.

What a spot to be in! All thought of bombing Aalborg was now completely out of the question. Here we were with about 200 miles of enemy territory to fly over, going along in broad daylight, all alone. If those boys in Norway hadn't much chance in formation our prospects were pretty small. A few farmers were kind to us; they waved, but that didn't do any good. One policeman was not so kind. I saw him pull out his revolver, take steady aim, but I think he must have missed. Our orders at that time were not to fire on anything in occupied territory in case we killed civilians. So we could do nothing about it.

We were flying very low and all the time our shadow flew beside us, dancing over the fields.

God did not mean us to die that day. Up came a fog-bank and we were safe. A few minutes earlier I had never been so scared in all my life. Now I had never been so relieved. Away out to sea we saw a Heinkel, but it had the legs on us and we couldn't catch it up. I think it must have been coming back from a shipping patrol. And four hours later we were circling Lossiemouth in Scotland.

Oscar had landed two hours before me. His attack had been successful. Rossy hadn't been too good. The flak gunners had been ready for him and gave him a tough reception at 800ft and he had got holed fairly badly. I was the failure and was furious with myself and everybody else, but when told that the compass in my aircraft had some 20 degrees deviation I quietened down. So that was the reason for our failure to keep on track. Then it wasn't Jack's fault. I went up and told him that I was sorry for swearing at him, and everyone was happy.

On my return to Scampton I asked Chiefy about the stiff controls and he found that one of the self sealing tanks had burst and was rubbing the control wires. Jack Kynoch had never noticed it, but without his strength I had found the going pretty difficult.

In the ante-room there was much joking at my expense, especially as we had been shooting a terrific line about our successful Middelfart sortie. Air Vice-Marshal Harris, who met us in the Mess, had a good laugh too. I was tempted to tell him about the compass, but it is said somewhere that a bad workman blames his tools. So we just sat there and took it.

The next night we went to Oslo Fjord to lay mines in the harbour. I had a pretty easy trip myself — but Joe Collier had to plant his vegetables within a few yards of a battleship and said that he didn't enjoy the experience very much. S/L Good, an Australian, was hit in the face and arms by cannon-shells fired at point-blank range, and owed his neck to his navigator's skill in pulling him out of his seat and taking over, an amazing feat carried out at 50ft at night while being blinded by searchlights.

Poor old Crappie Kitson had some trouble, too. His pilot, Svenson, a New Zealander, flew right over the battleship and got a packet for his pains. Crappie got shot in the face and lost both his eyes, poor lad. He was so full of life I felt quite miserable when I heard about it. Of all the things to lose, your eyes.

Oslo was a pretty hot spot all right. Apart from these instances everyone who went in got hit in some place or another. Three failed to return and Johnnie Johnstone crashed in England on the way home, killing the whole crew, including his second pilot, Taffy Vagg, the Welshman. Poor old Johnnie was married. I knew him and his wife very well. Next day it was a sad sight to see her, eyes rather red, collecting his kit from the Mess. These poor wives who live near bomber aerodromes undergo a continual strain. All day long they wait, knowing deep in their hearts that one day they will get the bad news, and when it comes they behave like thoroughbreds. I could write a lot about the wives, and perhaps I will before I have finished.

By now, the end of April, it was obvious that it was all over in Norway. We had begun to evacuate Trondheim. It had been found that it was just not possible to land supplies in the continuous bombardment. Our troops had had to retreat and now they were clearing out, poor lads. I pitied the PBI. They fight all wars, and have to win them, unless they go under. There can always be the air. There can always be the sea. But only the infantry can conquer territory, and only the infantry can evacuate territory at great loss of prestige and great loss of life.

In the beginning of May we made one more mine-laying sortie; the last for some time. This time it was Copenhagen, which as Snaith said, "Gibbo ought to know very well." This time Jackie excelled himself and we made the trip in six and a half hours. It was dawn when we came in; neither of us felt tired and we opened a bottle of beer to celebrate our success. After a while in walked Oscar.

"They are all back except Pitcairn. Nothing has been heard."

Old Pitcairn was very popular in the squadron not only because he was a sportsman, but because he was as white as a man can be, and we all sat around waiting for news. An hour passed, then two hours. Then, hesitatingly, from the east came the dull drone of an aeroplane making heavy going. It was a Hampden all right, a speck in the distance getting nearer and nearer. Then we saw that it had its wheels down, then we could read the letters. Yes — B-O-L — That was Pit all right.

"Good show, chaps," said Oscar. "Now we can go and have some bacon and eggs."

Later Pit told his story. When he arrived at Copenhagen he found that he could not open his bomb doors and after trying many taps in his cockpit he had pulled the wrong one. He had pulled the emergency undercarriage bottle, which not only blows all the hydraulic oil out of the aircraft, but also forces down the wheels. Then he found that he had done it. He had pulled his ladder right up. It was getting light at Copenhagen. He could not raise his wheels and he could not open his bomb doors, and worst of all he still had his mines on board, and so was very heavily laden. He had turned his nose for home, making an air speed of only 120mph. He had flown across Denmark in broad daylight and many Huns had come up to have a look at him, but seeing that his wheels were down, they had sheered off, thinking, no doubt, that he was one of their own. The journey across the sea had taken five hours. Poor old Pit, no wonder he didn't see the joke.

CHAPTER
FIVE

Balloon Cables and Bottles

Crosby was a funny type. For two years he had been my batman and had never put a foot wrong. He never even got browned off when I used to swear at him on certain occasions. He was a tall man with a slight deformity which screwed his head permanently on to one side. Born and bred in Lincolnshire, he had little if any sense of humour. Ever since the beginning of the war he had taken it upon himself to give me the news with the morning cup of tea, and so at 9 o'clock on May 10th, when his voice roused me, I was not a bit surprised to hear that Germany had invaded Holland. Reaching across my bed I turned on the radio and heard the full story. How our troops were rushing forward to save Belgium; how the Maginot Line was invulnerable and how at last the tank had come into its own. But the military commentator pointed out that no matter how far a tank advances it must always run out of fuel some time or, on the other hand, it may advance so far that it will be cut off from its main sources and can then be dealt with easily. He warned the public not to worry too much should a bulge develop in our lines; this was a case of enemy fighting behind enemy and both sides were running great risks.

The news quickly brought everyone to their toes. Nobody knew quite what to believe, as there had been so much wishful thinking during the Norwegian *débâcle*. And so everyone was prepared for the worst. All leave was cancelled and we had to be ready to take off at half-an-hour's notice.

It was three days before anything happened and then we got our orders. Some of the boys were detailed to attack Hitler's oil reserves well behind the lines. Myself and three others were given special missions which involved the Kiel Canal.

As we sat in the crew room we were told of the importance of the plan, how we might block all traffic if we were successful in doing our job thoroughly. We were also told the uncomfortable news that there were balloon cables every 300m all along the Canal, and that all bridges were very heavily defended with light cannon and flak. It looked like being a sticky target, and long were the faces of Oscar, Joe, Pit and myself as we smoked our last cigarettes. Suddenly Oscar began to write something on the back of a cigarette packet. It did not take him long, then he handed it to Harris, the Adjutant, an elderly man with grey hair, who had fought in the last war. "I want this will read in the Mess," Oscar said quietly, "if I don't come back.

You will do it, won't you?" There was an uncomfortable silence. I stubbed out my cigarette. Then we went into the night.

That trip was lousy. None of us got there and we all brought our bombs back. The weather was the trouble. Low cloud had been on the hills all the way and made it quite impossible to find a tree, let alone a canal.

Next day Pit and I volunteered to go again and this time we were lucky. It wasn't a tough trip at all and we completed our job in a highly successful manner, but in those days there was no such thing as constant aerial reconnaissance, and whatever good we had done will never be known till after the war. Anyway, despite all this we were all pretty pleased with ourselves, and the whole of A Flight went into Nottingham to get plastered at the "Black Boy".

Meanwhile things were not going too well in the battle of France. In Holland German troops were quickly overrunning the country. Parachute troops, dressed as nuns and Hula girls, it was said, came floating down into the fields and captured anything they saw. In France the bulge had developed. German armoured forces sweeping round like a cow-catcher were pushing miles behind our rear lines. They had attacked across the Forest of Ardennes and had driven the French back from the Meuse and the great fort of Sedan, which had collapsed under heavy dive-bomber attack. Their aircraft had complete air superiority in all directions. It was said that the French General Staff were asking Great Britain for more fighter aircraft, but we were loath to let our Metropolitan Air Force go — a wise decision, as things turned out.

We home-based bomber-boys had watched with a certain amount of trepidation the fate of our poor old Fairey Battles and Blenheims out in France. We had seen them hacked down one by one regardless of individual skill and bravery. There was the case of the Maastricht Bridge which young Garland dive-bombed with his Fairey Battle, earning a VC. This was a very gallant attack even though he perished in the attempt; but his soul must have shuddered when he saw the crack German engineers put up a pontoon bridge alongside his objective within a few hours. No, the thought of sending us to France did not appeal one bit, and apparently someone had some sense because they realized that we just did not have the necessary air superiority. And so our job was to fly out at night using the darkness to escape from fighters and using our night-flying skill to bomb accurately. This policy at the time seemed all wrong to armchair critics, but time has justified it. Those grim days and nights were the playing-fields of Eton to the would-be night-flying pilot. We learned the hard way, but we learned everything.

While the Dutch Commander-in-Chief was telling his Army to lay down their arms and to surrender to the Germans: while the battle of the Meuse was getting rather too far south for everyone's liking, the Air Force was not idle. Fighter Command Squadrons, of which the most famous were numbers 1 and 73, which included Cobber Kane and Co., were meeting fearful odds, but were acquitting themselves very well, shooting down four enemy for the loss of every one of their own. Coastal Command Ansons and Hudsons were watching the U-boats in the North Sea and elsewhere, and Bomber Command were getting down to the first big raids of the war. The objectives were the oil-tanks in the docks at Hamburg. None of us who sat around listening to the briefing ever dreamt that almost exactly three years later this city was to be destroyed by the same weapon, the bomb.

Snaith was speaking.

"Your target is the west side of the oil refinery at A.3, here on the map. Your bomb load will be 4 × 500lb bombs — fused instantaneous, and you will carry full petrol. You can attack at any height from which the target is visible, but remember the moon is in the south-west, so the best direction for attack would be to come in from the north-east side of Hamburg so that you can see the reflection of the water in the dockyards. Again I must warn you that on no account are you to bomb towns or villages indiscriminately. Only this target may be attacked tonight. If you cannot find it you must bring your bombs back. That is about all. You can fly to the target whichever route you wish and bomb at any time between 1200 hours and 0400 hours. Any questions?"

There was silence. Then he went on: "The Navigation Officer has got the maps ready, so you can all get down to working out your routes." He paused for a second. I think he wanted to go himself, but at that time Wing-Commanders' flying times were strictly limited. Then he smiled shyly and wished us good luck.

In came the Station-Commander and all crews jumped to their feet. Having told us to sit down he then described how we were going to help the situation in France by destroying Hitler's oil. There was no doubt that the offensive in Belgium was using up vast and prodigious quantities of this valuable fuel, and by bombing his supplies in the rear we would directly interfere with operations at the front. Such was the plan.

As Jackie and I wanted to get to a movie at Lincoln that night we decided to take off late. Our plan was to attack between three and four in the morning. We reckoned it would be getting light then and the glow in the north, coupled with the light of the moon, would make target identification very easy.

For a long time Jackie and I had been perfecting a dive-bombing attack in a Hampden. This consisted of a 60-degree dive from 6,000ft, pulling out at 2,000ft. We had found that we could get great accuracy and we also hoped that we would be quite immune from flak and searchlights. The only snag we had encountered so far, such was the speed we would get up in the final pull out, was that often the glass nose of the old Hampden would collapse, much to the embarrassment of the bomb-aimer.

The movie, *Babes in Arms*, was terrible, and neither Jackie nor I were in the right mood for it. When we got back we found most of the boys had gone; they all obviously had dates the next night.

Not long afterwards we were groping our way in the mist on the aerodrome, trying to find the flare-path. Then with a screech of brakes and the roar of the engines, old Admiral Foo-Bang, having first swung to the left in her usual style, lumbered into the air.

It was a clear night, and two hours later, above the hollow noise of the Pegasus engines, came Jack's voice.

"What height are we?"

"About 8,000ft."

"We are a bit low for oxygen, but I didn't bring my tube, anyway."

"Nor did I." This was Mac.

"Nor me," said Watty, the rear-gunner, making his first trip. Flying-Officer Watson was a newly commissioned armament NCO who had just joined the squadron as a volunteer air crew. He was a cool fellow but keen as mustard to do his bit against the enemy, and a very likeable chap.

"That's all right, chaps. We are not an oxygen crew," I called to them. We were proud of our crew and proud that A Flight were known as the low-level kings in the squadron. In most squadrons in those days there were always chaps who were willing to risk their necks and go in from a height from which they couldn't miss, and there was always the other crowd who used to stay high in the sky and drop their bombs at anything they thought they could see. Needless to say there was great rivalry between the two sides and many hot arguments ensued, but they all ended in the rash statement that the low-flying merchants would buy it, while the high-flying boys would live again to do another raid, a statement which has not been borne out by fact. To be successful, bomber pilots have to have a large amount of skill and dash; that is, if they wish to survive, and if they want to do any good work. This doesn't mean sitting up high, thinking one is safe, and of the bacon and eggs four hours later. Nor does it mean risking the crew's life unnecessarily. What it does mean is to try to get the bombs on to the target in the most expeditious way. Such was our creed at the time, and it hasn't altered very much.

Then we saw Hamburg for the first time. At first we thought it was another moon in the wrong place, just a small red sphere lying on the ground. When we got closer we could see the docks. Then we could see the town, a great sprawling mass spread for miles around, and at the northern end of our target we could see that one oil-tank was on fire. That was all, just one oil-tank; but the smoke reflecting the flames in many directions probably helped to magnify the damage. (This may have been the reason why most crews claimed the destruction of

129

the target, while the German radio said no damage was done.) This was the great snag in night bombing, and it was only when daily photographic reconnaissance came along that we were able to know exactly what we had done.

Anyway, the target looked to us to be well ablaze and great whoops of joy came from the front position. There were a lot of searchlights about clumsily fingering the sky, and there was plenty of flak being shot up in a sort of elongated cone directly over the docks. We had de-synchronized our engines to that unmelodious "Rhoom-rhoom" noise which we were told rendered searchlights ineffective, but all it did really was to cause unnecessary vibration on board.

There was more light flak here than I had ever seen in my life. Light flak is a pretty sight, curling gracefully up towards you, getting faster and faster as it comes until it goes by with a loud whistling hiss and a roar to explode a few hundred yards farther on. It makes a funny noise when it does that, a sort of "Bok-bok" noise. Each shell has a different colour and they are usually in the same order, and so they come chasing towards you — green, white, red — rather like a waterfall upside down. Yes, pretty to watch, even harmless, but if they hit you there is a noise like a crash of thunder; a rending of metal and then the tinkling crash of broken glass. Everything becomes bright red as your tanks go up, and your stomach suddenly feels hollow, then you begin falling faster and faster. You try to get out, but the wind keeps you in. You yell to your crew to bale out and all the time the light flak is still pouring into you. Then it is all over and you hit the ground. Petrol flames come soaring up into the sky almost ready to meet you as though to rocket your soul to heaven. Then all is silent save a dull red fire on the ground. Soon one of your boys will come along and bomb your fire, thinking it another military objective. Such are the thoughts that pass through your mind as you see the tracers curling up, and I for one quickly banked the other way.

But poor old Robbo of B Flight (P. L. Roberts, New Zealand) was not banking at all, when I last saw him, and he went down like a blazing fire-cracker. You have to keep moving the whole time when there is light flak around.

At last we were in a position about 1 mile north-east of the tanks and at about 6,000ft high. Down below I saw Peter Ward-Hunt of 49 Squadron going in at about 2,000ft and getting hell for it, but he got away all right. At the same time some other fellow was getting a few sundry shells lobbed up with him at some 15,000ft or so.

At last just underneath the port engine I could see the oil-tanks clearly. Yes, only one was on fire; the rest looked like silver golf balls in the moonlight. Then down went the left wing and we were wheeling into our dive. Down went the nose and immediately the altimeter began to whizz round backwards as the air-speed indicator began moving forward to hit a new high.

131

In the front Jack sat there all set, waiting for the order to release the bombs in a stick (these were the days when we had no automatic stick droppers but the bomb-aimer did it by pulling a thing like a cheese-cutter). I was watching the golf balls getting larger and larger in my windscreen. Watty was wondering when his hatch would blow off, and in the top Mac was wondering what it was all about. At last: "Bombs gone," I screamed at Jack. "Bombs gone." Later: "Did you see anything, Watty?" "Not a thing; I don't think they fell off." "They must have."

"No, they're still on!" This was Jackie. "I can see them."

When I had finished saying some very rude words about the hardworking electricians we began to climb up again. With a load on this was a long business, but we had to be quick because it was getting light. At last with engines red hot we reached 5,000ft. But when we got there we could not find our oil-tanks, as smoke from the fire had begun to blot them and everything else out. As we were circling round and round to avoid searchlights and flak I noticed a lot of balloons floating around above me — a not too pleasant sight. Suddenly on my right-hand side I saw what we wanted and dived straight for them. Because the dive was practically vertical we reached the phenomenal speed of 320 mph, and the pull-out was quite impossible, even though I put both feet on the panel, but she came out all right by using the tail-trimming tabs (which they say is very bad for an aeroplane), so quickly in fact that we all blacked out.

This time our bombs hit the mark and something burst in flames behind our tail. Then, because we had dived the wrong way, we were in the thick of it. Two thousand feet over the centre of Hamburg is not a healthy place. Flak was whistling all round us, making that aggressive "Bok-bok" noise. Then some broadbeam searchlights got us and we were completely blinded. Jack was saying, "Weave left, weave right," in front, but I knew he couldn't see a thing. I remember diving straight for a searchlight on the ground, firing my fixed Browning gun all the way down and yelling at the same time: "I'll get you, you bastard!" Then it went out and I hoped morbidly that I had killed the operator as well. I remember glancing to the right and seeing the starboard wing on fire. This was the end. We had better all bale out, and so I pressed the emergency "abandon aircraft" signal, but it wasn't working. Another look and I cursed myself for a fool. This was no fire, only a large piece of metal off the wing flapping in the light of an amber-coloured searchlight. I said to Jack, "I think we have been hit; she feels funny."

"You bet she feels funny, there's a few hundred yards of balloon cable on your wing," he answered.

He was exaggerating, of course, but we had hit a balloon cable and the "funniness" was caused by the damage to the rudders by flak.

At last we were out of it all, and save for the usual exchange of fire between ourselves and flak ships we reached the coast safely. It was good to see England down below in the early morning and someone said something about bacon and eggs in half-an-hour's time.

Sunny Scampton under Hugh Walmsley was a fine station. Everyone was very happy and everyone worked very hard, but the Station Commander had one bee in his bonnet. He did not like aerodrome lights; he hated them because he looked upon it as his own responsibility to prevent his station being bombed, and so instead of a flare-path for returning bombers, all we had to land on were two red lights, and this we had to do without breaking too many aircraft. On this particular morning it was foggy and we could not even see the tops of the hangars, so we were diverted to Abingdon, where we landed all in one piece, cursing the Station-Commander and his lights, and more than hungry for the bacon and eggs we had visualized two hours earlier.

Many boys had been well shot up on this raid, others had been wounded, but considering it was the first of its kind it had been successful. Most of them had gone in low to achieve their aim in the highest traditions of the Air Force. On the other hand, one Squadron-Leader had bombed from 16,000ft, and by excellent bomb-aiming was responsible for the fires which led us to the target. He was awarded the DFC.

And so ended a typical early 1940 raid on Germany. I have described it in full to show how different were the raids to come. These early raids were haphazard. We could choose our own route; we could bomb from any old height; sometimes we could carry whatever load we wished; we could go off at any time. We were individuals, but to tell the honest truth we were not very efficient, and out of the total tonnage of bombs carried to A.3 that night I would say that the actual amount which fell on the target might have been at the most 10 per cent.

A few nights later we went again to this place, but cloud was down to 500ft — below the safety height for bombing. Oscar was the only one to go below and his rear-gunner reported an oil-tank rise in the air behind his tail and well above him. Poor Dennis Field, I think, tried to do the same but didn't come back. He was a grand type. I spoke to his wife, Joan, next day in the Mess. She had been collecting his things, packing them to take home. I remember she couldn't find his movie-camera, and at last found it in his flying locker in B Flight Office. Joan was very brave, but then they all are.

The next few days there was a lull in operations; this was strictly enforced by the weather and nothing to do with tactical necessity.

Things were going badly in Belgium and France, but over in England fog came up regularly, as if by the will of God to cover our fields and to prevent us operating. But the Huns, in their limited way, began to roam around England bent on mischief. One formation of twelve Dornier 17's crossed the coast of Yorkshire at Withernsea and swarmed inland to the big bomber base near Morpeth. This was a fine station built on the same lines as Scampton, but the Dorniers did their work well. They knocked down all the four hangars and destroyed every other large building, including the Officers' Mess, the workshops and the airmen's cookhouse. The only thing they missed was the Sergeants' Mess, and this because they had no bombs left. They must have been pleased with themselves, this squadron. So pleased, in fact, that they, no doubt thinking our fighters were busy in the south, came back next day to give their undivided attention to the Sergeants' Mess, but this time the fighter boys were ready. Although the Sergeants' Mess was damaged, not one of the Dorniers reached Germany to report the fact. They were all shot down far out to sea. A few survivors were picked up by our armed trawlers, the crews of which were constantly asked the question, "Where did those fighters come from? We thought they were all in France."

As usual during these lulls we made the best of our time by going in to Lincoln. In that city is a pub of some notoriety, with a bar which some call the small bar and others the "Snake-Pit". In this den used to sit (they don't now, they've all been called up) young girls who spent their time with foolish young officers, tempting them, getting drinks off them; sometimes necking in the back of a car with them. We used to call them "amorous amateurs", but few of our boys would have anything to do with them, mainly because we were in good health and wished to remain so. One officer, whose name I shall not mention, however, felt different, and leaving our party went over and asked a thin blonde girl to have a beer. After a while, during which we noticed he was in earnest conversation with her, it was evident that all was not running as smoothly as usual. Suddenly there was an explosive, "Give me back my bloody beer," and he came strolling back towards us with his can and her half-drunk glass in his hands, while she rose and stormed out of the bar.

"What on earth's wrong?" someone asked.

"She won't play," said the young Romeo, drinking up his two cans.

"God, you're a dirty old —," growled Oscar. "Come on, Gibbo, drive us up to the 'George' — we can drink there until after hours and Jackie can hit the keys."

The night was pitch black outside, the moon had not yet come up. Driving with masked head lamps was no joke, as I had found out before. But this time I was seeing two white lines which disappeared when I closed one eye, a tricky and embarrassing situation. In the end I took off my masks and we shot off at an alarming rate towards the "George". The boys crowded into the back, singing bawdy songs. A policeman on lonely duty along the Wragby road must have been rather startled about that time when he saw a car shoot by, to the tune of "Whip her knickers away", and to the light of two, as they must have looked to him, searchlights. He immediately 'phoned the next man on duty along the road.

While this was going on, I was carefully keeping to the left of the second white line, while Oscar was yelling, "Faster, faster," in my car. Suddenly we came across a red light slowly waving from side to side in the middle of the road. The car wasn't taxed or insured; I knew that. I was also stinking; I knew that, too. I was also broke; everyone knew that, and so there was nothing for it. I stepped on the gas; how we missed the law I do not know. I remember his lamp going one way and his legs the other. Then we were a long way past and I switched off all lights and glided slowly into a by-road. There was dead silence; the boys knew how to play when the time came and no one said a word. We hardly dared to breathe, feeling like a submarine which has penetrated into Hamburg Harbour before daybreak.

For a full fifteen minutes we waited: then one by one we crossed the fields to the "George". The rest of the boys had arrived by then and there was a rip-roaring party going on when we came in. Later on in the evening I had the pleasure of buying a drink for a het-up country policeman who told me that he had nearly been knocked down by a drunken farmer coming back from Lincoln's market-day!

Although we had done nothing much at night for three or four days, during the day there had been some activity going on. Jackie, Dickie Bunker and Bill Tweddell had all taken on crews of their own to fill up the gaps caused by our own losses. This meant I was without a navigator, but Watty the rear-gunner said that he had done some in the year dot, and so I gave him his trial by stooging around in an Anson. He soon picked up the art of map-reading and it did not take him long to learn the rudiments of flying, so that he could take over in case I caught a packet. In all we put in fifteen hours in two days, which was quite a feat, especially as Watty was a man of about thirty, long past the age of learning things quickly.

On the last day of the lull I 'phoned Eve to come up and meet the boys, as there wouldn't be any flying that night. As is usual on all these occasions, things went wrong, and I was "dicing with death" the night she arrived, but my friend Ian stepped into the gap, and after they had watched me in old Admiral Foo-Bang take off with a lurch into the night sky, they went and had some dinner together.

The next few nights we alternated between Düsseldorf and the "George", Mannerheim and Petwood, Kiel (where we started some good fires — the best, in fact, I had seen) and Lincoln. You can't burn a candle both ends, and I was no exception. By the end of the month I was worn out, and Willie Snaith gave me a week's leave. The night before I went Harris, the Adjutant, came up and told me I had got the DFC, together with Oscar, Rossy, Bill and Dickie. This was good news and worth waiting for. There were smiles all round. Quickly I 'phoned Eve to lay on a big party at the "Snake-Pit." All the boys were to be there; it would be terrific.

Of the party I shall say little except that it was a good one; of the next day I shall say less. Bruce woke me up at about 9 o'clock.

"Good news about the boys," he said cattishly.

"What boys?" I was sleepy; I didn't understand.

"Oscar and Co. They've got the DFC."

I nearly asked him about mine, but instead reached for a paper. Yes, he was right. They had all got it except me.

I went to Brighton with Eve, disgusted that I had bought so many rounds the night before for nothing.

CHAPTER
SIX

Maximum Effort

Brighton was peaceful. In fact, just the same as it ever was — pretty girls with short skirts blowing in the sea breeze were still walking along the front, eyeing each man they passed with that well-known "I-don't-first-time-but-I-like-boys" look. Little dark-haired maids with the same black stockings with holes in the heels, and stained pinafores, were still serving tea in cosy but small restaurants by the sea. The boarding-houses were open, the beaches were packed. It was hard to realize that 100 miles away there was being enacted a grim drama, the one-act play of Dunkirk. Only the presence of soldiers and the barbed wire reminded one of the war.

My leave passed quickly, as lazy leaves do. All day long I lay on the beach with Eve and another girl, Doreen, who was in the same show. *Come Out to Play* was having its pre-London trial, and Jessie Matthews, the star, was pretty busy flapping around getting everything on the top line. I hadn't met many stage folk before, but I must say that, taking things all round, I got on very well with them, especially in the evenings when the bars opened.

On my last night I picked up Eve and a few other girls at the stage door and we were walking along the promenade when suddenly an air-raid warning sounded. A bomb dropped in the distance, one or two guns fired into the night and a parachute flare lit up the headland. And so we all went into the "Grand" to have a drink until the flap had died down. As usual in these places the lounge was congested with people. They had all congregated to listen to the 9 o'clock news. As we were standing there an Army officer came forward slowly, staring, his light blue eyes fixed on me like a madman. At first I thought he was drunk and prepared myself for just another row with one of those "brown jobs". But this poor chap wasn't drunk. He had had it. He had just come off Dunkirk that morning, after spending four days on the beaches, and was in as big a state of nerves as any man I have ever seen.

His lips began moving and at last he mouthed these words. It was the first time I had heard them, but not the last.

"Where was the RAF at Dunkirk?"

"I don't know; weren't they there?" I answered foolishly.

"They were — the Heinkels and the Messerschmitts, but not our fighters. I only saw one Spitfire in four days."

"Perhaps they were fighting the enemy elsewhere," I said.

"No, they weren't. We were bombed every hour. It was absolute hell. Bomb after bomb rained around us and we couldn't do a thing about it."

I let him ramble on; sometimes his voice got louder, sometimes died away. Now and then he stopped. He was almost talking to himself.

Suddenly the wireless pips sounded and Bruce Belfrage began reading the news. But still this man mumbled on, completely unaware that he was causing a slight disturbance. At last an old man who looked of foreign extraction got up and took the officer by the arm. "Do you mind if we listen to the news?" he said suavely, conscious of the fact that he had a sympathetic audience. The Army man blinked and seemed hurt. He couldn't quite understand what was going on. Now I had seen some sights in my time, but this one made my blood boil, and having gathered some Dutch courage from a couple of high-balls, this was enough for me.

I switched off the radio quickly and the room suddenly became very silent. Then I swung round on the old man. "Listen, you stupid old bastard," I said softly, though every man and woman in the bar could hear. "Do you realize that while you are here sitting on your fat behind, eating the fat of the land, there are a few men fighting for your plump neck? Do you realise that at this very minute the bomber boys are risking their skins trying to delay Hitler's advance, and far out to sea convoys manned by the Merchant Navy and guarded by His Majesty's ships are bringing in your food, and only 100 miles away over there an army, our British Army, is trying to get itself out of a mess caused by old men like you? Perhaps you don't realize that you're talking to a man who has just come away. He has probably seen things that you will never see in your lifetime, and you just want to sit there, thinking you are completely safe, and listen to the news."

After making this long speech, or something like it, I was completely stymied for anything else to say. So I gave him a dirty look and ended up weakly: "I think, sir, you are a complete bum."

Then I went out into the dusk, and as I went I heard the Army type still muttering: "Where was the RAF at Dunkirk?"

Next day I said a loving goodbye to Eve. She thought it was the last time she would ever see me; there were tears and for a moment I felt awful. But then the train started up and we puffed our way out of the station.

I was glad to be going back, for this seemed to be the wrong time to be on leave. The enemy would soon be only a few miles from our shores. Perhaps within a month he would be invading us. Then it would be a case of every man doing his utmost. And as we passed Grantham I began to feel quite happy.

The boys were sitting in the rest room when I arrived; some looked terribly tired because they had just done three nights running. Nevertheless, there was the usual chorus of rude greetings as I came in. The tension was there though, and Jack Kynoch and Sergeant Ollason both looked as if they could do with a week's rest. But who were we to grumble? Our job was easy compared with that of the Navy, who for nearly a week, backed up by volunteers, had fetched a large proportion of our battered Army back to England. And how about those fighter squadrons of the Air Component and the Metropolitan Air Force who had been flying sortie after sortie during the hours of daylight in order to maintain air superiority over the Channel? No sleep for them, just time to have a cup of coffee and perhaps a bit to eat while their aircraft were being refuelled and re-armed, and then up once again into the blue.

Suddenly I noticed two familiar faces missing. "Where's Ian and Greenie?" I asked.

"Missing two days ago," someone answered.

"What on?"

"Low level: Aachen."

"Hell! How did poor old Dell take it?"

"Damn well — the Adj. told her."

"Poor old Ian."

"Yeah; bad show."

"Yeah."

Suddenly Oscar came in breezily. "Hello, Gibbo. Heard the news?" he asked. He was always pleased to see someone back from leave.

"No, but I've heard enough. What's new?"

"Churchill has been speaking in the House of Commons. He says we have rescued 335,000 men from the beaches. I reckon that's pretty good when they only expected to rescue about 20,000."

There were murmurs of approval all round.

"What's he think of King Leopold?" asked Jackie.

"Thinks he's a bad type. He didn't say so, but said there is no reason why we should not form our own opinions on his surrender."

"That might mean anything. That's political language."

"Well, I think he's put up a black, anyway. He asked us to go in to save his country at the last moment. If he had had any sense he would have been in with us at the beginning." This was Tony.

"The Army are saying the RAF had its finger in over Dunkirk. What did Churchill say about that?" asked Ollason, changing the subject.

"He says it's all rot, the fighter boys were fighting like hell miles away. What better targets could there have been for the German bombers than the ships at Dunkirk? And what a mess they would have made if they had been let loose amongst them."

"I suppose a lot of bombers did get through," I said. "I met a chap at Brighton who said he saw nothing else."

"Well, that's pretty natural," Oscar pointed out. "When the boys had to refuel, they had to fly a long way back to their bases. In any case, they were out-numbered three to one, and so it is quite natural that a few bombers slipped through."

"Well, the Army are pretty browned off about it," said Bill, who had just woken up and was lighting his pipe. "I came up from Salisbury yesterday, and the chaps down there say it isn't safe to go into a

146

pub unless in convoys of two or three. The brown jobs are beating up anything in blue they can see."

"Oh, you can't blame them; they have had a hell of a time. They have been thrown out of Norway, kicked out of France. Where next?"

"God knows."

"First thing to do is to get a foothold somewhere."

"Yes."

"Oh, they've had a pretty tough break all right," said Oscar. "Being thrown out a second time is bad enough, but I honestly cannot see what went wrong."

Most flying fellows like to be armchair strategists, and Oscar was no exception. Getting out his cigarette case he began to expound his views.

"Norway was just a case of too many aircraft on the other side. We didn't have enough bases close enough to Norway to even protect our troops, but this time I think we had enough but didn't use them all in close support of our army. Like ourselves."

"But we would have been hacked down like flies," I pointed out.

"Well, we could have been protected by our Metropolitan fighter strength."

"Then the Luftwaffe would have bombed London flat."

"Maybe you're right," Oscar went on. He loved arguing. "Let's say we could have done this with more close-support aircraft but didn't have them available. After all, the shortage of aircraft and the right type of aircraft dates back to Swinton days. But to go back to the land forces. In the first case, if those petty neutrals had come in with us right at the beginning, the situation might have been different."

"That goes for Norway, too," said Bill.

"It will go for all neutrals forever," said Oscar, lighting his cigarette. "Then there was another snag. As soon as Germany invaded Belgium our armies rushed in to do their bit. However, they were too late to consolidate their lines of supply and the Germans were too quick for them. When the Jerries took Sedan and crossed the Meuse only a retreat right back to Amiens could have saved the situation. However, Weygand thought he could hold on and close the gap, but this type of blitz warfare was new to most of our commanders and strong point after strong point fell by the combined use of dive-bomber and tank. Moreover, the French soldiers, or some of them at least, surrendered on the slightest provocation. Then came the kick in the stomach when King Leopold surrendered and left us a gap of 30 miles along the coast to defend.

"I suppose there was nothing for it, we just had to fall back; in fact, right back to Dunkirk, having lost a good deal of our allied strength. I believe seventeen French Divisions went for a Burton, and of course the whole of the Belgian Army, and I think about 30,000 of our own. Taking things all round I think it was a complete débâcle."

"It was certainly that; but what's going to happen now?"

"Oh, I don't know. The French may hold out in the north until we can get a new army over."

"Perhaps, but it's not going to be an easy job."

"Churchill says we have lost all our equipment."

There was a long silence. We often used to have discussions about the war; this was one of them now. Someone was thinking of something good to say.

Then the door opened and Willie walked in. There was a scuffle as we all scrambled to our feet.

"Sit down, chaps." He was in a good mood. "Any of you fellows any good at billiards or other games of skill?" he asked, as he stood there, eyebrows raised. No one said anything; we weren't quite sure what he meant.

"I want two volunteers," Willie went on. Then he pointed to Pit and me. "You and you."

I groaned. What game could this be? I wanted to get cracking in the air, not playing billiards for some country fête.

Up in his office Willie took the lid off a small plasticine model. It was a miniature railway tunnel. He was serious now and began talking quickly.

"Your job tonight is to try out a new experiment that Air Vice-Marshall Harris has thought out. As you know, things have gone badly in France, and it is his idea to hold up the enemy attack by concentrating on severing his railway communications; the roads we are leaving to the day boys. As you know, the most vulnerable points of railways to attack are bridges and tunnels. The former are very

149

hard to hit, but the latter resolve themselves into a simpler problem. Just now I asked whether you played billiards. Well, actually, I meant snooker, and what I want is just that. I want a couple of fellows who will drop their bombs so that they roll into the tunnels and explode a few seconds afterwards. This, of course, will block the railway for quite a few days and in turn might have quite an effect on the amount of supplies the Germans can get through. There will be many applications to this game," he ended, "but I leave them to you to find out. Take-off will be at ten tonight."

No sooner had we left than a great smile lit up Pit's face. No snooker player himself, this was a game after his own heart.

We took off together and flew off across the sea, past smouldering Rotterdam on the left, across Belgium and badly blacked-out Brussels and on into Germany.

In fact, everywhere we noticed that the blackout was fairly bad and people were waving to us with torches. Away on the left an aircraft was being coned by searchlights at about 13,000 and being shot to hell by heavy flak. For some reason it had its bottom identification light on, and later we heard that this was some fellow in A Flight who had forgotten to turn it out after taking off. No wonder he told the boys, "You'd think I was the only aircraft in the sky . . ."

By map-reading carefully from canal to canal we at last came to our tunnel near Aachen. By now the

150

moon had gone down, so I released a flare. Like striking a match in the dark to see the way so suddenly we saw our tunnel clear and sharp in the yellow light. There was no time to waste, as these flares only burn for about three minutes, and so we dived into the attack. Down the railway lines we went like a high-speed train, and I noticed almost subconsciously that the signals were up. Then, when the cliff face seemed to be towering high above us, we pulled right up and at the same time let go a couple of 500-pounders. A few seconds later, during which we saw trees miss our wing-tip by inches, there came a welcome roar and turning round we saw the entrance to the tunnel had collapsed. This was fine and we still had two bombs on board. When we came to our next tunnel, about 10 miles farther on, we encountered a snag. The other reconnaissance flare would not fall off. This was terrible. It was too dark to see without one. If the armourers had heard even a quarter of what we said in that aircraft in the next few minutes, even they would have been embarrassed.

In the end Watty and I hit upon a plan. We flew down on to the railway line as low as possible and then I turned on my landing light, which lit up the permanent way enough for me to see the sleepers rush by. At the same time Watty held the Aldis light straight forward, acting as a spotlight waiting for the tunnel to loom up in its light. All the while the cliff face drew nearer and nearer at 200mph. For a few minutes we flew like this, watching the shiny surface of the railway lines, while I prayed there would be no night-fighters about. While we were flying along like a Brock's Benefit, some lonely soul opened up with a machine-gun nearby, but must have been squinting because it went about half a mile behind.

Then — "Here comes the tunnel. Bombs . . . bombs gone."

On the word "gone" I slammed the throttles forward and remember seeing the tunnel spotlighted in our Aldis lamp before I yanked back the stick. The old Hampden, relieved of her bombs, went up like an elevator, and we just cleared a 400ft cliff by a few feet. I remember this well because it was a white cliff with a chalk face, and we could see it quite clearly; eleven seconds later came that pleasant muffled crump, showing that we had reached our mark.

When we landed Pit had a better story to tell. He had been back an hour before and had had an even easier time, and in my opinion had done a much better job. When he found his tunnel he had noticed a train steaming into it. Full of cunning, he had quickly flown round the other end and by careful aiming had sealed it up: then he dashed back to the end the train had entered and had sealed down that entrance too. What a chap! Especially for a son of a Scottish Presbyterian minister!

There is an entry in my log book which reads: "June 13, 1940 — Hampden L.4070 — Pilot: self and crew — duty: bombing Ghent and England (nearly) — time: 7.15 hours."

This was one of those occasions when you nearly put your foot in it, but not quite. We were returning from a mission which involved the bombing of a German military headquarters at Ghent at dawn. Usually in these cases we used to set course from a target in a south-westerly direction, so as to arrive over Unoccupied France in daylight when there wouldn't be any air opposition. Often on these trips you could see the confusion of the refugees packing the roads, trudging their lonely way towards the south coast. When we had arrived at a safe spot in this unoccupied area we would then set course direct to England.

On this occasion, however, we arrived a little early and Watty thought he could make it direct with the hours of darkness available. So we set course straight to base, i.e. north-west. Soon we ran into low cloud and after a while passed over a concentration of heavy guns and searchlights. We thought that this must have been Dunkirk, and we then turned due west. As daylight came we got closer and closer to the ground, every eye looking in all directions for enemy fighters. We thought we were still over France, and there was still no sign of the French coast coming up. When it was quite light we began to distrust our compass and turned north-west, steering as far as we could judge by the sun. By now we were flying right down amongst the trees, everyone on board completely scared stiff. Suddenly an aerodrome loomed up in front, and I opened my bomb doors in desperation. If I was to

153

be forced down amongst the Hun the last thing I could do whilst still flying was to bomb a hangar, and we still had one bomb left. Just as my finger was playing with the button I thought I recognized the field. Yes, no doubt about it now. This was Harwell and this was England. I slammed the bomb doors shut and quickly turned on to a new course. After an hour we arrived at base to find that we were exactly three hours overdue. Most people thought that we had had it.

One Whitley pilot though wasn't so lucky and put up a real black. He did the same as I had nearly done, only this time he actually did let go a stick right across an English aerodrome. No sooner had he done this than both engines failed for lack of fuel. Quickly he slid his giant aircraft into a cabbage field and then proceeded to set fire to it, as one does on these occasions. When it was burning nicely he hid himself and his crew in a barn nearby, hoping to make a dash for the open country when night fell. Suddenly a Royal Air Force staff car drove up and out stepped a Group-Captain. Having watched the progress of the crew with binoculars from a control tower nearby, he had gone straight to the barn . . . I am told that the heat of the language from that wooden shack was only equalled by the heat of the blazing Whitley a few yards away.

The Germans, too, were quite good at this sort of thing. One crew, obviously not the very best types, got lost during one of their "armed reconnaissance" patrols. At last they came to South Wales and in the

154

moonlight saw the silver glow of the Bristol Channel to the south.

"*Ach*," said the navigator. "Good — English Channel."

The pilot turned south and after a while they came to more land.

Said the navigator again: "Good — France at last."

But he was wrong — this was North Devon. By now it had got light and they were getting low in their fuel supply, so they landed at the first airfield they saw.

And so, a tired Army gunner nearly asleep in his sandbags must have been rather surprised to see, at about ten past six in the morning, a Ju 88 make a perfect landing on No. 2 runway, then taxi up to the Watch Office. No doubt he immediately began to make out a report.

But the pilot was a stooge. Still thinking he was in France, he got out and walked to the control tower. Here an airman standing at the door failed to salute him, not being quite sure of the uniform and not certain of the rank. The pilot gave him a raspberry in German.

The airman was a keen movie-goer and suddenly realized. Out came his revolver and that was that. One more prisoner had been added to a long list.

Many stories such as this can be told, but must wait until after the war.

★ ★ ★

These were the days when we were working at maximum effort with very little sleep. It was a question of bombing as often as possible; as often as humans could possibly take the strain. And so the villages of Lincolnshire and East Anglia were kept awake all night long as the bomber boys roared off and returned from missions.

It was with regret that we watched dear old Willie Snaith leave us, this time for good. A new chap, Sisson, came along to take over the squadron. Sisson was a small, quiet man with a pleasant personality who did not say much. Meanwhile, the other squadron had also got a new CO called Gillan. It was Gillan who, in 1938, flew a 335mph Hurricane down from Scotland at the average speed of 408mph. For this he earned the eternal name of Downwind Gillan. He was a forceful personality and for sheer contrast the two were as different as chalk from cheese.

Each day while we were doing our best to delay the Germans' advance, Crosby would wake me at the usual time whether I had been up all night or not. That cup of tea was always welcome, but his voice got more and more doleful every day, his face longer and longer. Each day it was the same, there was no variation. He was pessimism personified.

On the 10th. "Italy's in, Sir. Shall I order breakfast, Sir?"

On the 12th. "Rouen has fallen, Sir. Do you want your best uniform?"

On the 14th. "Paris is out, Sir. You look a bit tired this morning, Sir." And so on.

Doleful days. Bad and black days. England had never sunk so low, and yet in some ways she had never risen to such a fine height, for it seemed that soon this little country would be alone defending the world against Nazi tyranny.

On the night of the 17th we listened to Churchill's broadcast to the people. Pétain had just sued for peace:

"The news from France is very bad, and I grieve for the gallant French people who have fallen into this terrible misfortune. Nothing will alter our feeling towards them or our faith that the genius of France will rise again. What has happened in France makes no difference to our actions and purpose. We have become the sole champions now in arms to defend the world cause. We shall do our best to be worthy of this high honour. We shall defend our island home and with the British Empire we shall fight on unconquerable until the curse of Hitler is lifted from the brows of mankind. We are sure that in the end all will come right."

Great words by a great man, prophetic words. But who could tell then that all would come right? It seemed practically impossible. It seemed that anything might happen.

To refer to a very different sort of personality we come to a large fat man, Hermann Goering, who had made millions of Reichsmarks by getting his fat fingers into such huge organizations as Krupps and

Linz. But Hermann was also, on the quiet, the proud owner of a small oil refinery near Hanover. In fact, it was his model refinery, not too large, not too small, but just right to bring in enough money to spend on his uniforms every year. It was said that the fat Marshal had built a canteen specially for his men with his name over the door in 9ft letters.

Naturally, this juicy target was not overlooked by the planners of Bomber Command, and one day in June it was with great pleasure that 83 Squadron received the order to destroy it.

We took off, well overloaded so as to do as much damage as possible, and three hours later clearly saw the target in the light of the nearly full moon. Rather like moths around a flame, we circled at 2,000ft, waiting for the right time. Walt Disney could not have created a better spectacle.

Pit started it off. We saw him running in, quite level, taking his time, and then his bombs crumped on to the foundry and sent what looked like molten metal spraying out in all directions. That started it all. The boys came romping in and soon the foundry area was one mass of bomb-bursts. One by one the buildings caught fire and glowed dull red like a smouldering charcoal fire 500 yards below us. But we waited, Watty and I. We had a plan. At last, when we thought that all the boys had bombed and gone home, we cut off our engines and glided towards the oil storage tanks. As yet no one had touched them, as these are not the most important part of an oil refinery, but what we wanted to see was a good blaze. When we were about 300ft high, Watty began to let go, trying, if possible, to put a separate bomb in each tank. Then, seconds later, there was a whoomph! and every tank blew up. The most wonderful sight that any man could ever hope to see, especially when you are responsible for it, and even more especially when they belong to Hermann Goering.

As I walked into the Intelligence Office later on in the morning, Oscar had just finished writing his report. I noticed he had put "Target destroyed", and this seemed queer, so I went up to him.

"What did you think of it, Oscar?" I asked.

"Damn fine blaze," unemotionally.

"But there wasn't a blaze when the boys left," I pointed out. "I know because I waited. We went for the oil-tanks."

"Well, what time did you bomb?" Oscar asked curiously.

"Twenty-five past one," I answered.

"So did I. And I went for those tanks, too."

Then I burst out laughing. So both of us had hit upon the same idea and we had both bombed at exactly the same time. It was lucky we hadn't both blown ourselves out of the sky. Three weeks later we heard from a reliable and secret source that Hermann Goering had moved his refinery far out to East Prussia.

Night after night it went on. Parties seemed things of the past, dreams of days gone by. All of us were averaging twenty sorties a month, and despite the fact that most of these were carried out at very low level the losses were not unduly high.

Nuisance raids on the Ruhr marshalling yards were the order of the day for a while, in order to delay German transport behind the lines, and as only about six aircraft were sent to each place the damage done by flak was considerable.

On one particular night Jack Kynoch, myself and Ross were sent to Soest; Oscar and three others to Gelsenkirchen, to try to destroy signal-boxes, which, after all, are the most vulnerable part of any railway. By flying with the hood open at about 500ft we at last got to the Ruhr River, turned left, found the Möhne Lake and, of course, 4 miles north lies Soest. We bombed from 600ft and nearly came to the end of a brief career there and then. There was much more flak than I thought possible in such a small place, and in a second I nearly had a baby as one shell took off the starboard wing tip, and then as we dived quickly for safety more shells pumped home, one severing both rudder cables. Getting out of the dive was quite a game without rudders, and why we did not hit a tall house standing at a crossroads I shall never know. Watty in the front said he thought I was cutting it a bit fine. This time I think perhaps he was right. The port engine had been hit and the oil pressure had dropped to 40lb per square inch. This meant if it failed, without rudders available, we would have to land at once. The trip home was a nightmare. Mac tapped out an SOS, the only one I have ever sent, so that should the engine seize we would be able to be "fixed" and perhaps they might be able to rescue us.

But all went well and we landed safely, our rudders still flapping uselessly behind.

Rossy and Kynoch had not been so lucky and had bombed alternative targets, but Oscar and the rest of the boys had done some good work at the other place, although they had paid the price and all their aircraft received many holes in odd places. Someone in B Flight had been so badly wounded that he had crashed while trying to land his aircraft and the whole lot had been killed.

Next night we went to another place on the Baltic coast called Wismar, where one of the big Dornier factories was situated, turning out seaplanes and bombers.

The Adjutant had just told me as I took off that I had been awarded the DFC, and I remember thinking at the time, this is a fine time to tell a chap a thing like that.

As it happened, the whole of our squadron reached and bombed the target, while not a soul in 49 Squadron found it. This was a great feather in our cap, but our rivalry was now disappearing with the coming of new faces.

The attack on Wismar was the same as all other targets, low level in the face of heavy light flak. My job, after I had bombed, was to beat up searchlights around the aerodrome. This was fine, and Mac shot out six, so he said, but when we got back both Pit's aircraft and mine had quite a few holes in them, and were both unserviceable for a week.

This was a memorable night, too, because there was a great argument in the briefing room when we got back as to who had started the only fire on the aerodrome. Sergeant Lister, one of the pilots, who had never started a fire before, kept on claiming it as his own, and on looking back I think he was right.

And so Aachen, Düren, Cassel, Amiens, and all the rest, and a few military objectives, such as aircraft factories, received half-a-dozen British bombers every night. Although the damage wasn't much, the strain on the crews was extraordinary, and some of the boys began to suffer from the first signs of over-strain and lack of sleep.

In the average Bomber Officers' Mess, what with batmen and waiters whistling, and banging doors, while penguins sing loudly in the mornings as they get up to shave, it was rather hard for the boys who had been up all night to get a good day's rest. To solve this problem and to try if possible to get the airmen amongst pleasant surroundings, a large country house had been requisitioned nearby: the idea being that the crews could sleep there and use it as a sort of club, while the officers were billeted in large country mansions all round the district.

It so happened, and not entirely by accident, that Oscar, Rossy, Jack, Tony and I were all billeted at a very nice old lady's whose name I shall not mention. She was tall and grey and psychic. She had a husband who was long since dead. Her house was one of the Lincolnshire paddock type with its own church and cemetery and acres of land; a fine rambling old place which had seen better days. I did not know what this lady's financial position was, but after a while I noticed she would be doing her own housework and that some of the chairs needed mending and that the carpets were frayed at the top of the stairs. Little things, I know, but whether I was wrong or not, I admired the spirit which enabled her to keep her home and her heritage going.

I am afraid we were not very good billettees; at least not very quiet ones. When we got back from a raid at night we were usually in very high spirits. Often we would make such a noise that we waked up the whole household. Often we played silly games in her garden, such as trying to plunge through the rhododendron bushes on bikes without hurting ourselves or rolling on the lawn in one great fighting mass cutting up all the grass, which must have broken her heart next day.

Soon I was to discover that this old lady was a firm believer in spirits and the occult. One night I sat up late with her talking about fear and faith and many other things until I had completely run out of conversation. I personally didn't have much to say on the subject, but she would ramble on for hours. In the end I stifled a yawn and went to bed, but not before she had confided in me that there were visible spirits in this very house, spirits which she knew by name and which visited her on occasion.

Having seen death hurled about in four dimensions, and not wishing to see the fifth, I grabbed my candle and went upstairs.

It was an old house with no electricity, so when I had blown out my candle and got into bed I lay awake thinking a long time about what she had said. At last the country air took effect and I went to sleep.

Suddenly, in the middle of the night, something woke me up. I did not know what it was and I didn't care, but feeling thirsty I lit my candle again and groped my way to the bathroom to get a glass of water. Now this was in the summer and it was a very hot night. On such occasions I sometimes sleep without pyjamas, and tonight was one of these occasions. As I was tripping my way back from the bathroom, quite unashamed in my nakedness, my candle blew out. I grabbed the banisters and gingerly began feeling my way back to the door. Suddenly, unmistakably, from the depths of the house came the gentle swelling music of an organ played softly.

I stood still. I was petrified. So these were the spirits. Then, as if someone had stuck a pin into my back, I made a dash for my room. I remember the first two steps — then, nothing, and I was falling head over heels into space.

When the noise subsided I realized I had fallen downstairs. Cursing, I began to crawl my way up. Suddenly at the top appeared a queer figure in a nightcap and old-fashioned nightgown. It was the old lady. A querulous voice broke the silence. "Is that you, John, is that you?" she called out. She was peering into the darkness down below.

By now rather ashamed of my lack of clothes, I at last managed to blurt out that it wasn't John and that it was me, and would she kindly leave the candle at the top of the stairs so that I could find my way to my room.

When I at last got back into bed again Jack and Tony came in. They had just come back from a late raid and both had had a few glasses of beer.

"Nice organ in that church," said Jack to Tony.

"Yeah, good organ that. I didn't know you played so well."

I nearly leaped at them. So it was they who had been playing the organ in the middle of the night in the old chapel. And to think that for a moment I had been scared!

Next night John, with a very large lump on his head, was bombing Lorient making great efforts to keep inside four dimensions and not to slip into the fifth.

CHAPTER
SEVEN

Sustained Effort

By the beginning of July most of the bomber crews were just about all in. Lack of sleep night after night has a cumulative effect, and soon tempers began to get frayed and quarrels were picked on the slightest provocation. Many of the boys, especially old Jack Kynoch, would use one of the finest old British traditions to the full; that is, grumbling about everything: the weather, the aeroplanes, the bomb load, even the war.

However, had we been more wide awake we would have realized that the change of policy in our bombing technique was slowly making itself felt in Bomber Command. Up to now we had done our best to support land operations indirectly by concentrated attacks on military objectives in the rear, but France was now going under. Military objectives could no longer aid actions being fought at the front, and slowly but surely we began to bomb Germany on an organized pattern; part of a long-term policy. These co-ordinated blows were to fit into a big jigsaw puzzle of an offensive which was not to last one year, nor even two, but perhaps four.

And so plans were changed. The Ministry of Economic Warfare had long consultations with the Chief of Bomber Command, and later orders were given out to Group-Commanders to hammer away at dockyards, at oil, at ships and at submarines. In these dark days this was our only offensive against Germany. Soon it was to become complementary to many others.

On July 5th the Pétain Government in Vichy broke off diplomatic relations with the British. No sooner had they done this than they laid the tortured, innocent people of France open to air attack as well. These men of Vichy, thinking no doubt that the days of Great Britain were numbered, were only too ready to flirt with their new German mistress. And so the factories of France began turning out goods in the shape of lorries, tanks and guns for the Reich.

One clear night in July, the skies of southern France reverberated with the din and heavy hum of many twin-engine bombers. I was in one of the leading aircraft and had been told to be extremely careful not to bomb French civilians. Our target was a lorry factory on the River Loire. As this was well away from any nearby town it seemed that we would be able to lay it flat without hurting anyone.

As we neared Nantes I saw the whole town lit up like peacetime. There was no question of blackout; they just weren't expecting us. And even later, on moving down the river some distance towards Lorient, we at last came to our factory, and here we

167

found the same thing. It was just one blaze of light. It was pleasant flying over a lit-up area so different from Germany and reminiscent of the good old days of peace.

After a time we circled until we were joined by the other aircraft. From about 2,000ft — which is, after all, only 700 yards — we could quite easily see people moving around the factory roads in the light of the arc lamps and wondered when they would begin to take to their shelters, because we could not possibly bomb them before they had gone down below. Someone dropped a bomb in the river to let them know there was a raid on and to try to hurry them away from their lathes and furnaces. Then it started. Panic reigned down below and for about twenty minutes one by one the lights of the factory began to go out. Someone even opened up with a machine-gun. It soon appeared that the place was quite empty. Then the boys proceeded to knock it flat.

On this occasion no one saw my own bomb-bursts, a sure sign that they fell in the river, and so old Watty, for the first time in his life, had under-shot.

On the way back we passed over St Malo. Only two years before I had spent a very nice holiday here, and I couldn't believe that we were now returning after such a mission. But it was lucky for the world that we were in a position to do these things.

The next night someone managed to get some flak down there, but whether it was manned by French Quislings or Nazis I do not know. Anyway, it was very inaccurate.

When this area had been heartily bombed, the boys moved further south to Bordeaux. Here an attack on the oil-tanks at low level by about twenty-four aircraft burnt for two weeks. Rightly had the rear-gunner of the leading aircraft claimed that the target had been destroyed. However, most pilots had been taught not to believe the rear-gunner, because usually he is over-enthusiastic. After all, the pilot is always responsible for the final report and has to put his signature to it.

I know of a good instance where a certain pilot put up quite a black by making this mistake. He was in my squadron (no names, no pack drill) and had been detailed to attack a factory near Strasbourg. It was a normal trip and everything went fine. There wasn't much flak and the bombing raid was made at extremely low level. As they turned away the rear-gunner reported flames and sparks up to 1,000ft and, of course, saw the tall chimney fall down. Next day when the pilot made his report out he merely wrote "Target obliterated" and strolled off to the Mess to have his morning can of beer. Later his CO sent for him while he was having his lunch. He was quite pleasant but a bit plaintive. "Look," he said. "I know you have a good record, but why on earth did you claim to have destroyed that target last night?" The pilot was incredulous, he did not quite understand what the CO meant. Then the CO went on: "You say that sparks and flames rose to 1,000ft, yet your Flight-Sergeant has just come in here and told me that you brought all your bombs back, except for a can of incendiaries."

This story has two morals: 1. Never shoot a line until you have made certain your bombs have dropped; and 2. Never believe the rear-gunner.

Another time, when attacking the *Scharnhorst*, which was lying in dry dock in Kiel harbour, Jack Kynoch bombed from 16,000ft. When he came back his rear-gunner reported two direct hits near the funnel, one near miss on the dry dock and one in the water. This rear-gunner must have had mighty good eyes, because we were trying at the same time to dive-bomb the thing with a 2,000lb armour-piercing bomb from 6,000ft, and each time we couldn't see a thing. In all we made six dives and on the last one that great bomb fell off too late and dropped into the middle of Kiel town. This, of course, may have killed some civilians, but it was purely an accident, as we had been told carefully to avoid the town.

One thing puzzled us that night. We had not hit any balloon cables and surely such an important harbour would be absolutely bristling with them. Two weeks later we found out why. A high-flying Blenheim brought back some good pictures of Kiel after our attack, indicating that there had been a gap in the balloon barrage about a quarter of a mile wide, and by sheer luck each time we dived we had gone through it. Why there should have been a gap no one ever knew. Perhaps least of all the Germans. The photographs also showed something else, that the *Scharnhorst* had been hit six times by small bombs. So perhaps that rear-gunner did have very good eyesight!

This sustained effort was very much easier than the other thing and everyone began to quieten down. We would fly one day and then have perhaps two days off. It was quite a pleasure to be able to go out to Lincoln again; perhaps get tight on the first night and rest on the second, ready for operations on the third. Mull, Rossy and I would often go to the celebrated Theatre Royal in Lincoln City, watch the first house of a road show, which was usually lousy, and then drink till 10 o'clock in the "Crown" afterwards. A pleasant way of spending an evening and not too hectic.

Life became quite orderly and we felt rather like businessmen who spend their days in a year doing regular things. At the same time tempers calmed down and nerves became normal, and everyone was quite happy once more.

Every night between 100 and 150 bombers would leave England bent on bombing missions over Germany. Their course would take them over separate areas far and wide, from Denmark to Southern France. For these were the days when raids were spread over a period of the whole night, so that the sirens would blow everywhere all night long, causing as much disruption to war production as possible. For instance, in the vast steel mills in the Ruhr, scared workmen would be forced to leave the furnaces; in time the crucibles would cool down, the steel would harden. It would take some time to drill it all out.

Enemy night-fighters were practically non-existent, or at least we thought so, because they had no method of detection. But, on the other hand, German flak was extremely heavy and very accurate; it ought to have been because they had been making guns for eight years. One of their favourite tricks was to put a box barrage just above you which would creep down on top, forcing you to get lower and lower until you were in range of the light flak guns, where the searchlights would grab you, and you would be very lucky if you got out without being hit several times. Even in those days their method of detection was very sensitive and often above the clouds. It was nothing to see a shell burst 100 yards away dead level past one of the wing-tips. But despite this night-bombing losses were very low, about 3.5 per cent. On the other hand, accuracy was very low, too, not many bombs actually reaching the target. So both sides were satisfied.

Therefore, for good or ill, every night when the weather was fine German sirens would wail in Hamburg, where the *Tirpitz* lay, in Wilhelmshaven, where the *Bismarck* was lurking, in Kiel, home of the *Scharnhorst* and *Gneisenau*, and in many cities from Aachen to Frankfurt.

On some occasions when conditions were ideal severe damage was done; other times, when cloud blocked all chance of getting a pin-point, probably no bombs dropped within miles of their objective. The Germans, too, were beginning to lay out dummy cities, with dummy factories burning furiously inside them. Often a very heavy weight of bombs would fall around these places, while the Germans fired anything but dummy flak at the bombardier. But sometimes, strange to say, these dummies helped. There was one near "X", a huge affair which looked almost too absurd for words; everything was set out in typical Hunnish fashion in straight lines and squares. The procedure here was simply to navigate to this place, which could be seen miles away, then, knowing that "X" was only 18 miles south-west, the rest was comparatively easy.

These trips to places inside Germany often meant spending a long time over enemy territory, especially in slow aircraft like Hampdens. Because we had no real navigation equipment, except sextants, which very few navigators knew how to use anyway, we would often stray off track and blunder over some enemy strong point and get heartily shot out of the sky for our pains. To overcome this snag many contrivances were devised, but the one which worked best of all was to carry the Luftwaffe emergency cartridge which signifies an aircraft in distress. Whenever their defences opened up we would fire one of these, and as soon as the red sparkling light left the aircraft in a gentle curve

173

every gun and every searchlight would immediately pack up. The layman would think that such a trick could only be used once, but we went on using it for months. I think the explanation of this was simply that at that time the Luftwaffe in Germany was all-powerful and the simple rather brow-beaten Reichswehr AA gunners lived in constant fear of shooting down one of their own planes.

And so, with that new-fangled device "George" flying the aeroplane all the way back from Mannerheim, it was quite pleasant to sit there and eat oranges while the rear-gunner periodically fired off one or two of these cartridges.

Towards the end of July word got around that a lot of Germany's armament reserves were being stored in scattered hangars in the Black Forest. A plan was accordingly set afoot to destroy these and other weapons and also Hitler's wood supply. Scientists put their heads together and soon the weapon was evolved. For some curious reason they named it a "razzle." It consisted of two square sheets of celluloid about 6in long, and in the middle, surrounded by damp cotton-wool, was placed a piece of phosphorus. The idea was a simple one; the razzle fell into a wood or on to dry grass, the cotton wool would take about fifteen minutes to dry, the phosphorus would begin to smoulder and set light to the celluloid, which would burn with a very fierce flame for about ten seconds. Naturally the art of dropping this was called "razzling."

These razzles were always carried supplementarily to the bomb load, and no special mission was ever planned which would involve razzling alone. Mostly the pilots were told to arrange their routes to a target so that they passed over a large portion of the Black Forest or other forests in Germany, when they could be dropped out at will. Large conflagrations were caused which burned for weeks on end, for the summer was particularly dry at that time. To my mind the idea was quite a success, but one pilot, so the spies told us, made a navigational error while flying above the cloud and dropped his razzles in the middle of Bremen. The citizens of that gay city, having received a few leaflets the night before, thought this was more British propaganda coming down from the skies; knowing full well that the Gestapo's eyes were everywhere watching their movements, they stealthily crept along the streets, picked up the razzles, stuck them in their trousers pockets and took them home to read . . . The results must have been embarrassing.

Oscar, Rossy and I were having a good laugh about this story one day sitting on the lawn of our baronial hall when Jack Kynoch turned up.

"Hullo, chaps. I have been posted."

"Where?" asked Rossy.

"Cottesmore."

This was an operational training unit.

"Who else?" Oscar asked.

"Only Sergeant Ollason and myself. I don't know why. I suppose I am being rested or something.

Well, I must rush off and pack now. Cheerio, chaps."

And with these words Jack went off on his bike to the main camp. "That's funny," said Oscar. "I hadn't thought of a rest. I thought we would go on forever."

"Me too."

"And I reckon I could go on forever, too," Oscar went on. "Anyway, I think I have got the answer to this night-bombing racket. As long as you keep alert the whole time and keep as far as possible out of defended areas, except over the target, there is no reason why you should not do a hundred trips. What do you think, Rossy?"

"I like high-level attacks," Rossy replied in his Australian dialect, "or else it must be the very low-level prang; but the main thing, without a doubt, is to keep right on the track."

"I agree," I said. "But, of course, it takes a lot to beat a dive-bombing attack for sheer safety; the only snag is that you have to rely on the rear-gunner to find out where the bombs went."

"That's OK," said Oscar, rudely; "they will always shoot a pretty good line for you."

Rossy laughed, probably thinking of the chap in B Flight who had bombed Strasbourg.

"But seriously," Oscar went on, "if you are really in the know in this game, there's sweet FA danger to the whole thing."

"Well, there's always the chance of a lucky hit."

"Yes, but it will have to be pretty lucky to hit me," said Oscar, lighting his pipe.

Just as he spoke a tremendous explosion came from the direction of Scampton, followed by a column of black smoke 3,000ft high.

"Christ, what on earth's that?"

"That wasn't an aircraft."

"Come on, let's see."

When we got up to Scampton we found all ground personnel emerging from their shelters. At first we thought they had been bombed, but later a calm WAAF in the operations room told us what had happened. Eighteen magnetic mines in the bomb dump had just blown up and she said that the stones were still falling five minutes afterwards. It was certainly the biggest explosion I had ever heard.

At this time Hemswell had just carried out an attack with twenty-four aircraft on a very special military objective on the Ems Canal. They pressed home their attack from very low level. The raid was a success in so far as it destroyed one bridge, but it was necessary to destroy the second one which carried the Dortmund Canal over the River Ems. This bridge, of course, is very vulnerable to air attack, and when Hemswell carried out the raid it was practically undefended. However, there was every indication that the Huns had now put in a few searchlights and plenty of light flak all round to see that the attack was not repeated. Scampton, being at the time the best Station in our bomber group, was, therefore, given the job of trying to destroy this important military objective.

Two teams, consisting of mixed crews from both squadrons, were selected; one team consisting of "Babe" Learoyd, Pitcairn-Hill, Joe, Oscar and Mull, and the other made up of five equally good pilots as a sort of second eleven.

Training was carried out on canals in Lincolnshire the same width as the bridge which we were going to attack. Plasticine models were made and careful study was made of the lie of the land around this objective. During one of the practices Mull and I changed aircraft at the last minute. I was fairly proud of Watty as a bomb-aimer and was glad to see that during our attack he dropped his bombs exactly in the right spot. At lunch later on it was a bit of a shock when the Armament Officer came up to me and told me I had dropped the bombs on the bank, and had narrowly missed blowing his foot off. This was Mull flying in my aeroplane.

And so we trained on in moonlight until both teams were highly proficient. At the beginning of August everything was ready. Learoyd made a reconnaissance and found that the defences were fairly hot. In his estimation the job had better be done soon or not at all.

As it happened I went on leave down to Cornwall just when everything was being prepared. On my birthday, August 12th, they set out. While I was drinking beers with the yokels in a pub down in Boscastle, Pitcairn, leading Learoyd, Mull, Rossy, and Matthews, was droning his way towards his objective.

Much has been written about this attack, but there is no doubt that it was a very gallant effort. Pitcairn went in first, dropped his bombs in the right spot and got shot up very, very badly by the light flak defences. Next came Rossy. He went in low, and the next they saw of him was a flaming mass on the ground. Poor old Rossy was killed. Then came Mull. His port engine was set on fire, but he managed to climb up to 2,000 and was able to bale the whole of his crew out. Then came Matthews, and he too bombed accurately, but had to return on one engine. Lastly came Learoyd; in the face of blinding searchlights his bomb-aimer managed to put his bombs in the right spot.

Next day photographs were taken of the objective. The raid had been a complete success; the bridges had been breached and all the water had flowed out of the canal. This must have been a serious impediment to Hitler's barge transport.

Learoyd was given the VC, Pitcairn the DSO, and when they found out that Mull was alive they gave him the DFC in his prison camp.

This raid was noteworthy because it was one of the first attacks of its kind during the war. A special attack trained for by crack crews; a completely successful attack planned by men who flew.

It was the first of many.

CHAPTER
EIGHT

Battle of the Barges

Down in Cornwall the air was good. Sitting back in my comfortable bed each morning I would look out of the window and try to realize that at that very moment the grimmest part of the Battle of Britain was being fought. Then we would go down and have breakfast and eat good food, and afterwards walk along the windswept cliffs, watching the pounding seas and trying to forget the thunder of enemy flak.

The papers rolled in about lunch time and each day I could read about the blitz on England which had just started. Everyone remembers those early days. How on August 8th Marshal Goering sent his vaunted Luftwaffe towards London, rather like an armada Napoleon would have given a fortune to control. There were hundreds of bombers flying wing-tip to wing-tip in close formation, covered by a few fighters; later a few bombers would make hit-and-run raids covered by hundreds of fighters.

But they were being driven back. Everyone knows how our aircraft industry produced our fighters and equipped them with a new constant-speed propeller which made all the difference to the actual fighting.

Everyone knows how our fighter boys went in. Standford Tuck, Douglas Bader, Shorty Lock and the rest of them, rallied their squadrons and went into the fight with their country at stake. They acquitted themselves well, these boys, and fought in the finest of all traditions with their backs to the wall. This battle, one of the most important ever fought, ended in a trouncing defeat for the Luftwaffe.

In the operations rooms great men watched the thin blue line slowly retreat, even as far as London, but it was never broken, and in the end it began advancing over the stratosphere towards Dover. We, like the infantrymen of old, had held the Hun and then threw them back over the other side of the Channel decimated and beaten, never to come back.

It was a great story, of which we should all be proud. Many speeches have been made about the boys concerned, many classic utterances published, such as Winston Churchill's — "Never in the history of human conflict have so many owed so much to so few". Songs were written and danced to in London night clubs to celebrate the victory, but let us pray, here and now, that those men will be remembered for ever; and especially in ten or twenty years' time.

While all this was going on I was slowly getting fit by sunbathing and even sometimes slipping into the cold Cornish sea, afterwards drinking quiet cans of beer with the locals in the Wellington Hotel at

Boscastle. I did not feel the same as I had at Dunkirk. This time I knew that reserves were fast coming in; I knew that if they needed me they would quickly let me know. This was the time to rest, and I made the most I could of the chance. But at last it was over, and at Bristol we stood on the station, Eve and I, saying goodbye. Many were doing the same all round us, young people saying pre-invasion goodbyes, holding each other close and looking into each other's eyes before going into the unknown. For we were not to know that the Luftwaffe had been completely defeated; we were quite ready for the invasion. All of us had heard grim stories of the Nazi occupation of France, how they ruthlessly achieved their objectives; how callous and cruel they were as conquerors. We all knew that if they set foot in England it would be the same, or worse.

At times like these one doesn't know quite what to say, and I am not very good, anyway, at saying these things, but I remember looking Eve straight in her shining eyes and holding her up to the railway carriage while the porter went running up and down the platform blowing his final whistle.

"Well, one thing, darling: if they invade Wales I will come straight down and take you away," I whispered, not quite knowing how I'd do it; "just send me a telegram and I will be there."

Then there was a shrill whistle, a clanging of doors, and we began to move. Eve faded out of sight, tears streaming down her face.

Back at Scampton the sun was still shining; it was still hot, but there was a difference. A great change had taken place, at least it seemed so to me, from the Scampton I knew two weeks before. Rossy and Mull had gone, and so had some of the other boys. Sergeant Ollason had gone to his OTU, Learoyd was running round as PA to Brooke-Popham, and even some of the WAAF officers had been posted. It was a funny, depressing feeling, coming back after such a glorious leave, and a horrible feeling when I found that I was on Ops that night.

But Oscar was there as usual when I went into the Flight Office. "Hello, Gibbo," he said. "We are all going to Lorient tonight, not much of a trip, just to lay mines off the U-boat basin; it ought to be pretty cissy because they have only got a couple of guns there."

"Thanks, Oscar. Are all my crew back?"

"Yeah, they are all here, but I'm having Watty — my navigator was hit the other night. You can have the new bloke, Sergeant Houghton."

"Well, thanks very much," I said, feeling damned annoyed, as Watty was such a good navigator and I had got used to him. But as it happened Houghton was very good and it was poor old Watty who was to be unlucky.

It was a simple trip, and although we were laying mines very close to the shore the flak did not bother us much, and the whole squadron did a good job of work. Afterwards we looked around for some E-boats which we were told were operating in that area. We turned out to sea and stooged around with our navigation lights on so as to lull all and sundry into believing us to be friendly aircraft. Suddenly, in the long silver reflection of the moon in the calm water we saw one going at a rate of knots for a small harbour in the Ile d'Eu; and Houghton pressed the button. However, at times like this, when bombing wasn't a highly organized affair, we weren't sure of our height and Houghton certainly wasn't sure of our level, and so the 2 × 250lb bombs fell within a few yards but did not hit him; whether we damaged him or not we couldn't say, but there was some happy chatter on board as we turned for home.

But even better was to come. As we crossed over Cherbourg on the way home an aircraft passed us going in the opposite direction with his navigation lights on. This must have been a Hun which had been bombing England. Quickly we whipped around and by pushing the old Hampden to the limit so that she shuddered and quivered at the unknown horse-power she was developing, we at last caught him up just near to Lorient. For a while we flew in formation, about 50 yards away, trying to make out what type of aircraft it was, but the night was dark. At last, through the welcome beam of an enemy searchlight, we identified it as a Dornier 17. Moreover, both pilots on board seemed very happy; they had their full cockpit lights on and we could see them inside sitting motionless as they, no doubt, thought of the ersatz coffee and bacon and eggs they were going to get in a few minutes' time.

184

In the rear both my bottom and top guns slid slowly over to the starboard side and I told Mac to take careful aim. Then I counted slowly.

"One — two — three," and then I yelled: "Let him have it, Mac."

There was a quick staccato roar as all four guns belched out tracers and the Dornier dived to the ground with one engine on fire. In doing so he flew low right over Lorient Docks, where his own flak, no doubt thinking he was one of ours, gave him a pretty good pasting, and the last we saw of him was a flaming mass going down behind some trees. Bomber Command credited us with a probable when we got home.

Next night, August 26th, came the first raid on Berlin. Great excitement was caused when the target was announced. We had been waiting for this for a long time. Now we were going to get our chance. Many pilots who had been given an off-night immediately began to plead to have themselves put down on the list of the first crews to bomb the German capital. Even Downwind Gillan took an aeroplane over from one of his youngest pilots in order to be one of the first over the big city. But whoever chose August 26th chose a night when as good a head wind as any faced our medium-range bombers.

The raid was in fact lousy. There was thick cloud over the target itself, and I don't suppose more than ten bombs actually landed in Berlin. On the way home the Germans, in their methodical way, had laid a line of flak which stretched in a straight line from Berlin to London and the going was very heavy. Many aircraft landed in the sea on the way home, and even in our own squadron we had three incidents. Tony Mills ran out of petrol off Flamborough Head and took to his dinghy with his crew, who were all violently seasick; Pitcairn-Hill, who was always doing things wrong but was always getting his bombs on the target, thought that he was going to be unable to make land and slid his Hampden into the sea opposite one of HM Trawlers 30 miles off Grimsby; a Canadian, called Pitt-Clayton, pulled off a dead-stick landing in the middle of an East Coast minefield and had to sit in his aeroplane for a long time, not daring to walk across the sand dunes himself in case he trod on one, while those on land watched him, not daring to walk out until a coastguard, who knew a channel, drove up and rescued them.

As soon as I landed I got my aircraft refuelled and took off to look for Tony. We were in the air six hours, but never saw a thing. When we finally landed back at Scampton I was annoyed to hear that he had been picked up a long time ago, having seen me pass over him twice, and was at the moment having a party with the boys in Grimsby.

Some nights later Joe Collier undershot when landing and crashed, giving himself very severe concussion. The next night Dickie Bunker crashed in a field near Norwich and split his skull open. Gradually our numbers were dwindling, and out of the great bunch of boys who had started to fight a war against Germany, only Pitcairn, Oscar and I were left.

Meanwhile in Hamburg harbour, where there is always a busy hum of activity from the shipbuilding yards, sat the *Tirpitz,* a great battleship of some 45,000 tons, having the last fittings put on before she was to sail out on the high seas to challenge the British Fleet. Many heads in the Admiralty were put together to think out some method off disabling her before she made her first sortie.

Our capital ship situation was not good at the time and the war in the Mediterranean had seriously embarrassed our strategy. Someone had heard of our dive-bombing attacks, and on our off-nights it fell to some other boys and myself to take off early in the morning and make a dawn dive-bombing attack on the *Tirpitz* and return in time for breakfast.

Usually we would split up, some going to Wilhelmshaven, where the *Bismarck* was lying, and others to happy Hamburg. But these attacks were never much good, and owing to the fact that the bomb never fell off when we pushed the button it was lucky if we ever put one within half a mile of the dock she was lying in.

As we flew above the clouds in these early mornings over the cold North Sea, it seemed to me that the very anvil tops of the cumulus storm-clouds were all pointing the way to Germany, as if to say,

187

"That is the way; that is the way to Germany, and you won't come back." Now and then a flash of lightning would make me jump vertically in my seat as at the same time I went into a vertical turn with Mac shouting: "Flak, flak," in the background. I was getting nervy, there was no doubt about it; this bombing was beginning to get me down.

Sometimes over a German city we would make a half-hearted attack, knowing well in our hearts that we had not done our best. Even when back in bed I could not sleep, but used to lie awake at night tossing and turning, thinking of the noise of the engines and that bok-bok noise which was always in my cars. And when I did dream it was always slow-motion dreams of balloon cables, thick ones, like tree-trunks, which I would get past by landing my aircraft in the middle of Hamburg and cutting them down with an axe, then flying home as if nothing had happened.

In the middle of one night Gibby, a B Flight rear-gunner, came into my room when I was having one of these nightmares. Although I don't remember anything about it, he told me afterwards that I yelled at him to get out at the top of my voice for about five minutes, and he thought I was a raving lunatic. If ever there was such a thing as a war of nerves, then some of us in 83 Squadron were certainly beginning to get affected.

Meanwhile, although everything wasn't going dead according to plan for the Hun, he hadn't been exactly defeated in the air. No doubt Goering thought that in a few weeks' time we would come to our last reserves, and then Hitler could establish his headquarters in Buckingham Palace and the Marshal himself could take over the Savoy Hotel. In other words, the plans for the invasion of England were still on.

All the military strategists in Germany knew very well that the first thing on the programme was to obtain complete and absolute air superiority over the Channel ports. Then it would be possible to launch an invasion force, consisting of many thousands of 2,000-ton barges which would sail across one dark night, covered on either side by submarines, minesweepers and E-boats. Then, with the dawn of a September morning, unload under cover of air superiority. Once the bridgehead had been established, airfields would be improvised on the beaches and in the fields, consisting of wire-netting strips, and these no doubt would ensure the forward air support for the Invasion Force.

Marshal Rundstedt, who commanded the Invasion Force, must have known that our Home Guard had not yet been equipped and that our Army was being reorganized and rebuilt. Like Napoleon, Hitler came all the way from Paris one sunny day to gaze at the white cliffs of Dover with powerful binoculars and survey his next victim.

By the beginning of September unusual activity was noticed on the canals in Germany. Barges of all kinds began to make their way to most of the invasion ports; many of these were ocean-going barges with 200-horse-power engines, capable of ploughing through the seas at 10 knots. They were laden with high explosives, tanks, field- and anti-aircraft artillery; troops stood by in the dockyards, waiting for the order to set sail. Everything was ready. Every port from Antwerp to Dieppe was packed like lumber floating in a river with thousands of these invasion barges. The Huns knew, of course, that our meagre bomber force would attack them. Light flak guns were brought from far and wide to put up a cordon of steel which would ensure that no bombs could be dropped within miles; flak towers were erected, balloon barrages were put up.

At the beginning of September the Battle of the Barges began. It went on day and night, Blenheims, Hampdens, Wellingtons all taking part in low-level attacks which not only destroyed many barges on the spot, but also killed many troops whose billets were in the warehouses nearby.

On one of these raids on Antwerp I flew for a while alongside an aeroplane which was on fire. It was a nasty sight because I could see it was one of our own. As flames and sparks came out like the wrong end of a rocket hanging in the air, I saw one chap bale out and land in the river, and I remember hoping that he could swim.

When we got back I asked young O'Connor, a Canadian boy, what sort of a trip he had had. He did not say much except that he had caught fire over the target and had got hell from the light flak. Later, I heard that Hannah, of our squadron, had been awarded the VC for his attempt to stamp out the flames with his bare hands.

Two nights later we went again to Antwerp, and this city, with its heavy flak defences, shot down one of the few left. I saw him flying straight and level over one of the basins; taking his time about his run, making sure that all his bombs went into the right spot. Then he blew up — and Pitcairn-Hill had gone to join his forefathers.

These raids on the invasion ports were organized to destroy as many barges as possible. Each squadron was given a port which was to be considered its own particular port and the pet baby of all concerned; each crew was given a basin; in each basin there were so many barges, sometimes 200, sometimes even 400. Bomb-loads were organized so that the maximum amount of damage would be done per aircraft. Many small bombs were carried, even hand-grenades, which would, at least, do the job if they hit the right spot.

After each raid a reconnaissance was made, and the CO would call all crews together. "I have got some pictures of C Basin at Antwerp. Yesterday there were 400 barges there; to-day's reconnaissance shows 350. Who is on C Basin?"

Some pilot would shuffle to his feet.

"Well, you sank fifty, you and the rest, but that is not enough. You have got to put all your bombs in that basin, not a stick starting on the edge and then doing its job, but every single bomb. Otherwise those bastards over there are going to come and invade us, and then you will have to fight with your bare hands."

Then we would go off again. Of course, sometimes this didn't work very well. In my particular basin — a thing shaped rather like a heart in the middle of Antwerp dockyards — I once gained 100 barges, and neither the CO nor anyone else could tell me that I was responsible for them. Taking things all round, we were sinking them fast despite all the anti-aircraft fire they could put up against us. But our losses were heavy and we all knew that we would have to win the Battle of the Barges before they started to move out. There were rumours that they actually had moved out and that we had sunk them. There were rumours that thousands of German soldiers were buried on the east coast of England; soldiers who had been hit by Bomber Command, who had been drowned and washed ashore. These rumours were untrue, and no one in this country will ever know anyone who saw a dead German soldier, although many a man will claim to know someone who knows someone else who buried one.

On September 15th the fighter boys pulled off their greatest victory. They shot down no fewer than 185 German aircraft for quite a small loss of their own, and no doubt after the war it will be known that the number destroyed was far greater.[1] It was the victory of superior fire-power, of superior aircraft, of superior men.

On that night we made our biggest raid on Antwerp. It was the night of the full moon; many barges were sunk, many blew up, destroying others around them. They were full of stuff and we could see, there and then, there was no doubt about it, the Germans were ready.

Flying low around these docks that night we could easily see the tanks on board, the guns on mountings at the stern of each invasion craft, the tarpaulins over sinister objects on the docks. "Der Tag" was drawing near for the Hun, and September 15th was, perhaps, the day when they realized that it would be no use.

From now on we stepped up our trips to maximum effort and all our nerves seemed to vanish in the heat of the battle. It reminded us, perhaps, of those dark days in June. On September 17th we heard on the wireless Mr. Churchill's report on the war situation in the House of Commons. The Italian Army had begun to advance in Libya, the two British platoons which had been holding Sollum had been withdrawn, but the enemy had still to reach our main line of resistance. He went on to warn us all that invasion might come at any moment.

---

[1] Publisher's note: The true figure proved to be considerably less.

Many will remember a few days after this a great invasion scare which swept the country. This may have been caused by one lonely Coastal Command pilot on his moonlight patrol over the North Sea who made a slight error of observation. He was flying some 100 miles out from England, when glancing down he saw to his amazement many dark shadows moving on the sea. There were a few clouds above him, small clouds, but he did not notice these and immediately wirelessed back that the invasion was on.

Immediately everyone stood by. Fighter boys were aroused from their beds for a day's hard fighting, bomber pilots stood by till dawn, and it was only a subsequent reconnaissance by a more experienced pilot which revealed that the "barges" in the sea were merely shadows of the small clouds reflecting on the water.

After the flap had died down there were a few sardonic laughs in the Mess, but we knew it would come some day, and although we thought we were ready, we were not quite so sure about the rest of the country.

A few days later the AOC decided to give the squadron an extra night off duty. I was scared stiff that I would have to go on one of those lonely dawn missions to Hamburg to do a bit of divebombing, but luckily this did not happen. Jack Withers and I took ourselves to a quiet "flick" in Lincoln because we knew that we would probably be on next afternoon. But Oscar, Tony Mills and a newcomer called Barker, whom we nicknamed "Colonel" for obvious reasons, took themselves to Nottingham, where the story is that they got very drunk.

Next day we were on again for a large raid on Antwerp. As I was walking across the hangar, having fixed up the crews and ready to take Houghton up to the Mess for a cup of tea, the Flight van drew up outside with the screeching of brakes. Out staggered the boys, somewhat the worse for wear from their night off. One was in a belligerent mood and ready to take a swing at anybody, but Jackie quickly ran forward and slapped him back in his van and drove him up to the Mess, where, with the help of a few more of the boys, he was tucked safely into bed.

Meanwhile, Tony Mills came into the Flight Office.

"Hello, Tony. You're late."

"Yeah, I know. We had a hell of a party."

"Well, that's OK; you're not on tonight."

"Oh yes, I am. I'm all right."

"Like hell you are! You're going to bed."

The "Colonel" joined in. They were both as high as anyone, in the sort of mood when they thought they were all right and very keen to fly. There was quite an argument. At last Jack and I with much diplomacy persuaded them that it was a cissy target and only the new boys were going, plus ourselves, to show them how. They were pleased then. Tony said:

"I would have been damned annoyed if you had kept us off because we went out last night."

And they departed to the Mess, their honour satisfied.

And so off we went each to our own basins in Antwerp. Once again I had the pleasure of hearing that crump, crump, crump just behind my tailplane as our bombs went off. Then, that illuminating flash which lit up the ground all round as some ammunition barge exploded. But this time something happened. There was a rending crack and a noise like the crash of thunder. At first I didn't know what had happened, and was rather frightened that Houghton in front had been killed. Then, as one does on these occasions, I suddenly realized that something was wrong with the aeroplane; she was flying in a queer way. There was no rudder bar. Then Houghton told me what was wrong. He had to crawl up to do so because the intercom had gone. A shell had entered by my feet had got the toe-strap on my rudder bar and then had hit its pivotal point and knocked it spinning forward on to Houghton's head, where it had laid him out. Quite an unlucky shot.

When I got back to Scampton F/Sgt Langford examined the damage. I remember his words very well.

"Cor, sir," he said, "that's bloomin' providence, that's what I call it, bloomin' providence. It missed your foot by half an inch."

I did not know quite what to say, but Houghton was up to the occasion and he replied, sardonically:

"No it wasn't, Flight; it was just a question of having short legs!"

Strangely enough the lad who had been put to bed was up when we got back and extremely rude. I think he was rather annoyed about his behaviour and didn't like someone taking care of him as we had. When Houghton told him about our trouble he just looked queer and said:

"What the hell do you need rudders for, anyway? You never use them, you know that, you old lineshooter."

There was an awkward silence from the boys all round. Even the Intelligence Officers felt something was wrong. I thought for a minute I was going to say something really bad, then I realized that we were all tired out, and so I walked out of the room without saying another word.

The next night we went to Berlin. This was a big raid; the biggest so far of the war. About 200 aircraft were engaged and it looked as though it was going to be a good prang on the German capital. As we were standing around, ready to take off, I wanted to go up to Oscar and wish him "good luck", but he hadn't said a word to me all day and I knew he was furious, so I went to my aircraft and took off.

It was one of those trips which were so common in those days. Cloud all the way, flak all the way; no one knowing where Berlin was, our loop bearings continually being jammed by the enemy and general chaos all round. Needless to say, we had to bomb at the end of our dead reckoning position where we estimated Berlin might be. Down below were several American journalists, and one of them, William Shirer, said afterwards that not many bombs actually dropped in Berlin itself. I can well believe it.

On the way home there was another head wind of gale strength, so we came back at 1,000ft with our radio shot away. As I walked into the briefing room quite a few of the boys had already returned. Jackie Withers had had some trouble with flak over Hanover and had had to return early on one engine.

"Oscar's had it," he said quietly and rather strangely, as I opened a bottle of beer.

"What do you mean?"

"About half an hour ago he sent out a signal, saying that one engine had been put on fire over Bremen and that he was baling out. Later another message came in that he was trying to get home. Since then there has been silence."

"Did the messages come in strong?"

"Yes. Gorwood, his radio operator, was tapping them out as if nothing had happened."

"Well, we had better get on to the Rescue Service and see if we can get anything."

We waited all night; we waited until the grey darkness of the early hours became purple, then blue as the sun rose in the east over Lincoln Wolds and it became daylight. But Oscar never came back.[1]

And so I went to bed. I was the last one left, the last one out of a bunch of boys who belonged to 83 Squadron at the beginning of the war, to fight until the end of Hitlerism. They had all fought well, but they had paid the price. Some were prisoners of war, I knew, but many were dead. As I lay in bed thinking, I knew I was lucky to survive, but it would come to me any day now. We would go on and on until the whole squadron was wiped out, then there would be new boys to carry on our traditions, new squadrons, new gadgets and new ground crews to crack jokes with us as we took the air. I did not see any point in living. For the moment I didn't even care about Eve. All my friends had gone now — there were new people — different — with different views on life, different jokes and different ways of living. I was the last one left.

Houghton and I made one more dawn attack on Kiel. This time we carried a flare on our 2,000lb bomb so that we could see it go into the sea. It missed by some 200 yards, so the rear-gunner said, and as we got hell beaten out of us for our attack, I swore then and there, at that moment, that I would never bomb the *Scharnhorst* again. It seemed so foolish to go there all alone. It seemed that we were the only ones fighting the war for England when

---

[1] Publisher's note: S/Ldr Bridgman survived, to be taken prisoner.

you sit up there on top of a cone over a great harbour surrounded by coloured lights and smelling the flak. You feel a long way from home, you feel you want to get back, you feel you never want to go again. And when you do come back it gets you and you want to have another crack. God knows why.

Once again we had to spend two hours over Hamburg city, dropping a bomb every thirty minutes in order to cause despondency and lack of sleep to the dwellers down below. Needless to say, we came back dithering wrecks. Never had so many guns fired at so few.

It was after this, when we were all sitting in the Mess, that Harris came in and read out Oscar's will. Someone switched off the wireless; there was silence save for the clinking of beer cans being put down on tables.

"Squadron-Leader Bridgman," began Harris, "asked me to read this out if he failed to come back from a raid. As you know, that has happened. So here goes."

I looked across at Jackie Withers nervously; this was one of the moments when I would have preferred to be elsewhere. Then it began. He had left little things, such as his pipes, to Jackie, his notebook to me. He had asked one or two of us to write to his mother occasionally and — "to __ __ of 49 Squadron, the biggest lineshooter of all, I leave one hearty kick in the crutch to be delivered by John Kynoch, who is the strongest man I know."

But John Kynoch wasn't there, nor was the lineshooter.

There were one or two more raids. A few attacked the Channel ports. Others, some 300 strong, consisting of all types of bombers, made their way to such cities as Bremen, Kiel and Wilhelmshaven. Even now a change was apparent. In fact, some organization was being revealed. True, we could still choose our own routes; true, we could still bomb at any height we liked; but now the best crews began to carry flares to light up the target. Bomb-loads were scientifically worked out with a view to causing as much damage by incendiaries as possible. Bomber Command was getting organized; it was getting itself fit, it was beginning to shape itself for the years to come. But the German Bomber Command was already organized. Hitler, in a passionate speech to the German people, swore that he would raze every British city to the ground. From sundry bases in France they came, flying high and fast to begin a series of attacks on London. Such attacks made everyone's blood boil. What could we do about it? We were still told to bomb military objectives and to keep our bombs right on the target or not to bomb at all.

One night, however, the mother of one of our sergeant pilots was killed in an air raid on London when a bomb came through her window as she was lying asleep underneath the stairs. He came to me that afternoon; his eyes were wet, but he was not crying. He wanted to come with us that night, to avenge his mother.

Such a spirit spelt doom for German cities in 1943 and 1944.

The Battle of Britain and the Battle of the Barges drew to a close. The long arm of Bomber Command had begun already to reach far into Germany to smash war industries. We must never forget the boys who took part in those battles. We must never forget that they laid the foundation for all that was to come. It was a great victory and one of which England should forever be proud.

When the fighter boys showed the world that they possessed undisputed mastery of the air over the Channel and Great Britain, and when the twin-engine bombers gave the barges such a packet, William Shirer, in his *Berlin Diary*, wrote of the bombing of the Channel ports, "But from what I saw of these bombings myself and from what I have been told by German airmen, I think it is highly improbable that the German army would ever be able to assemble in the ports of Boulogne, Calais, Dunkirk, Ostend or on the beaches, enough barges or ships to launch an invasion in the force that would be necessary."

Thus checked, after many days of continuous defeat, the Hun gave up his idea of invading England for a whole year and turned the might of the German army elsewhere. Future historians will say, and rightly so, in my opinion, that the

Battle of Britain, coupled, in a lesser degree, with the Battle of the Barges, altered the future of the world.

CHAPTER
NINE

Interlude

When the Battle of Britain ended with the Luftwaffe beaten and baffled, thanks to the British aircraft industry and a few hundred pilots, new developments began to take place elsewhere. Italy, like a hungry Jackal, looked round for some easy prey and found it, so she thought, in Greece. Immediately our forces in the Mediterranean, already hard-pressed, were dissipated even more by the formation of the third expeditionary force in just over one year.

While all this was going on, an interlude was taking place in Lincolnshire. This took the form of a bloodless battle royal between two age-old rivals — the Bomber Barons and the Fighter Glamour Boys. No lives were lost, no one was even injured (by a miracle) in this fight, but much cunning was used to bring about the defeat of the enemy. Like many battles, it ended with both sides saying they had won. To many it was known as the Battle of the "Snake-Pit" and will, no doubt, go down in Air Force history as such.

Since the earliest days of the RAF there have always been two very different breeds, different both by temperament and by virtue of their jobs — the bombers and the fighters.

During the lull in between wars, the latter had it all their own way. At Hendon air displays everyone thrilled to the aerobatics of four Hawker Super-Furies as they looped and rolled in perfect box formation. No one noticed the heavy bomber pilot, except perhaps to say with sympathy, "Look at that poor bloody bus-driver."

With the advent of new and fast fighters such as the Hurricanes, there was much talk in the newspapers of "young supermen who had to be corseted, so fast do they fly".

All young would-be pilots at their flying training schools clamoured to be put on to single-seaters. Only a few, the very best, the cream of the Service, ever got there. One and all hero-worshipped the white-overalled Squadron-crested youth who had just stepped down from a Spitfire. If he had lowered himself out of a Handley-Page Harrow, they would have merely turned away and said to themselves: "Poor sucker! he must be a Ham."

Anyway, compare the thrills of flying in formation, beating up each other and ground-firing on fixed targets, to the drab training of the "Hams" — straight runs over a camera obscura and level bombing from 10,000ft.

Even in the cities, the fighters seemed to have all the fun, walking off with the women and drinking

205

the beer, mainly because their stations were always close to a town, while a bomber base is miles from anywhere.

Naturally all this irked the boys of Bomber Command quite a lot. They began to take an active dislike to the flying-booted, scarf-flapping glamour boys; many a rude word was spoken between the two in practically every pub between Biggin Hill and Edinburgh.

Much of this rivalry may have arisen from the last war, when the feats of such great men as Bishop, Ball and McCudden captured everyone's imagination, while a bomber pilot hardly ever got his name in the papers.

Not surprisingly, the fighter boys became very cocky and full of their own importance, and the bus-drivers began to get quite an inferiority complex, knowing, as they did, that only the very best of them could be considered really good pilots.

Then came the war.

At first everything was forgotten in the common desire to beat the enemy. But as time wore on a few loose-fingered fighter boys would shoot down the odd bomber, and feeling began to run high again.

The trouble was that neither appreciated the other. The, fighters never escorted the bombers, the bombers never saw the fighters in action. And so came the battle of the "Snake-Pit."

What precipitated the battle no one will ever know. Probably too much beer on both sides; anyway, the whole thing started in the small bar.

Next day three Hampdens took off from nearby Waddington, laden to full capacity with lavatory paper and old leaflets. As they were circling to gain altitude, a few miles away lay the aerodrome at Digby, an old fighter station from the last war. Two squadrons were stationed there at the time, a single-seater Squadron No. 141 and a twin-engined Beaufighter Squadron, No. 29.

While the fighter boys were having their lunch, they were surprised to bear an angry snarl of engines. The three Hampdens were beating up the place in no mean style. As they ran out of the Mess, their mouths gaped in astonishment. No Hampdens were to be seen, but the sky was full of lavatory paper, floating quite slowly down on to their airfield. Quickly the Flight-Commander swore that reprisals would follow. Being fighters, they could not carry a sufficient quantity of paper, but they soon hit upon a plan. Phase II would soon be in operation.

Next day there was rain and flying was cancelled. The bomber-boys of Waddington sat around in their crew-rooms, having a good laugh about their successful venture the day before. They felt good; why, last night even the "Snake-Pit" had been clear of glamour boys. Everything was fine.

At about 11 o'clock a Black Blenheim with no squadron markings landed on their field and taxied up to the control tower.

"Hullo, Control," it called. "This is Group-Captain Biggleswade from Bomber Command. I have an important message for OC 144 Squadron. It is very urgent. Will you send him out to this aircraft immediately?"

In a few minutes the Wing-Commander's car appeared around the perimeter track and soon he began to climb inside the Blenheim. No sooner was he in than a bag was snapped over his head and willing hands dragged him back into the spacious rear of the aeroplane. At the same time the Blenheim became airborne with F/L Sandy Campbell of A Flight 29 Squadron at the controls . . .

At Digby the Wing-Commander's instructions were simple. He was given a long stick with a spike on it, and was politely asked to go around and pick up all the paper his squadron had dropped the day before. When this had been done, he was returned to his base as expeditiously as he had come.

From then on the war raged fast and furious. Both sides had attacked, and had drawn blood. Plans were made for the third phase.

A few days later, Digby entertained a few Mess visitors. There was a padre from a Scottish station, an engineer officer and a few others. They hadn't much to say and didn't stay very long. They had, they said, to catch a train from Lincoln. Half-an-hour after they had gone someone noticed that both squadron crests had disappeared from the hall. Now, all squadrons are very proud of their crests and most of all, perhaps, are fighter squadrons. Feeling ran high in the Mess, cars were sent to chase the padre and his gang, but no one was found.

At Waddington the crests were received with pleasure. They were set up against a tree in the Officers' Mess garden. Then all the boys gathered around with beer mugs, waiting patiently. The camera was adjusted, everything was ready. Then the camera clicked.

Next day, as mysteriously as they had vanished, the crests were returned. But stuck to the notice-board was a picture; a picture which nearly sent the whole of Digby raving mad.

This was an outrage. Threats were hurled across the ante-room as the Digby War Cabinet met, when the bar opened, to discuss the situation.

Only two cans had been knocked back before the master plan was evolved. It seemed a cinch.

Back at Waddington, the bomber boys were puzzled. Nothing had happened for a few days and they had begun to wonder why. Next second they didn't have to worry any more, the fighter boys had come.

Screaming across the hangars they came in close formation, one jerking the motionless windsock into life, so close did he go, vapour swirling from his wing-tips. For a quarter of an hour the beat-up went on, and even the bomber boys came out of their ante-room to have a look, admitting it was the best they had ever seen.

Suddenly they vanished as quickly as they had come with a final dive by the leader at the boys standing on the Mess lawn.

It was a good beat-up, but what was the point? Nothing had happened out of the ordinary. One by one the barons went back into the Mess.

When the time came to go to work they soon discovered what had happened. There were yells of chagrin throughout the bar. While they had been outside watching the beat-up, some smart type had slunk into their cloakroom and pinched all their hats.

Now a bomber boy is proud of his "operational" peaked cap and wears it on every occasion, because he thinks he looks a stooge in a "fore-and-after". This manoeuvre by Digby successfully kept the bulk of the barons away from the "Saracen's Head" that night, and the fighter boys had the place almost entirely to themselves.

But worse was to come. Next day a Beaufighter shot up the Mess and cascaded the whole load of headwear into the mud. Immediately there was a rush to lay hands on and identify each other's hats, but the fighter boys had played their cards carefully. All nametabs had been removed.

From now on, the battle began to reach a climax; little moves were made by each side which caused inconvenience to the other. For instance, one fighter boy was going to rub out the white line in the middle of the road which leads from Lincoln to Waddington. The barons relied a lot on this white line, especially when returning from a sortie to Lincoln. They began to regard it as rather like "being in the beam". So much so that one fellow had a white line which went up the stairs and led into his bedroom. But this glamour boy had an even more diabolical plan. His intention was not only to rub out the correct line, but to paint in another which would gently swerve off the road and up a large oak tree.

Such a move would have been detrimental to the war effort and was sadly abandoned by all concerned.

It was at this juncture that the respective COs took a hand. The barons, vastly superior in numbers, had begun to threaten the glamour boys that they would de-bag everyone of them who came into the "Saracen's Head". Fearing, no doubt, that trouble would be caused by the civil authorities if this happened, and scared stiff that both sides might hurt each other, both Station Commanders gave an order to cease fire. The battle ended on that day.

As a Scampton boy, I wasn't really mixed up in the whole show, but now and then I had been around in the "Snake-Pit" when some fighter boy had come in wearing a roll-neck sweater. My part in the war had been brief, merely to be slightly rude to fighter types on certain occasions.

Despite this, my hand wasn't quite as steady as it might have been when one day in October I received a blunt telegram from the Air Ministry.

"Report to 29 (F) Squadron Digby for Flight-Commander (Flying) Duties. FORTHWITH."

CHAPTER
TEN

29 Fighter Squadron

It was a rainy, murky day in mid-November when Runt Reynolds,[1] a pal of mine from Upper Heyford, flew me in his old groaning Anson to bleak Digby Aerodrome. Here Lincolnshire is at its worst — a vast area of flatness, spreading out towards the East Fenlands of the Wash. Hardly a tree breaks the horizon, hardly a bird sings. Now and then large numbers of rooks croak their way above the barren earth. These are constantly being hacked down by ardent farmers.

On the aerodrome not a soul was in sight. The aircraft were all covered up and the windsock hung water-logged and motionless from one of the hangars. As I stood and watched Runt take off to climb towards the sunny south, I felt very lonely standing here, surrounded by a few suitcases, my worldly possessions. For a minute I wished I had never volunteered to be transferred to fighters, but that I was still residing in a warm OTU where life is

---

[1] Now Wing-Commander Reynolds, DSO and Bar, DFC and Bar.

pleasant and where I had a lot of pals from bomber squadrons.

I asked the first airman I saw the way to 29 Squadron offices. He was a friendly soul, as all airmen are, and soon we stood in front of a little wooden shack with a white notice on the door. I noticed it was peeling slightly and the door didn't fit very well either. All the notice said was "CO and Adjutant: 29 Squadron," and underneath was the cruder and more direct "Knock and Enter."

I went in. When my eyes had pierced the thick clouds of pipe smoke I saw a small man, a Pilot-Officer, walk towards me out of the haze. Sam France was the Adjutant. He was a man of about forty who had flown in the last war, but looked younger. It was nice and warm in his office and he was friendly. He held out his cigarette case.

"Good afternoon, sir. You're F/L Gibson, aren't you? Group told me you were coming."

"Yes. How do you do? Miserable day."

"Certainly is, sir. I am afraid the CO is away at the AOC. He will be back about tea-time."

"Good. What is he like?" Everyone asks this when posted to a new unit.

"A wizard type and a good pilot. He has put you in charge of A Flight, sir."

"Fine."

I was a bit puzzled, him calling me "sir" the whole time, and asked him why. "Well, this is a Fighter Squadron, sir, and you are a Flight-Commander and as such you are treated in the same way as a Squadron-Leader in a Bomber Squadron."[1]

"I see. How many aircraft are there in each Flight?"

"Normally ten, but we are converting to Beaufighters at the moment and everything is upside down. We have three detachments at various places all round the country. There are two chaps at Turnhill to defend Liverpool; two at Kirton for Hull, and two at Wittering for Coventry."

"What are the rest doing?"

"Oh, the rest are here converting oil to Beaus."

"This is a night-fighter squadron for all purposes, isn't it?" I asked.

"Yes, day and night. We operate in all weather: during the day when the Spitfire boys can't cope. Things are not going too well at the moment though. We haven't got anything much in the way of control and the airborne intercept devices are not working very well, but the technical blokes say they are coming along fine."

I didn't know what he was talking about. Fighting procedure was obviously very different from bomber. I thought I had better change the subject. I would find out about control and other stuff later.

We went on chatting for quite a while. He told me that we were operating from a little aerodrome near the village (of Wellingore) which, for some reason,

---

[1] A Bomber Flight is commanded by a Squadron-Leader, a Fighter Flight by a Flight-Lieutenant.

was called WC1. That our Mess was in the village (at a place called The Grange). The corporal in charge was an ex-London chef and so the food was excellent. This suited me because in the last week or two I had become engaged and meant to bring Eve up here when we were married. Before he could tell me any more, Charles Widdows strolled in. He was the Squadron-Leader, and looked like it. In fact, I thought him a little pompous at first, but soon got to know and like him very much indeed. He was one of those officers who had been in the Service for years and regarded it as his career. He was very pleased to see me and began to ask many questions about the bomber war, and to find out my ideas on night-fighters. As I had never seen one I didn't have any.

When they had fixed up all the paperwork, I was driven over to the Mess. This turned out to be a pleasant old country house set in its own grounds. Inside there was a pleasant warm atmosphere, no doubt due to low ceilings and log fires. It was an ideal house to enter on such a miserable day. But my reception was anything but warm. In fact, it was somewhat chilly. As we entered the anteroom I noticed a few chaps sitting around; all dressed in the conventional attire of the fighter-boy — flying-boots with a couple of maps stuck in the top, roll-neck pullovers and/or sweaters, no ties or collar and, of course, dirty tunics, with top buttons undone. Personally, I like this type of dress; it is comfortable and when one has to be leaping into the air at odd times of the night it is sensible. I felt a little embarrassed standing there looking like Little Lord Fauntleroy. As Sam closed the door there was an uncomfortable silence. Then he spoke to the whole room.

"Er, er, this is Flight-Lieut Gibson, the new A Flight Commander." Another silence. One or two put down their papers and said: "Wotcha," and "Hi'yer." Then buried their noses once more.

Someone yawned.

It was obvious that these boys weren't pleased to see me, and I knew why. I was a bomber boy. Someone got up and walked out of the room; he was a fat man with a black moustache, whom I later got to know as Peter Kells. Later he came back and without saying a word picked up his beer and walked out again, slamming the door.

This was a highly embarrassing situation, and having just come from a squadron where everyone was very friendly, I nearly asked the CO if I could be posted on the spot. As Sam and I were standing by the fireplace saying very little, a long, lanky fellow who had a pleasant grin on his face turned up.

"My name's Graham-Little," he said, without ceremony. "I have just come too. Have a drink."

This was a welcome break, and I spent the next hour talking to him. His father was an MP, but he seemed more proud of the fact that he was one of the best skin-disease specialists in the whole country. "Very useful around here, you know."

It seemed that the squadron consisted of a few new arrivals and some old hands, who had been flying around the night sky never shooting anything down and always grumbling about the hardness of their work. Graham, introduced me to some of the newer ones. There was Ken Davison, a barrister; there was young Victor Lovell, who had just left school, and another tall, good-looking boy called Robin Miles, who I think had been a tea-planter in Burma. These fellows were all right, and we had supper together. Sam was right about the chef: the steaks were wonderful.

After supper Sam suggested that we should go and have one at the "local", and here he told me the story.

"In the first place," he began, "you don't want to think that the squadron is bad just because of your first welcome. The trouble is, as you know, that these boys are very browned off; they have been flying since the beginning of the war in Blenheim aircraft, never shooting down anything, and watching all the other squadrons get the gongs. Then, of course, there was that 'war' between Waddington and ourselves, which doesn't help matters, and above all, I am afraid they dislike bomber boys at the moment. The other great snag is that by coming here you are taking over A Flight from a very popular chap called Wynne, who has got to drop his acting rank. This has upset the boys quite a lot." There was a funny feeling in my stomach as he went on:

218

"As I am a slightly older man than you, the best advice I can give you is to take things easy; they'll soon get to know you and everything will get smoothed over."

He went on talking for a bit and then I went to bed. As I lay trying to get some sleep in my new surroundings, my thoughts were very mixed. No one minds a new job, but it is a bit tough to start off on the wrong foot. But at last I turned over, thinking of the days when I would be married to Eve and would be able to have a little home life, which I had missed so far.

The next day was my own, but that night the Huns began to come over in swarms to bomb some Midland town, and Widdows took me to the operations room. Operations rooms have been described so many times that I certainly won't try to do so here, but broadly they consist of a large sound-deadened room in the middle of which is a large table on which is drawn the sector map. WAAFs sit around with earphones on their carefully done hair, working small flags which indicate the position of enemy aircraft and, of course, our own fighters. Some of these girls are extremely pretty and have in Fighter Command been known since time immemorial as "the beauty chorus". As they worked the flags, I noticed there was a small board attached to each, indicating the height at which the aircraft was flying; a small arrow indicated its course.

Sitting on a raised dais watching the whole show was the controller, whose job it is to talk to the fighters and vector[1] them on to the incoming bombers. I couldn't help thinking, as I watched these little green flags move inwards towards the city of Sheffield, that they were like so many green slugs, slugs of death. And as our red fighters moved in between them here was the last thing in modern warfare: the last word in efficiency.

However, it seemed that although the controller would tell a fighter that the bandit was only a few miles in front, no one ever saw anything; the night was too dark and the sky was too big. Much technical development would be required before we mastered the night bomber.

The controller this night was the Duke of Newcastle, a Squadron-Leader and a very likeable man. He was a good-looking man and I noticed that all the girls had quite an eye on him. He gave me a terse description of what was going on. "Now and then," he said, "you will hear me say to an aircraft: 'Hello, Bad Hat 14. Transmit for fix,' and you will hear him count 1 to 10 quickly and then switch off. While he is doing that, these three radio-fixer stations get bearings on him which are plotted on that table over there. This plot is then handed to me and to those girls working on the main table; they then adjust his position into its right spot and I tell him where he is, so that should he get lost, he will

---

[1] Steer.

know what course to steer for home. Of course, you can see the snag," he went on. "Although the fixing procedure is very quick, there is still a delay of a minute or so, and four miles in the air is a very great distance to see; that is why we are not having much success."

"But can't you put up more fighters flying one behind the other, so that one is bound to see him?" I asked.

"No, I'm afraid that this method of control isn't accurate enough. Besides, there would always be the danger of someone shooting down his friend."

"How about searchlights?"

"Well, they do their best, but they rely entirely on sound for their directions and usually illuminate the fighter flying behind."

"Not so good."

"No."

And as I watched the green swarm slowly cluster around Sheffield, hang there for a few minutes, then disperse again to the coast, I realized that these raids were being carried out by the GAF almost without loss.

After a few days I began to settle down. When the boys had got over their first reactions to the revolting idea of having a bomber pilot as flight commander, they seemed to me to be quite normal types. In my flight there was Dave Humphries, who got on well with the ladies; there was young Anderson, who wasn't fond of women at all; there was a little man called Munn, who was always grumbling, and there was a very nice fellow called Buchanan, whom we nicknamed Jack; Graham-Little, the lad who had first spoken to me, was also one of the boys. He spent most of his time prowling around with a .22 rifle, looking for hares.

The days passed fairly quickly, as I was working pretty hard, getting used to radio-telephony procedure. Air firing wasn't much of a snag, as we used to have a front gun on the Hampden, and though I wasn't good, I was not completely bad.

The Beaufighter was the new aeroplane of the day. It possessed a terrific punch in its armament of four cannons and six Browning guns, but these often used to freeze up, because as yet we had no cockpit heating. For its size the Beau was very heavy and its wing loading rather on the high side. For this reason the CO insisted on all pilots carrying out a lot of day flying before trying to fly it at night, especially as our landing run at WC1 was only 1,000 yards.

On November 22nd there is an entry in my log book which indicates that a Blenheim, flown by myself, took off from WC1 to land on Cardiff aerodrome with P/O Lovell as a passenger, and in the duty column are three great words: "To be married!" The only other comment I should like to make is that this was due to the courtesy of Cox and King's Bank, London, who granted me an overdraft of £5 for the occasion.

We returned from our honeymoon and tried to get a house in the neighbourhood. It was quite

222

impossible, and at last we put up at the biggest pub in the village called the "Lion and Royal". Its chief distinction was that it possessed a bath. Although it was pleasant to live with your wife on these occasions, I used to feel very sorry, as I would come back for lunch every day and find her sitting there all alone in our bedroom, the only room available for her, trying to keep warm in front of a gas fire, waiting for me. Lonely because there had been no one to talk to the whole morning. Some wives have to go through quite a lot to be near their husbands.

Christmas drew near, and I began to operate at night. As there were very few of us in the squadron who were in a position to fly the Beau at night, it was a question of being two nights on and one off. Although we rarely did more than four hours' flying each night, it was an awful bind having to sleep in the operations hut on the aerodrome with all one's heavy flying kit on, feeling dirty and unshaven. By the end of two nights on, one's bathwater was quite black.

One particular night, I remember, the Huns were bombing Coventry. Everyone will remember the occasion because it was one of the first heavy raids made on a provincial town. I was above and saw it burn, and the only consolation was that I had seen Kiel burn better. There was very little flak, in fact none, but No. 5 Bomber Group had put in the air about fifty Hampdens whose job was to circle the city at 500ft layers, above the city, and shoot down any twin-engine aircraft they saw. As there were about two hundred Huns as well floating around the night sky, someone thought that someone might see something, but this did not occur. I never saw a Hampden or a German bomber the whole evening, and this convinced me once and for all that the night sky is very, very big.

Another time we went up to defend Sheffield, which was getting bombed, but instead were directed to Manchester. At this critical moment the radio telephony failed. Cloud that night was down to 500ft everywhere. We wandered around England all night, trying to find a flare-path, and I was just about to bale out when I saw an old Anson go in to land. By following him in and landing on the other side of the flare-path we just managed to scrape down. It was a lovely feeling to stand on Mother Earth again; being lost is not a pleasant feeling.

Naturally, I arrived back at WC1 next morning but no one had bothered to tell Eve of my misfortune and I found the poor girl almost in tears, not knowing what to do. I am afraid she thought I had had it.

Fighter stations are excellent for parties, and they know how to throw them in a really big way. There is always someone on a fighter station who knows some star in London who will bring up a really good show. One particular night a famous strip-tease artist was billed to appear in the Officers' Mess to give us an informal dance. Naturally everyone turned up. Unluckily, she caught cold or something, and couldn't be there; but someone else filled the bill fairly well. We had gone to this party in a convoy of three cars.

The snow was just beginning to fall as we went on our way, but it didn't seem very heavy. When we left, however, at about 3 o'clock in the morning, the leading car led us down a country lane, which began to get deeper and deeper in snow. Then a blizzard started up. Suddenly our wheels began churning and we realized we could go no farther. Quickly we tried to reverse, but this was no use and we were stuck. From the other two cars we heard coarse words in the distance, which indicated that both were in the ditch. It was a pitch-black night and we were about 3 miles from any sign of habitation. With Eve and the other girl in their flimsy evening dresses which Dave Humphries and I had gallantly supplemented with our tunics, the prospect of wading thigh deep in snow for 3 miles wasn't very pleasant, but it had to be done. It was a question of "march or perish". That journey took two hours and I never want to see icicles hanging off my wife's nose again.

Another time we went into Lincoln in my new car which I had bought with some of my short-service commission gratuity and, of course, the darned thing conked out with about 6 miles to go on the way home. We had to spend all night in the car and I have never been so frozen stiff, except perhaps on certain occasions in Beaufighters. When it got light a meat-van came along and we rode back to our pub hanging on hooks beside large sirloins of beef, but the temperature inside that meat-van was tropical compared to what it had been a few hours before.

During all this time London had been getting its nightly blitz. There wasn't much flak and, taking things all round, I think the civil population were getting decidedly jumpy. I remember one occasion when I happened to be in London while it was getting a packet. The train I had come up in was three hours late, and it was about 2 o'clock in the morning when I tried to get a room in the Station Hotel. They had only one room at 24s 6d which struck me as being too high, so I made my way to a tube shelter. As I walked along the rows upon rows of huddled figures, crouching on each side, I was aware of a certain animosity in the crowd. Suddenly one woman yelled out at the top of her voice, "Why don't you get up there and fight those bastards?" I quickly turned and ran up the stairs again, not wishing to be torn limb from limb.

It was miserable wandering around London with the bombs crumping down, and I couldn't help thinking how much more pleasant it was to be up above in a warm cockpit thinking of home in a few hours' time. Yes, London was taking it all right, but I prayed in my heart that the Hun wouldn't go on bombing London forever because something was bound to happen.

Meanwhile, the Beau wasn't behaving itself. Although I never had any trouble with the Beaufighter myself, it had been a bit troublesome with other pilots. Don Parker, one of our fellows, himself an ex-bomber boy, had to bale out when an engine caught fire. Another time the CO was flying around above Northampton when suddenly one engine started banging at about 8,000ft. He immediately throttled it back, then the other went. He started pulling taps and juggling petrol-cocks, but was unable to do very much about it, and so gave the order to bale out. The observer, sitting in the back, was a bit slow and caught his feet in the rear escape hatch. When Widdows looked round to see that he had gone safely, he was astonished to find him lying on the floor doing his best to free himself. During this time the aeroplane had lost some 5,000ft in height. Old Charles then put up a very good show. He climbed back into his seat and although he didn't have time even to put his feet on the rudder bar, managed to pull off a good landing in a field with the aid of his landing lamp, missing some high-tension wires by a few feet. By his quick action not only did he save the life of his observer, but also brought the Beau down in more or less one piece, and thus enabled the experts to solve the mystery, which turned out to be some trouble with the blower.

But despite the small trouble we had had, other squadrons had begun to look upon it as a suicide ship. There is a story that one particular squadron in the north had got to the stage when they almost refused to fly it. They said that it stalled too quickly and that it was unmanageable in tight turns. They were sitting about one foggy day on their aerodrome when there was no flying possible, and were discussing the subject heatedly, when suddenly a Beau whistled over their heads at about 100ft, pulled up in a stall turn, dropped its wheels and flaps and pulled off a perfect landing on the runway. Naturally, this attracted a lot of attention. They all thought that this pilot must have been one of the crack test pilots who had come up to show them how. As it taxied up to the watch office, they all crowded around to get the gen. However, a lot of faces dropped to the ground when from underneath the Beau crawled a figure in a white flying-suit, capped by blonde, floating hair; it was one of the ATA girls. I am told that this squadron had no trouble from Beaus from that day on.

Time marched on. We had to wait for the scientists and the Boffins to complete the trials on our new weapons. They were coming along, there was no doubt about that, but as yet they weren't perfect. And they had to be just right if we were to beat the night Hun.

Many fantastic ideas were being put forward. Don came into my office one day and told me about one.

"Here's a chap with an idea to beat the night raider. He suggests we cover England with motor-car headlamps which will dazzle the enemy bomb-aimers."

"What a cock-eyed idea. How about the cost?"

"Oh, he says it can be done pretty cheaply."

"Well, what about the radio beams? The Hun doesn't aim much with the human eye; I think he relies more on wireless. That's why he can hit a city above the cloud."

"Yes, I thought it was pretty silly myself," Don agreed. "The trouble with these old boys is they don't think in terms of modern science."

"Then there's the other old chap who believes in flares," Jack Buchanan said. "He wants us to go around the night sky in Fairey Battles, towing a flare behind like a match-flame in a cathedral."

"All right if there were enough of them."

"Yeah, but there's not."

Arguments and discussions would often take place at length, but it always boiled down to the same thing. The night raider must be beaten by the night-fighter. And we had a long way to go.

Meanwhile, the lowly Italian was finding that war was not all fun. In Greece they were being driven back everywhere. Those tough little fighters had already captured Argyrocastro. In Libya we had begun to advance again, under General Wavell, who seemed to be in a hurry. Sidi Barrani and Fort Capuzzo fell in a matter of days, yielded thousands of willing prisoners. No — it wasn't all fun for Mussolini; even his internal politics weren't too good. Badoglio had resigned.

But each night whenever the weather was reasonable the Huns droned over, intent on destroying Britain, city by city. We were always up, leaning forward in our cockpits, eyes pressed against the armour-plated windscreen, trying to see something. One night I actually did. We thought it was a Blenheim, and as Robin Miles was flying in one we thought it would be a good idea to shake him. We slunk up behind, then turned on our landing light. Quickly I grabbed the twister ring on my firing-button, but it was too late. Spotlighted in the beam was an iron cross and a very startled W op. AG of a Ju 88. Then it had gone, before either he or I could fire a shot. His pilot put her into a dive which I prayed he wouldn't pull out of. But apparently my prayer failed.

Towards the end of the year I had a chance to fire at my first enemy aircraft. It was one of the flare droppers over Hull, and I could see him quite clearly as flare after flare emerged from his bomb doors. I was so excited for the moment that I took bad aim and missed, but he jettisoned the rest of his load into the Humber, and I landed feeling very pleased with myself. It was obvious that I was a very bad shot, but at least it was a beginning.

CHAPTER
ELEVEN

Dusk Readiness

The beginning of the year was marked by bad weather. Everyone in Lincolnshire will remember the continuous fog which lay on the ground for practically three weeks. It was, in fact, only possible to fly one night sortie throughout the whole of the month. The bombers, by landing on bases far from those from which they set off, had been able to get a few hearty punches in at the *Scharnhorst* and *Gneisenau*, which were lying at Brest. As I watched them drone overhead I couldn't quite honestly say that I would like to have been with them. But there was plenty of day patrolling for us, and as the Hun used to spend his spare time coming over England under cover of cloud and bombing whatever he could see, we would be up day after day trying to intercept them on the way home. Often these patrols would take us far out to sea, sometimes as far as the Dutch coast. But the great trouble was that as soon as his reargunner spotted you the bandit would disappear into a cloud. This misty weather was bad for morale, and everyone began to get very browned off.

In order to raise some spirit in the squadron, the CO decided to have a squadron party in the City Hall at Lincoln. Everything was organized so as to make it one of the biggest parties ever. Needless to say, it was a great success — even when someone passed out on his face in the middle of a cabaret and had to be carried out by two airmen. The only snag about the party was that it didn't make a very good impression on the Lincoln Watch Committee, who wrote a letter saying that never again must such parties be held in the City Hall.

With the coming of the good weather in February the squadron began to get really down to work. The Beaufighters were now running smoothly. A new sort of operational control had been introduced which could put the fighter on the track of the bomber, and yet another innovation had been devised by the scientists. This was a very secret weapon which cannot be described in full until after the war, but roughly, it consisted of two teams — a pilot and the observer. It was the pilot's job to fly carefully on instruments, while the observer sat in the back twiddling knobs and working dials "picking" up the bandit ahead. When he had got within a certain distance he was able to give the pilot such directions as would bring the fighter within a few hundred yards of the bomber. It was then up to the pilot's eyes and his good shooting.

To carry out training we used to go up in pairs and fly hour after hour with about three operators on board who would each do an hour's work. At first the operators, as they were called, seemed to have no idea at all, but we all had to be very patient, and after a time some of them began to get very good. This went on day and night for the next two months.

Meanwhile the Huns were still coming in and training was complementary to operations. About six of us used to stand by every night in our dirty little operations hut waiting for the order to take off.

One wintry morning at about 7 o'clock we went up after a Heinkel 111 which had dropped some incendiaries near Grantham. As he was flying very low, about 500ft, there was nothing much we could do to intercept him except follow the advice of the controller from our radio fixing plots, but after half an hour, way out to sea, I suddenly saw him about 800 yards ahead, just moving from one cloud to another. Eight hundred yards is, of course, a long way even for cannon, but we gave him a squirt and as far as we could see nothing happened. When we landed, however, they showed me the radio plots which indicated our tracks converging on to one another and the exact moment we had opened fire the bomber had made a large circle and disappeared. Naturally we did not claim anything because no one could honestly say that it had been destroyed, or even damaged.

Another time Don Parker, in a daylight patrol, was actually vectored on to a bomber high above the clouds. It was a Junkers 88, but the pilot was good and had dived so speedily for the cloud that

233

Don was unable to follow. This was the great limitation of the Beaufighters in daylight operations. At night it was good because it could slink up behind, unobserved, to deal the death-blow. By day it could always be seen, and provided that the enemy pilot took good evasive action, he would usually get away.

All this involved about sixty flying hours a month for each pilot in the squadron and was not without casualties. One pilot with a crowd of radio observers on board went into a wood upside down. Jack Buchanan mistook his air speed and stalled when coming on to land and crashed on the edge of the aerodrome, a burning mass. Another young pilot, Paul Tomlinson, who was never very fond of the Beau., crashed while taking off at Digby. The whole front of the aircraft caught fire, but the ground crew were up to the occasion. Led by F/Sgt Pease they dashed out and despite exploding ammunition hacked away at the fuselage until someone could get in and pull him out. Poor lad, he was coughing and spitting out black smoke for the next week.

I was never very squeamish about bodies, but one night Dave Humphries and I saw a sight which made us both turn and run. It was stormy and had been snowing, when suddenly a Wellington returning, no doubt, from a bombing mission tried to land on our flare-path. For some reason or other something went wrong and the great Wimpy crashed into a field and burnt up. Dave and I went out to look for it next morning. We were the first there and the wind was whistling fiercely, sending up snow-flurries round each foot as we tramped across the fields towards the gaunt skeleton of the Wellington, its tail fin sticking up in the air like an accusing finger.

As we got closer and closer we could smell that unpleasant smell of burnt aircraft, but when we got really close we could see quite clearly the pilot sitting still at his controls, burnt to a frazzle, with his goggles gently swaying in the wind hanging from one hand.

Without a word we began to retreat and were back in our operations hut within a few minutes.

As February turned into March and the snow melted away there came the full moon. We had fifteen crews ready to operate. It looked as if the Hun was going to begin bombing again after the short lull, and we were all looking forward to doing some really good work.

Widdows shot down the first one, a Junkers 88 which crashed in a field near Louth. A few hours later Bob Braham[1] had an exciting combat with a Dornier 17, which he chased down to sea level and watched blow up. I myself didn't have any luck that night. My special device was working badly, and when my operator gave me directions to go up I should, in fact, have gone down, with the result that we lost every Hun that we were vectored on to.

---

[1] Now W/Cdr Braham, DSO and Bar, DFC and two Bars.

A quick night-flying test next day put that right and that night off Skegness I saw a fat Heinkel flying north. He didn't notice me and I dropped down into the darkness of the land which formed the background. I knew he hadn't seen me, but I could see him clearly — a black smudge against the stars. I adjusted my parachute harness and safety straps, then carefully turned on my ring eight and closed for the attack. When the centre spot was right in the middle of the Heinkel I pressed the button . . . Instead of a blinding flash there was nothing. The Heinkel flew on and I throttled back to avoid over-shooting; in doing so flames and sparks spat from my exhausts and I swore, anxiously hoping that he wouldn't dive away. The next time I got into position, I pressed the button again. This time only one cannon fired and again nothing happened. There was no return fire, so I reckoned my first burst must have killed the rear-gunner. The third time we got into position, no cannons fired. I began imploring Sergeant James to get one going so that I could finish him off. But it was some ten minutes before he was able to do so. The Hun, meanwhile, had turned out to sea and began diving for home.

It seemed quiet and ethereal up there, man against man. At the time I wouldn't have exchanged places with anyone else in the world. This, in a way, was better than a bombing mission; the only thing was it didn't happen often enough.

At last James got one cannon going and we aimed at the port engine. As shell after shell banged home there was a yellow flash. Sparks flew out and the engines stopped. Then we aimed at the starboard engine, and this stopped within a few seconds. And the great Heinkel was careering down towards the earth at 120mph. Someone baled out, but we were a long way out to sea.

We followed it right down, and watched it land in the sea off Skegness pier, but I don't know to this day whether that Heinkel landed itself or if at the controls there was some wounded Hun trying to pull off a safe landing.

When I first saw him I had screamed over the RT full of excitement. When he was gliding down completely helpless I felt almost sorry for him. The whole combat had taken about twenty minutes, but Sam and I had no idea of time. We were so excited we could hardly speak, but both of us made a complete mess of the next interception.

That afternoon we collected the whole of the Heinkel tail assembly as a squadron trophy. Sam France and I drove over to Skegness. There we met the Chief Constable.

"Looking for your Heinkel?" he asked.

"Yes. Any bodies?" asked Sam.

"One. A Hauptmann with the Iron Cross. He's in the morgue. Head nearly shot off by a cannon shell. Care to see him?"

I was nearly sick. But I wanted the Iron Cross to send home to his people.

"I'm afraid that's been pinched: his watch, too. Talk about vultures. I've got some men out trying to find who did it."

"Anything else?"

"A rubber dinghy in good condition. You can take that if you want."

"Thanks."

I've still got that dinghy, and sometimes, when basking off the sunny shores of Cornwall, I still wonder if some dying German airman made a vain attempt to save his life in it.

That was all we got for that moon party. Three destroyed, but it was certainly the beginning of things to come.

When the moon ended there was a squadron party to celebrate, and it was no mean party either. A large silver mug was bought on which were inscribed the names of the pilots concerned. It was the duty of those pilots to drink this mug full of beer without stopping — a job much harder than shooting down a Heinkel.

The party was a bit too good, really, because it had a sequel for me in court. All I had done was to take off my headlamp masks, as I had done once before in order to get home safely, but this time they got my number. Graham-Little and Ken Davison gave me plenty of advice, but the police had me in their grip and there was no way out.

Eve and I went to court and appeared before a magistrate who looked like Colonel Blimp. He was a tall man with a large moustache and a bald head, and sat eyeing us from the bench with his spectacles as though we were objects of curiosity rather than offenders against the law. I had told Eve I would do all the talking. My defence was simple; I merely stated that the visibility was down to 400 yards, which is termed "fog", and that in order to proceed safely on my way I had taken off my headlight masks. This was a fact. I could have brought a meteorological officer along with me to prove it, but instead had to listen to three policemen get up one after another and say that it was a clear night. Suddenly Eve spoke up from the back of the court. The magistrate was very pleasant. He let her say her piece, and no sooner had she done so than he tapped his hammer and said: "You are fined four pounds five shillings. Will you pay now or by cheque?" I paid by cheque.

This little clash with the law quietened us down a lot. Eve and I spent our evenings off going to quiet flicks and sometimes listening to the wireless in our miserable bed-sitting-room. By now our pub was beginning to get us down, neither of us having ever lived in anything like it before. However, the news was good. The Italians were being given a tremendous pasting on all sides. Abyssinia was going; they had lost Benghazi. British Somaliland was recaptured. In fact, Il Duce's Empire was about to drop off like a ripe plum. Moreover, there was a rumour that we were going to move south to defend London.

Working hours in a night-fighter squadron were easy, taking things all round. Each morning we could lie in bed and take it easy till 11, when flying began. It was quite pleasant, reading the good, optimistic news in the morning papers and drinking tea brought up by Mine Hostess.

However, one day she put up a black. We had been given some smoked salmon, a rare delicacy, and Eve decided we would have it when we returned from Lincoln that night.

When we entered the pub at about 9 o'clock we asked if we could have our salmon.

"I think so; it's nearly ready." She went out to the kitchen

"Nearly ready!" Eve's face began to drop.

With a "Git out of my way, Artie" to her youngest offspring, in came mine hostess with a tray. *She had fried our salmon in batter*. Eve nearly fainted.

By now we could intercept often enough on practice nights, but this didn't mean we would get the enemy. When it came to the actual thing, something always seemed to go wrong. Either the airborne detector apparatus would fail, or the RT would get jammed, or the cannons wouldn't fire, and if all these were working, there would be no Huns about. It was a depressing job and everyone had to be very patient.

Cockpit heating had been introduced and this worked very well. It was pleasant to sit up there and listen to the directions of the controller.

"Hullo, Bad Hat 17. This is Digby Control. Bandit approaching you from the east. Vector 09 zero, Angels 15, about 10 miles away."

A little later:

"Hullo, Bad Hat 17. Bandit 3 miles from you. Prepare to turn sharp to port on 270 degrees. Angels 10."

Then would come the order to turn, and with full throttle the Beau. would swing around in a vertical turn and wait for further instructions. Then:

"Hullo, Bad Hat 17. You turned rather late. He is now about 4 miles ahead and slightly to port. Vector 425 for two minutes then back on to 280 degrees. Buster."

This meant that I was going to get myself into position and at the same time would have to go much faster. All those who have sat down below and listened to a night raid will often hear a very high-pitched, buzzing noise rather like the sound of an angry bee. This noise is usually a fighter trying to chase a bomber. After a while the Controller would come on again.

"Hullo, Bad Hat 17. He is now about 1 mile ahead. Prepare to use your apparatus. Let me know when you have got anything."

You immediately throttle back and adjust your speed to one which you think will be overtaking him very slowly. Then your radio observer begins to work the dials at the back. After a while he will probably say: "OK, Pilot, I have got an indication. He is straight ahead about a mile and a half." And then a series of quick directions will gradually bring you into a position, from which you should see him silhouetted the night sky.

Yes, it is pleasant sitting there warm and comfortable, eating the odd spot of chocolate, waiting for a sight of the enemy. The big moment comes when you see him.

Once we were put on to an 88 and I had got exactly to this moment. I quickly swung to the left, as I was told he would he slightly on my left, but on looking the other way I found that we were flying practically alongside him, and he saw us and disappeared. Another night we got so close that the operator said that we would collide any minute, but I couldn't see a thing. In desperation I fired all four cannons into space to try to make him fire back at me, and immediately back came the tracer from his rear-gunner from far below; something again was wrong with our airborne apparatus. This time the rear-gunner paid for his folly though, and I saw a lot of cannon shells pump into him before he managed to escape.

It was all a question of trial and error, and, I am afraid, a lot of trial and a lot of error. Many times our night-fighter aerodromes would get bombed. Often lonely Junkers 88 would sit above our flare-path at night, waiting for us to land, and would try to shoot us down. I myself had an affair of this kind with a Junkers 88; we had been returning from Manchester, where we had seen "sweet nothing" except a lot of inaccurate flak, and were circling

242

WC1, looking forward to bacon and eggs and coffee. I called up the control and asked them if there were enemy aircraft about.

No, there were no enemy aircraft, they said.

This was fine. So I turned on my navigation lights and began the approach. Down went the wheels and flaps according to plan. Meanwhile, down on the ground, watching events, but unable to do anything, as there were no RT facilities, stood Charles Widdows. He had been looking at a suspicious aeroplane which had been floating around for some time. Now he saw it get into position behind my tail. When about 50ft off the ground the Junkers 88 let me have it. But he too was a bad shot and all we did was to crash through some trees on the far side of the 'drome, although one cannon shell went into the radio operator's leg and wounded him.

These things were happening every night and so there was nothing to shoot a line about. Sometimes, though, the intruders got more success with the bombers over their own aerodromes. In fact, Scampton a little later was to have quite an eventful evening. First of all an intruder tried to do the same thing, but got shot down for its pains, and rolled in a ball across the middle of the aerodrome. Then Tony Mills, returning from a mission, happened to collide with one of his own aircraft directly above the 'drome and both crashed in flames, everyone being killed. The final curtain came when a Hampden opened its bomb doors at the dispersal point and a 40lb fragmentation bomb fell out, killing three people. There were fifteen bodies in the mortuary that night.

One night one lone Ju 88 spent about two hours over Lincolnshire, prowling up and down between Hemswell and Cranwell, sometimes having a bang at a bomber, now and then getting among the "Oxfords" at that very famous flying school. Each time his route took him over a certain fighter station. There, the Station Commander stood on top of one of his hangars and watched, swearing loudly each time he came over. He was a last war pilot and had won both the DSO and DFC flying camels in France. The sight of this Ju flying unmolested over his 'drome on this bright moonlight night irked him considerably.

At last he could stand it no longer. He ordered a Hurricane to be started up.

In its cockpit he sat, waiting patiently for the reappearance of the Hun. At last it came along, flying north at 2,000ft. He took off.

Almost immediately he intercepted and got into a position astern for the kill. With memories of the sky above Amiens in 1917, he pressed the button. Nothing happened. Again. No cannon even clicked. He swore down the RT, but this wasn't working.

Suddenly the Hun turned out to sea and he followed it for some twenty minutes, all the time trying to get his guns to fire, but, needless to say, in vain. Regretfully he turned around for home, breathing dire threats to those on the ground.

Some say at this station that you could hear him shouting when he was coming in to land. Others say he put every armourer on the station under arrest. Whatever happened, he was very annoyed until the Squadron-Commander turned up. "Did you turn the ring, sir?" he asked politely.

"What ring?"

"Why, the safety ring on the gun-button, sir. The guns won't fire unless you turn it anti-clockwise, like this — then press like this."

Four cannons roared healthily into the night.

The Station Commander went very red. He had tried to fire his guns in the "safe" position.

The rest of the story must remain untold.

After a while the aerodromes of Lincolnshire were right in the front line. We had to change the flare-path, amidst exploding bombs, on many an occasion; often bombers returning from raids in bad weather would crash near our landing ground and our ground crews would put up magnificent shows trying to get the air crews out in a hell of blazing ammunition and bursting bombs.

These were the days, too, when the fighter-bomber feud closed down. Escorted by scores of Hurricanes and Spitfires, our new heavy bombers had made a worthy attack on Brest. It was a complete success. The fighters protected the bombers, and the bombers flew through heavy flak to do their job. Both sides came back swearing to high heaven about the prowess of the other. They were blood brothers at last.

★ ★ ★

Meanwhile, a word about security. Most people will have seen a poster depicting a young airman talking to a dumb blonde who tells the story to a not-so-dumb redhead — thence to the spy; underneath is the legend "Careless Talk Costs Lives".

Many, like ostriches, like to bury their heads in the sand and say, "This can't happen in England". To these people I would like to tell this short story, of how such a thing did happen. At least, I think it did.

It was in the days of sweeps, when vast formations of Spitfires would patrol up and down the Pas-de-Calais area, looking for trouble. Sometimes they found it, sometimes the never saw a thing.

One day, in the early evening, I was having a quiet glass of beer in a certain pub. The bar was crowded mostly with RAF types, but with one or two civilians thrown in. Suddenly, my companion saw a fighter boy across the bar.

"Hullo, old boy. Have a beer?" he called.

"No, thanks. I'm on a big show early tomorrow."

There was a hushed silence. Everyone had heard with a certain amount of uneasiness what had been said. Some were in the "big show" as well. Then the bar became alive with conversation, and the incident was forgotten.

Next day they went off. Flying high in tight formation they crossed the coast somewhere between Dunkirk and Ostend. Behind, criss-crossing from side-to-side, flew the weavers, whose job was to keep a continual watch behind and to cover the rear of the formation.

Suddenly — "Bandits diving astern" came the cry. Out of the sun came the Me.s, and fifteen of our boys failed to return. Later, I read the Intelligence report on the raid. "It would seem," it read, "that enemy knew we were coming from sources other than radio. Some information must have leaked out." Next night I looked for the boy who had talked, but he was one of the fifteen.

As on a cloudy day, when the sun has been shining for a few minutes, then goes behind a storm-cloud and it begins to rain . . . we in England began to face bad news once again. First, the Germans retook Benghazi. Then began a long retreat for the tired, supply-starved British Army. Then Hitler invaded Greece and Jugoslavia. By the 10th of April the British and imperial Forces were in action over the entire Greek Front. Exactly seventeen days later Athens fell, and a day later, to the fanfare of trumpets, Hitler announced that Marshal Rommel had entered Sollum.

At home the Luftwaffe was doing its best to carry out Hitler's threat. Coventry, London, Birmingham and Plymouth all received the fury of the fire-bomb. Many were unprepared for such a blitz and severe damage was done. Sometimes whole blocks would be burnt-out shells with the coming of daylight.

Britain was getting it. And taking it.

The papers demanded reprisals. "Bomb Berlin," they shouted. "Bomb Berlin."

We did, on the 17th of April, and thirty-seven of our bombers failed to return out of a couple of hundred. The trouble — icing.

No, we had a long way to go before we could reply in strength, but the might of our bombers was growing day by day. Some said we would have a thousand before the end of the year. Mr. Churchill said, "We will bomb the German enemy in ever increasing measure."

He spoke truly.

With the sure knowledge that one day we would be able to repay the compliment tenfold, we night-fighter boys did our best to protect our kith and kin down below, but we had to be patient. These were dark days, but perhaps they would get darker. Invasion time was looming up. We could only sit and wait. Sometimes a little tired — because, although this night-fighting business had nothing of the strain of night bombing, it was, when the blitz was on, quite a hectic job.

By the end of April, Charles Widdows came in with good news, the first we had heard for some time.

"Good morning, chaps," said he, puffing at his pipe. "I have new gen for you. We are going to be moved out of 12 Group down to West Malling in 11 Group. As you know," he went on, "West Malling is in Kent and there ought to be bags of activity down there, especially as we are entrusted with the direct defence of London."

In a week we had gone, and although we were not to know it, we were going to be very disappointed.

CHAPTER
TWELVE

Find the Hun

West Malling is in Kent, near Maidstone. Of all the airfields in Great Britain, here, many say (including myself), we have the most pleasant. It is near London (one hour by Southern Railway) and it is also near the sea. Its location in the middle of the hop country makes it extremely attractive to Air Force fellows. For in this country are many pubs, and good ones at that, and the inmates are fine types who have toiled and cherished their land for many centuries. The local people are kind and generous, probably because they saw the Battle of Britain rage above their heads, and know more than most what the Air Force have done for this country.

The Huns in 1940 had done their best to destroy Malling, but it had been put up again quickly, this time amongst the trees, which made it hard to be seen from the air. Natural camouflage is always a good thing. Usually contractors insist on cutting down the trees around an aerodrome site, all except those which lie directly in the landing path. There is a well-known story which got around about that time which, I believe, originated from this aerodrome. Workmen had been imported from the North to do the renovation, and these were always grumbling about their pay and the long hours they had to work. One day a particularly badly shot-up Spitfire pilot landed there after a rather tough sweep. On his way to the watch office an old labourer stopped him. "How did you get on?" he asked. The Spit boy told him; they had a cigarette together, and the conversation drifted to the subject of pay.

"Well, how much do you get?"

"About six pounds a week," the boy answered. "How about you?"

"I get eight pounds," replied the workman, "but, of course, I work through alerts."

But Kent in the beginning of May is a sight to be seen. No one could have given this fair county a better name than the "Garden of England". As we flew over the orchards on our way to the 'drome we saw the apple-blossom was out. White and fragrant, it gave the impression of newly formed snow. One by one the orchards came and went in continuous panorama, some large, some small, but all owned by the men of Kent. Now and then an oast-house would flash by. This is where the hops are dried, and they say you can feel tight on the smell alone if you stay in long enough. And all over the country was the Mark of the Beast — thousands of bomb craters that had left their holes in the white chalk, dropped in neat sticks miles from anywhere. This, we found out later, was known as the jettison area where many a windy Hun, pursued by fighters, would pull the plug, then leg it for home across the Channel.

Then there were the trees, green, impassive and tall, miles and miles of them. It takes more than a bomb to shift trees, and these had been here for hundreds of years and meant to stay. Green trees, green fields, green England. A lovely sight. We were glad, as we roared over the 'drome in a tight box, to be here.

It did not take long for us to settle down. Wing-Commander Wilkinson, the CO, a nice chap, had everything fixed. Our quarters were in the old Maidstone Flying Club clubhouse, comfortable and warm. He had taken over a fine Victorian country house, known as The Hermitage, which was to be used as an Officers' Mess; the ground crews were put up in an older castle nearby, and they were all very enthusiastic about it too, especially when they compared it with their drab quarters in Lincolnshire.

That night we stood by, but the weather was bad and Group released the squadron at about nine. Down to the "Startled Saint" we went, complete with ground crews, to sample the beer; it was good and everyone was happy.

The next night the Huns began to give Liverpool a week of blitz. In doing so, their route to the target usually took them over our sector, and we were ready. For a few nights we were unlucky, but then came the night. Above Brighton six of us circled, waiting . . .

Then:

"Hullo, Bad Hat 25. Biggin Control calling. We have some customers for you. Vector 180 degrees to meet them across the Channel. Angels twelve. Buster."

I heard Dave acknowledge the message and thought, lucky devil, he is going to get first chance.

"Hullo, Bad Hat 13. Biggin Control calling. Vector 170. Bandits." That was Graham-Little.

"Hullo, Bad Hat 34. Vector 130 degrees. Angels twenty. Bandits' course zero-four-zero. Stand by to turn."

One by one the boys were pulled out of their orbiting positions to chase the unseen enemy. I sat up there, cursing, waiting for my orders, impatient to be given the chance. Sergeant James, my radio observer, sat in the back, silently chewing gum.

We listened to the other voices, coming over the RT.

"Hullo, Bad Hat 25. You are right amongst them. Flash your weapon."[1]

"Hullo, Bad Hat 34. Sharp turn on to zero-zero-zero. He is 1 mile in front."

"Hullo, all Bad Hat aircraft. Bandits going for Liverpool — rough course three-four-zero. Stand by."

Still no orders; round and round I went, getting almost dizzy. It was a lovely night, clear as a bell and just a small new moon. Ideal. But we must wait. Wait for orders.

---

[1] This means "Use A.1."

I pictured the Controller sitting at his desk 100 miles away. On his table all the green slugs were moving north, amongst them a few red flags; that was us. He must have been harassed at all the activity, hoping that he was doing the right thing. He wasn't a pilot himself and hadn't flown much. He had a tough job.

Suddenly:

"Tally-ho, Tally-ho." This was Bad Hat 34, a new fellow called Lance Martin.

"OK, 34. Good luck. Listen out."

"Listen out."

Silence in the air for ten minutes. Then:

"Hullo, Control. 34 calling. It was a Wimpy, blast it. I nearly cracked him down."

"OK, 34. Stand by."

Another problem for the Controller. What was a Wellington doing here? Was it friendly or was it one of ours flown by a German crew? They say they had captured some in Libya. What was he going to do? What must he say?

"Hullo, 34. Identify and challenge."

"OK, Control. I have; it's friendly."

"OK. Listen out."

Plenty of OKs in this night RT, but the Controller wasn't worrying about this. He was cursing Bomber Command to all and sundry in the operations room. Why must they let their ruddy Wimpies fly around amidst Huns on a night like this? If they had to fly high, why couldn't they keep on their identification lights? He picked up the 'phone to have a word with the operations room.

The air was full of radio background "mush" and now and again came an odd order from below. An unreal scene, a scene engineered by science. This was the twentieth-century war. The war of electricity.

Still more jabbering.

"He's 4 miles in front. Buster 34."

"OK."

"Flash your weapon."

"Flashing weapon."

"Hullo, 13. Any luck?"

"No, nothing yet."

"Hullo, 25. Return to base."

"Bad luck."

"Hullo, Bad Hat 16. Change to button D and call Ragbag."

Alan Grout, who was sixteen, acknowledged and then went off the air. He had changed his frequency to receive instructions from an advance control point known as Ragbag. Alan was new, a pleasant chap, who seemed to fly well. I wished him luck.

We were still circling Brighton. Away on the left I could see the searchlights flickering above Southampton, now and again supported by the odd amount of flak, nothing much, just a few shells. Away in the distance a red ball suddenly appeared in the sky. At first it looked like a flare, but soon we could see it was moving slowly — terribly slowly — then sparks began to come out from the back. So this was an aircraft on fire. Gradually the ball began to lose height, taking its time, but all the while going towards the ground. It had flown on like this for what seemed a lifetime, but actually perhaps for two minutes, and it suddenly got bigger and something fell off behind, a wing, maybe. Then it was all over. It began to plummet down towards the earth like a rocket, leaving a long trail of white sparks and exploding Very lights. Was it a Hun? Perhaps it was one of the boys? Then it hit the ground with a tremendous yellow-orange explosion which lit up the countryside for about five seconds and then died out. All that was left was a dull red glow like a piece of red hot charcoal, burning solitarily in the darkness below.

If it had been a Hun there should have been a few incendiaries burning around the wreckage. But maybe he had already dropped his load. Maybe someone had shot down that Wimpy. Maybe everything. Anything can happen up here. Then:

"Hullo, Bad Hat 17. Are you receiving me?" This was me. "Yes, loud and clear," I replied, waking up.

"Press button B and call Kenley Control."

On my left was a little box which has various buttons on it, just like an ordinary radio. I pushed, and immediately heard the voice of the Kenley Controller. A deep and hearty voice, as though he had just had a good dinner. He was talking to someone else.

"Well done, Binto 40. Return to base. Nice work."

So it was the other squadron which had just had a kill. I called up quickly, anxious not to miss anything.

"OK, 17," came the fruity voice. "Vector 180 degrees."

When we were in mid-Channel:

"They're still around you. They're coming in droves and convoys, crossing the coast at Hove."

I nearly expected a voice to say "Square four", but nothing happened.

"OK. Shall I orbit?"

"Yes, orbit and flash your weapon."

We circled to the left, James in the back working his instrument, watching carefully, ready to shout instructions to me at the first opportunity.

"Any joy, Bad Hat 17?"

"Nothing yet, listening out."

"OK."

It was then I saw it. A black shadow with flames spitting out of the twin exhausts. He wasn't coming directly towards me, but rather more from left to right. For a minute I felt rather like one does when driving a car. You see another chap coming towards you, and you hoot your horn wildly to tell him to keep to his right side. A funny feeling of alarm, and I felt my thumb tighten against the gun-button as if to do the same, but there wasn't much time. A hard kick on the rudder-bar brought the Beau into the right position and I squinted through the ring-sight. One ring deflection. No, give it two. I didn't know much about this deflection business, anyway.

"Look out, Jimmy," I found myself whispering, thinking for a second that the bandit might hear me, rather as one does, or might do, if you were slinking up on a sentry from behind.

Then my four cannons and six machine-guns blazed into the night. The effect was startling. An enormous explosion rent the air and it became, quite suddenly, as light as day. For a moment I was rather stunned by what had happened as I watched my victim fall quickly towards the earth. We were away out to sea. No one had baled out. Even if they had, the sea was pretty cold.

I felt pleased and worried at the same time. Pleased to have shot down something; worried because I didn't know what it was. James was more excited than I and kept yelling at me from the back. Then a sort of anti-climax came over us both, and we wanted to land quickly and tell the boys all about it.

As we crossed the coast again:

"Hullo, 17. Bandit 4 miles ahead. Angels 10."

We were at 18,000, so I put down my nose to gain speed. The Beau began to whistle (no wonder she is called "whispering death"). Then a yell from James.

"OK, Pilot; he is straight ahead — a little below."

We were now going quite fast: air speed about 330. I had to wind the trimming well to keep her in her dive. Then I saw him. He was going like a dingbat for Southampton at about 6,000ft. But just before I could press the button, he suddenly rolled over on to his back and dived into a small village, a mass of burning incendiaries. We had followed him right down to the ground, and the explosion blinded us completely and at the same time rocked our wings, as though to shake them off.

It was some time before I could regain contact with Kenley. At last, when we had climbed enough, I told them the story — how the thing had pranged without my firing a shot.

"OK," came that voice. "I think she must be yours."

"But I didn't fire a single shot!"

"I know. Ring me up when you land. Press button A and request a homing bearing. Goodnight."

We flew home puzzled. Both combats — if you can call them such — were not organized as they should be, but complete flukes. We felt lucky and a little ashamed.

Next day, as usual, all pilots who had flown the night before reported to the Intelligence Officer. Unlike some RAF Intelligence Officers, F/L Hickman was intelligent. Unable to fly himself because of his eyes, he did everything humanly possible to help us pilots. Moreover, he was young and could drink beer.

"Well, chaps," he said as we came in, "last night was pretty good. In all eighteen Huns were brought down: a high percentage of the numbers involved. It looks as though we are getting somewhere at last."

This was true. I noticed one or two of the pilots fidgeting, anxious to get into the air to test their apparatus, ready for the night's work. I think

Hickman noticed this, too, because instead of his usual résumé of current troop movements on the world map, he came right to the last point.

"Last night," he went on, "some of you were unlucky. Humphries's apparatus failed in the chase. Gordon Clegg got shot up by another Beau, and his observer's leg has just been amputated; he is doing all right, though. Martin's RT packed up, but the searchlights helped him to get home. The only real combat of the night was by Bad Hat 17."

"Pretty lucky," I murmured.

"Yeah, but your first one is confirmed by the Home Guards and Coastguards at Selsey Bill, who saw it fall into the sea at the exact time you yelled to the controller. So that's all right."

"How about the second?" asked James.

"Well, this is the tricky part. First Fighter Command told us to credit you with both, so that the Gunners wouldn't claim it. Now we have heard that not a gun fired at it in the whole neighbourhood. So the AA boys are not claiming anything. But another fellow in the squadron at Tangmere says it was his."

"Probably was. It certainly wasn't mine."

"Then you don't want to have anything to do with it?"

"No."

"Well, wait till you have heard what I have got to say. The crew of four baled out and were interrogated. They all say, independently, that they were first attacked by a twin-engine fighter which did them severe harm but did not send them completely out of control. They therefore abandoned the idea of bombing Liverpool and decided to drop their incendiaries on Southampton. It was while they were running in that something hit them and knocked off their wing. They have no idea what it was, but say they had to bale out in a hurry. Someone gave the pilot a cup of tea in the farmhouse where he landed. He was pretty shaken."

"Well, I think it should go to the first pilot," said Graham.

"I agree," said James.

"Well, it is a mystery which may never be solved, but I think that's the best plan. That's all, chaps. Good luck tonight."

James and I walked out feeling good. We were both pleased that our first one had been confirmed, even though it had been so lucky. It was a great job, this night-fighting business.

The last few nights Liverpool had got it badly. The fires that were started, despite the valiant efforts of the NFS, were still burning the next night, and all the Hun had to do was to aim at these. The resulting devastation was appalling. But by shooting down a large number during the time of the blitz, we had diverted the bombers to a route which took them far away from our sector up the Irish Sea; not all of them, but a few. This, being a longer journey, at least reduced their bomb-loads slightly, which, of course, gave Liverpool a slight break. But those that did fly up the Irish Sea managed to evade most night-fighters, although the few operating from the Isle of Anglesey did get one or two. This journey up the Irish Sea, it was said, resulted in Dublin being bombed.

When Liverpool had been left battered, the German Bomber Command laid off. They had done their work well, but had misjudged the calibre of the North-country Englishman. Although some ugly stories got around about the morale of the blitzed citizens, it left that city in the mood of war, a grim mood, longing for the day of reprisal. But except for the daily news of the bombing of Brest they had a long time to wait.

A few nights later the Luftwaffe sang its swan song of night bombing over the Houses of Parliament. The House of Commons was hit. About 250 long-range bombers swarmed over the capital at two-minute intervals, crossing the coast at all points between Dungeness and Beachy Head. They flew high across the coast, dived inland towards London to make their bombing attack and came out low. I think that was partly to avoid night-fighters and partly to avoid collisions. All had the same tactics; all did the same thing, and they received a severe rebuff. It was a full moon. Ideal for the fighter. Thirty-three failed to return, many others were damaged.

In my squadron Alan Grout got two, Bob Braham shot another one down over Croydon (his third) and others had combats. It was an eventful night and one which marked the turning-point of the air war over London.

I flew that night. I saw London burn, but it didn't seem too bad. Many bombers were dropping their loads far short amongst the suburbs, some even as far out as Dorking and Guildford. The bombing wasn't concentrated. If it had been London would have looked much worse. One load which fell in a wood in Alton burnt for a whole week, doing no real damage. No doubt some German observer claimed this as an aircraft factory burning.

The flak over London was really terrible, not enough of it and not even accurate. All we fighter boys used to take no notice of it at all, knowing that it would be extremely bad luck if it hit us. I remembered from my bombing days that even a French village would push up more. This wasn't the fault of AA Command so much as, the fact that the Germans had started making guns eight years before us. But, nevertheless, if we were to be really successful in the night-fighting game, we would have to be backed up by real anti-aircraft ground defences which would prevent the Hun from straying around too much. Army gunners and searchlight crews at that time were always annoying the night-fighter pilot by their optimism. Often they would claim to have done their stuff on the flimsiest piece of wishful evidence. All we knew was that it would take a fighter to stop the night bomber, and so were very careful in what we said. Every piece of information was analysed, checked and re-checked.

Each combat was carefully thought out. Could it have been better? Could our equipment have worked in another way? These were all filed into a master plan which eventually made Night Fighter Command what it became.

But I shall not say much of May 10th/11th. My log book tells the story. Here is an extract:

Date	a/c	No.	Pilot	Observer	Duty	Time up
May 10th	Beau	2250	Self	Sgt James	Night defence London. We saw four Heinkels. Cannons jammed each time.	3.40

(There was also a very rude word written in the Remarks column, but this was blacked out by the CO with an appropriate note.)

The entries read on:

May 11th. Tested cannons out at sea. No good.
May 12th. Tested cannons. Only one fired.
May 13th. Tested cannons. None fired.
May 13th. Tested cannons. None fired.
May 15th. To test cannons. All fired OK.

And the reason? Not the cannons at all, but a simple electrical solenoid in the firing-button becoming unserviceable. Sergeant James, who had, of course, been responsible for the interceptions, was furious! Four Huns! For months we had stooged around, thinking ourselves lucky if we saw one. Then we had seen four fat ones with bomb-loads on, and they had all got away. We saw them — unlike most things that got away.

Despite our failure, the whole night's work was a great success for the defenders of the night sky. The percentage shot down was high and, despite what Goebbels said, they never again came over in strength on a bright moonlight night.

The rest of the month of May passed without incident. Few enemy aircraft crossed the coast, and although we never even dreamed that we had driven them away, everyone was puzzled as to their whereabouts. The weather was good, but the Luftwaffe seemed to have disappeared. Then came the news of the invasion of Crete.

We all thought that they had all gone down there for their summer holiday and to take that island in their stride. Many sea-minded men were saying, "It is impossible. Hitler's really bitten off too much this time." But air power conquered Crete in a few days by combined use of parachute troops, glider-borne troops, anti-flak fighters and bombers.

The Luftwaffe had not gone to Crete for we got the answer a few weeks later. Every night we had stood by at dusk, in readiness, in our club quarters, waiting to take the air. The first one off usually patrolled up and down the French coast, ready for the early bird, but never saw a thing. These stooge patrols were browning us off, and sometimes we were even scared of being smacked down ourselves by a German night-fighter. Each morning I would cycle home to our little cottage, where Eve had breakfast ready for me. Her eyes would light up when I came in. "Any luck?" she would ask. "No, nothing about."

"Well, here's your breakfast. You can have it in bed!"

Then in between clean sheets to snatch a few hours' rest before getting ready for the next night.

But on June 22nd some of us had gone up before dawn to look for that odd Heinkel, making his early morning shipping recco. When it got light we landed back at base and the Spitfires took over. Graham was standing on the doorstep of the clubhouse, looking terrible. He had just got out of his sleeping-bag in the Readiness hut; his eyes were red (four hours' night flying), his hair looked like a mop and his face was covered with oil (unserviceable windscreen spray). We had all been on three nights running, and he hadn't shaved during that time. So you can imagine the rest, a grim sight to see so early in the morning.

"Hullo. Heard the news?" he asked, knowing that I hadn't.

"No. Been stooging around for the last two hours."

"Germany has invaded Russia."

There had been rumours of this for the last few days, so I wasn't too surprised.

"So that's where all the Huns are."

"Must be. We may as well pack up for a few weeks," said Lance, who had just landed.

"No, we can't. Our spies say the Huns are going to intensify their mine-laying in the estuary, so that we cannot get supplies up to Russia. We have got to get going at low-level interception. It is going to be a tough job."

"Which?"

"The mine-laying interceptions, of course."

By then the morning papers arrived, and I pounced on one and took it home. Some said it would all be over in a matter of weeks. Russia's show against Finland hadn't been too impressive. Others said that Hitler was too late: the winter would begin long before he reached Moscow and he would perish like Napoleon. Only one paper made a really accurate statement. If, it said, Russia could survive the first hundred days, Germany would have had it. By then the Soviet would have been able to mobilize her full manpower reserves, which were prodigious, and even the might of the Wehrmacht would be halted.

During the next few days events moved quickly. The Russians became our allies. Brest-Litvsk and Riga fell as the Hun tide of terror moved slowly forward. Marshal Stalin broadcast his famous scorched-earth policy to his people. By the 7th the Russians had fallen back to the Dnieper, but left a trail of desolation behind them in their retreat. Another milestone in the war had been reached.

The Russians were now friends and allies of the British people, who were left blitz-free for many a moon. Most night-fighter squadrons now had plenty of time to perfect the new devices which might be able to beat the night-bomber, while we took up our role of anti-mine layers.

The enemy minelayers were hard to beat. They left their coast, flying low and fast until they came to a point about 30 miles from England, when they would climb up to about 4,000ft, get a quick radio position, then dive down again to drop their mines. With our existing equipment it was necessary to make our interception at the exact place where they began to climb. Needless to say, this was very difficult. Moreover, it involved flying to almost unheard-of accuracy. When we were told to lose height at 250ft per minute, we had to do so; if we did not, we would lose him. If we were told to fly 180 ASI, it meant that exactly. A special RT station was fixed up on the Kent cliffs which could talk to us as far as the Dutch coast. Beside it was a special station which could "see" us almost as far. Day and night we began to practise, often within sight of the enemy coastline, often intercepting ourselves, but sometimes practising on enemy shipping raiders. Now and then the enemy would send up a fighter which would listen in to our frequencies and not only would follow the directions of our controller but would begin to chase us, with the result that it became a game of grim hide-and-seek among the low-lying clouds off the Dutch coast.

On our station, while vast changes in the British Cabinet were being announced, we, too, had our reshuffle. Charles Widdows took over the station. A new Wing-Commander, Ted Colbeck-Welch, became Squadron-Leader; he was a pleasant fellow with an outstanding personality and a nice wife. Bob and I were each given a Flight, at the same time being promoted to Squadron-Leaders.

A few days later the squadron had its first success at this new game. Bob got one near Southport, flying at 6,000ft. All its mines blew up and it fell, a blazing wreck, into the sea. A few minutes later James put me on to a Heinkel at 4,000ft, and after a two-second burst it caught fire and spun in off Sheerness. A third was shot down into the marshland near Harwich by another squadron. Considering this was about 20 per cent of the number sent over, it was a very good night, but the sky had been clear and the visibility good. Our next step was to do the same thing in bad weather.

Robin Miles and Lance Martin both did the trick within a week. Both had seen the glow from the enemy's exhaust underneath the cloud. Both had taken careful aim. Both Huns were blown up, and both Robin and Lance celebrated.

One of the survivors was interrogated by a special chap on the Station. I saw him in the Mess afterwards. He was fuming.

"I've never heard such a line of bull in all my life. The fellow must have been absolutely crazy. He said the Russians would be conquered in a month's time and Hitler would be in London by the end of the year."

"What about America's supplies.

"He said we're losing nearly all of them to the U-boats."

This was partially true. The U-boat situation was critical, but, like us, Coastal Command was still persevering with the unseen enemy. An electric device was coming along, and they thought they would soon have the answer.

"Did he say anything else?"

"Nothing else," the Intelligence Officer said grimly, "except to tell me that if I could put in a good word for him and get him to Canada, where he seems to think he could escape easily, he would see that I was well treated when the Germans marched in. I nearly smacked his teeth in," he murmured, taking a long swig at his can.

So those were our enemies. Cocksure, brutal and full of graft. No wonder they stink.

As the summer began to pass away, something began to stir within me. God knows what it was. I was very happy in the squadron; they were an extremely friendly bunch with very high morale. There was no cattishness; no one talked about the other, and there was no jealousy. They loved flying and could do it well. They liked parties and, of course, they could do that very well. Night-flying was good fun and not too dangerous. There was absolutely no nerve-strain, and I felt I could go on for ever. Leave came regularly and frequently. Only last month Eve, Dave and I had driven down to St Mawes in Cornwall, where our antics in a sailing-boat made the local sailors grin. They would spit and say, "You may be able to fly a Spitfire, but you bain't able to sail a ruddy boat." This was true enough, so we never argued; that was one of the reasons why we always had our Heinkel dinghy towing behind us, so that if anything went wrong we could always bale out. Needless to say it was a good holiday.

Our Station, under Charles Widdows, was happy. He and Nicky, his wife, knew how to entertain. The parties in the Mess were prodigious. No one even minded when Nigger, my new and lovely Labrador pup, would let himself go over the Mess carpet. A great flyer was Nigger; he used to go up on nearly every patrol. I think it made him thirsty, and he loved beer.

The local people had by now got to know us. Everyone wanted to have us, with our wives, in for a meal. Such names as Sheldon and Bincham were by-words in the district, and more than that, in our squadron the latter used to have the boys in every Monday night. I would usually work it that my Flight was "off" that night, and we would go there in a convoy of cars up the winding hill to Ebbor House. There the beer flowed easily. Songs were sung. Lance played the piano well. A few men like Ken could do little acts, such as reciting some of Noël Coward's masterpieces in a certain manner, arousing great enthusiasm. These were really

271

enjoyable days, and no matter what happens, I should like to record that in many ways they were the happiest I have ever had. But, somehow, in the back of my head was that little bug of restlessness.

The enemy bombers had almost ceased their activity, both by day and night. Now and again they would come over to make quick attacks on our coastal towns. At one time they began to send Junkers 87s, making their first reappearance since the Battle of Britain. One night they came a little too early, when it wasn't yet dark, and I had the good fortune to damage two of them. A lonely watcher on the cliff said he saw one go into the sea, but it was never confirmed.

New devices were being fitted up in our aircraft which enabled us to land in fog. Bob Braham once went up when the visibility was no more than 300 yards. I did the same when it was about 600 yards, and found no difficulty whatsoever. Other devices were on the way which would enable us to shoot down enemy aircraft when they were flying very low. We would practise with these a lot and became, in the end, very successful.

Good fun, but it wasn't enough. That is why, towards the end of November, the duty pilot in Scampton Watch Office was surprised to see, at dusk, a Beau pull off a mediocre landing by the old A Flight dispersal point. He immediately picked up the 'phone and asked for the Mess.

Jack Kynoch, now a Squadron-Leader, met me in the hall. He was back on Ops again in the same old squadron, but a lot of the old faces had gone. Gillan had transferred to Fighters and had been shot down on his first trip. "Colonel" Barker had failed to return a few nights before. Jackie Withers had been killed by one of our own night-fighters. Charles Kidd had pranged himself in a Manchester. In fact, all of them: Tony Mills, young Dixon and the rest — that is, nearly all — just weren't there.

"Things are getting tougher there now," said a fellow called Ord, in answer to my question. "The flak's about the same, but those searchlights are absolute hell. They have put up a huge belt to cover the Ruhr, about 20 miles wide, from the Dutch coast down to Paris. We all have to go through it, both on the way in and on the way out. In fact, there is no avoiding it. A few say go in at low level, but none of us can fly high enough to get out of the beams; besides, the Hampden's getting pretty worn out."

"How about targets? Do you still go for military objectives?"

"More or less. We have given up that old idea of bringing the bombs back if you can't see the Primary. These days we are given an aiming point in the middle of an industrial area; the idea being that even if the attack is scattered, some worthwhile object will be hit."

"What sort of numbers are sent out now?"

"Oh, about 400 if it's to be a good prang. It would have been much more if it hadn't been for the Middle East offensive."

"I suppose that's about 800 tons?"

"Yes, about 800 if a few Stirlings are with us. We can carry 3,000lb to the Ruhr now, because we knock off petrol."

"Good idea! What about accuracy?"

"Well, some aircraft are fitted with cameras to show how we have got on. The effect of searchlight dazzle, coupled with decoys and deceptive fighting, and, of course, the flak, makes a good attack almost impossible, except on bright moonlight nights. The trouble is the weather is so bad, and we have to dive below the cloud if we want to do any good, but it is often so dark down there that we can never see the aiming point. More often than not bombs fall anywhere within 10 miles."

"Well, what do the cameras do?"

"As yet only a few carry them. We all take our turn. The idea is really to find out who are the best crews, so that they can go in and light up the aiming point, if possible with an incendiary load, but even if that happens the Hun will put up dummies which will look just like an incendiary light burning on the aiming point, which is, of course, miles away. I have carried one of these cameras, and the results have been startling," he went on. "Some chaps who come back shooting a hell of a line find they have taken a photograph of open country miles from anywhere; that's happened to me."

"But does the photo show where your bombs fell accurately?" I asked.

"To within a few hundred yards. When you press the tit a flashbomb goes off at the same time as the bombs; it explodes at about 3,000ft and lights up the ground while the camera shutter is opened for just about the right time. It is quite simple, really."

"I should think a camera fitted to all aircraft will not only increase bombing accuracy, but will make sure that all crews press home their attacks," said my observer.

"That is just what it will do," the bomber pilot went on. "But there are several technical difficulties. However, the Boffins[1] are hard at work. What we do really need is a new aeroplane. These old Hampdens . . ."

We talked on for an hour or two, then went down to the flarepath to watch the boys take off. They were just the same. They still hit that large ridge in the middle of the field and jumped into the air prematurely, as if someone had kicked them in the pants; there was still the same little crowd of boys who weren't going, to wave them off from the first flare; the same spirit — the spirit of pioneers of an offensive.

Then I jumped into my sleek black Beau, which looked so handsome amongst those flying suitcases, pressed the self-starts and we were off.

My journey had been really necessary. I was convinced that it was Bomber Command for me any day.

---

[1] Scientists.

★ ★ ★

A few days later Bob got another one. By now he was getting really good, and the way he handled his latest success showed that he was going to be a past-master at the art of shooting down Huns.

The Bandit had been flying far out to sea, just above cloud, now and then darting into it, probably as some gunners in the back saw a star and gave the alarm. Bob, on his way out to intercept, had noticed that the cloud broke some way from the coast. When his observer, Gregory, gave him a contact, instead of trying to close immediately, and therefore risking the chance of having a quick squirt before the Hun dived into the cloud, he told him to lay off. They followed about half a mile behind for some fifteen minutes, then the cloud broke. The rest was simple.

Bob was a dead-eye Dick as far as four cannons were concerned, and the Hun blew up smartly.

But no such luck for me. I flew on night after night, never seeing any more. Once I did see a Heinkel going in the opposite direction just below me. I tried to turn, but it was no use, the thing had disappeared.

Each time I was on these stooge patrols I used to get more and more fed up. Poor old James in the back would take a whole harangue of "this being a waste of time, etc. etc." Each night I would long for the minute when my wheels would touch earth again, so that I could go back to see my little cottage.

Flying is great fun if there is some point in it; if something's going to happen. I don't think I should ever be able to take the long hours of Coastal Command, where boys have to be on the top line for sometimes eighteen hours, or even more.

And so came December. The third milestone of the war had arrived rather slowly, and very unexpectedly. On December 7th the radios of the world blared out the news that while negotiations were being carried on in Washington to make quite certain that Japan would not enter the war, she carried out a dawn attack on Pearl Harbour that Sunday morning. It was an attack aimed well below the belt, but, nevertheless, total war is all below the belt, and Big Powers have to realize this.

The general feeling among the boys was — good. Thank God the whole world's in now. There can't be any more surprises in this war now. Three milestones had passed; the last would be Victory. News began to pour in through the ticker tapes of London clubs, as quickly as it could be tapped out: to be read anxiously by members who had all returned, now that the blitz was over. They crowded around — knowing that history was being made.

On the 10th the *Prince of Wales* and *Repulse* were sunk by the Japanese. On the 11th Germany and Italy declared war on the United States. A few days later Hitler, no doubt not satisfied with the events in Russia, dismissed Field Marshal Brauchitsch, while Mr Churchill crossed the Atlantic Ocean to confer for the second time with President Roosevelt.

On the 24th Benghazi was occupied. This was the only successful offensive waged by the British at that time; next day Hong Kong was forced to surrender. Many Canadians were taken prisoner.

And so the year came to a close. But there was worse news for me. I was playing billiards while standing by for "dusk readiness" in the clubhouse. It was an important game because we had all got very good in our long hours of waiting, and this time I had half a crown on to win. Suddenly Ted Colbeck-Welch came in.

"Hullo, Guy," he said. "I have got some gen for you."

"Oh yes, what's that?" I asked, eyeing a pocket cannon I was about to pull off.

"You're being posted to an OTU," he said. "You're being rested."

"Rested!" I nearly yelled. "But I came on to night-fighters for a rest. Group must be barmy."

"It's not Group," said Ted. "it's Fighter Command who feel you should be. You've got to go."

I knew that Ted wasn't joking, so I picked up my cue to finish the game. But from then on I couldn't play another shot. Rested in an OTU! What a thought! I would ring up Bomber Command tomorrow. Then I could go back on to Ops. But you cannot play billiards when thinking of these things. I lost half a crown.

CHAPTER
THIRTEEN

The Heavy Brigade

AOCs, Group-Captains and the rest of them are very fine, powerful fellows; there is no doubt about that. By merely pushing a button they can launch into the air hundreds of aircraft to obey their immediate command. If the wine last night was good and their liver this morning bad, they can in one quick second give an order which will parade thousands of young airmen in best blue; all standing stiffly to attention, each one thinking the old thought, So this is an inspection. They can post men from John-o'-Groats to Baghdad. But when it comes to altering a posting, then it is an entirely different matter.

"Ah! we must be careful here," says one.

"Must not put our foot in this," says another.

And the final result is nearly always the same — nothing happens. And so it was with me. A journey to Fighter Command brought no joy. A quick flight to Grantham, which used to be the Headquarters of No. 5 Group, was a waste of time. It looked as though I would have to go to the OTU.

My last week in the squadron alternated between Bob and me trying to "pull as many strings" as possible, a run of large and extensive farewell parties. I was sorry to leave fighters and very sorry to leave the boys. Someone said something about my taking over the squadron when I came back in six months' time. Ted hadn't been very well and might be rested himself about then. But I didn't intend to come back. Night-fighting was all very well, but it meant too much patience for me. I should think single-engine fighters are good, clean fun if you are lucky and a good shot. The best thing of all would be train-busting in Hurricanes, being both fairly safe and effective, but night-fighters were different. In a year's work, involving about seventy night sorties and thirty day patrols, I had in all seen about twenty Huns. Of these, I had opened fire on nine. Obviously I was not a very good shot. And bombing was still in my blood.

Many people have asked me which I prefer, bombers or fighters. The answer is obvious. They have also asked me many times what is the essential difference between the two. I may be wrong, but I think it lies in one's mentality and personal make-up.

But first let's separate the day-fighter from the night-fighter. The former is usually a single-engine flyer; the pilot has no responsibility save for his own skin and, of course, the responsibility which all team work involves in aerial combat. He does not have to undergo an awful lot of training. His is a happy-go-lucky existence, for the very reason that to him flying is fun, even though sometimes casualties are high.

In the case of a night-fighter crew we have a highly skilled team, working together, pilot and observer. A Spitfire boy will always avoid flying in cloud, as it involves instrument-flying, but a Beaufighter pilot has to fly on instruments, often from the moment of take-off to the moment of landing. He has to spend most of his time practising both by day and by night. This involves a lot of hard work and practice, but he must be patient. For this reason, many night-fighters are ex-flying instructors with plenty of experience, perhaps married with a family, who wish to do their bit for their country, and a grand job they do too. And speaking of casualties (in Home Defence Squadrons, anyway) due to enemy action, I would say that his is the safest game of all. On the other hand, there is always the eternal enemy, the weather. Most people will agree that night-fighters have to fly, from take-off to landing, in worse weather than any other airmen. But provided the pilot can fly on instruments, it is not a dangerous job.

The degree of danger varies, of course, with the position of the squadron. Some squadrons hardly ever cross the sea, while we at West Malling spent most of our time stooging up and down the enemy coast at a time when we had no dinghys fitted to our aircraft, so that, should anything go wrong, we would have a long way to swim home. Even so, during the whole year I was with the 29th we had only one casualty due to enemy action. He was a radio observer who flew with Charles Widdows. They had over-shot when attacking a Junkers 88, whose rear-gunner had given Charles a good squirt. Then everything happened at once: an engine stopped, the radio inter-com. went, Charles was wounded and the observer baled out. Unfortunately they were 50 miles out to sea. Charles put up a very good show in bringing his battered aircraft all the way back to base on a dark night with no instruments. And he didn't know, until he landed, that his fellow had baled out.

But the weather killed quite a few — Alan Grout, Robin Miles, Sergeant Freer and some others — all through the unlucky roll of the dice. Most of them bought it in the high ground near West Malling.

Yes, the night-fighters' job was to beat the weather and to fly on instruments; they had to be good, if they wanted to survive.

Now let's take the bomber pilot. Here we have men with responsibility. They have a crew of about seven chaps, all of whom depend on the captain for their lives. They fly aircraft weighing about 30 tons and costing £35,000 sterling. They have to combine the skill of the night-fighter with the guts of the day-sweeper. They face all the hazards of bad weather, icing and low cloud. They have to endure the sagging effect on morale of high casualties due to enemy action, they have to wait weeks, perhaps, to know what has happened to their comrades; and all the time weighing on top of them is a deep sense of responsibility.

Perhaps that is why some bomber pilots are a little quieter than others. Perhaps that is why they stand in a corner of a bar, smoking their pipes, reserved and cautious. But not all are like that, especially the fellows whom I mix with. "We must never let our job get us down," they say. Nevertheless, they don't go around dressed like film stars, because the nature of their job is such that it can only be done by iron discipline and good morale. Good leadership will produce the latter, but discipline has to be made. Many members of bomber squadrons when they first arrive think that except for flying, life is all honey. That is not quite the case. They soon find that the other members of a squadron, feeling as they do that they captain the "little ships" of the air, like to take a pride in their appearance; they like to keep their offices clean and tidy; their gardens growing; their aircraft polished. Such spirit breeds efficiency.

That, I think, is the difference between the two.

Some will have wondered why during my association with both types of pilot I have made so much mention of parties and of beer. The reason is simple and true. In a squadron the boys live, eat, sleep and face death together. Some are lucky and keep going and sometimes finish their tour of operations, others don't. If the lucky ones who get good at the game were to sneak out on their off nights with some girl, perhaps to a quiet movie, they would never get to know their squadron, and the squadron would never get to know them. The younger members would do the wrong things at night and squadron spirit would die. However, the one and only plan is to go out with the boys, drink with them, lead them into thinking they are the best; that they cannot die. Get them away from the atmosphere of "Yes, sir," "No, sir." But make sure that atmosphere is very much present next day; be polite, listen to advice. The specialists in the squadron usually know much more than you. Then you will have high morale and a keen team spirit. Huns will be shot down; bombs will fall on the target.

Having risen during this war from a Flying-Officer to a Flight-Commander, I knew such doctrine to be right. I had served under all types — quiet, noisy, mousy, forceful. But of all these men, Ted Colbeck-Welch was the boy who knew the game. Although I hadn't been extremely successful during my time in night-fighters, I had at least picked up some very useful tips from him on how to run a squadron in a happy way. And, moreover, the whole of Fighter Command is the same. It is a very happy Command.

And now I was leaving to go to an OTU. The idea was extremely distasteful, and I felt sorry for myself.

The weather was quite unflyable during the last week, and so the farewell parties to Dave, myself and Bob were on the hectic side. The final one came towards the end of the year, when the whole

Station, including friends and wives, sat down to a Christmastide supper in the main Mess.

From then on it was free for all, and certainly the most outstanding party of all times in that district. Faces were blacked with cork, lipstick was used with abandon on all the unwary. The "kneeling-behind" trick was performed again and again. Those from outside who had never seen anything like it before, looked on, amazed that human beings could act in such a barbaric way. But here was steam being let off, steam which had accumulated for a long time, owing to the Huns' inactivity, and I shall leave it at that, because I think enough has been said.

Next day the boys spent about an hour trying to wash my face. My wife had imprinted with lipstick two large question marks on either cheek during the latter part of the night, which looked very funny at the time, but next day it wouldn't come off. They even tried to use petrol, but it was no use. That afternoon I reported to Group-Captain Fullergood at the OTU with a chapped face and two faint red lines still discernible. However, it was New Year, and I think he put it down to bad liquor, because he didn't say anything.

Days at the OTU passed slowly into weeks. I could never say I was happy, but Fullergood was an ideal CO for the job, and life was not unpleasant.

But the news was. We had started the year full of hope. The Russians had begun their counter-offensive against Kharkov and simultaneously

General Auchinleck's advance into Libya went as far as the capture of Benghazi; then both petered out. And while the Germans in Russia held their hand till the spring, the Afrika Korps began to counter-attack almost immediately, throwing us back as far as Gazala.

They had brought up a lot of reinforcements since the last battle. Now and again I met a few boys who belonged to the Desert Air Force. They said that the going was pretty tough. Dark days were ahead, there was no doubt about that.

We had little to set against the heavy disasters which befell us in the Far East. The crippling of the American Fleet in Pearl Harbour, coupled with the loss of the *Repulse* and *Prince of Wales* off the Malayan coast, had left the Japanese complete masters of the Pacific Ocean. With almost everything in their favour, they had landed troops in the Philippines, the Dutch East Indies and the Bataan Peninsula. The Allies fought well against tremendous odds, especially the Dutch, but it was no use; they were slowly forced under.

Then came the black week in February. Profiting by the treachery of Siam and the submission of French Indo-China, the Japs swept down on to the Malay Peninsula. There, the great fortress of Singapore, built solely for defence against the sea, surrendered unconditionally on February 15th. Many white people vanished never to be heard of again. This was the greatest blow to Britain since Dunkirk — a blow against Britannia who used to rule the waves, against all free people fighting a long uphill battle.

The loss of prestige would have been almost unbearable had not another incident occurred during the same week. After a year of continuous bombing, the *Scharnhorst* and the *Gneisenau*, accompanied by the *Prinz Eugen*, had left their refuge in Brest and had steamed up the English Channel to their home ports in Germany. Immediately a storm of criticism swept the country. A vote of censure was demanded against the Government. First Bomber Command, then the Navy, then the Tories all got their share of bombastic language in editorial columns. Insolent cartoons appeared in our national papers. In America the people who had not yet got accustomed to their new Ally waxed furious. In Berlin they chuckled and waited for the summer.

Of the two disasters, I know little of the first, except that some men came back with horrid tales of inefficiency and apathy on the part of all concerned. One day we will know the truth, but let judgment be suspended until after the war. But of the escape of "Salmon and Gluckstein", there is a small story to tell.

In the first place, these two ships were bombed both by day and by night as often as possible during the past year. "Why," asked the man in the street, "hadn't they been hit, or even destroyed?" The answer is simple. The crews couldn't see them. Moreover, not only the glare of hundreds of searchlights, but the many decoys, coupled with thousands of flak-shells filling the sky above the very small target area, made it virtually impossible even to hit the docks, let alone the ships. Even when our bomber formations had bombed Brest by day, the Germans would fill the whole area with thick yellow smoke, which completely hid everything from view. When I say that in order to get the bombs anywhere near the docks it was necessary to do a five-minute timed run from an island nearby, it will perhaps be realized why no serious damage was done. However, they were kept in port, probably by blast damage, for a whole year — thus saving many a "murder" on the high seas.

On the day of their departure, which was carefully timed to coincide with some very bad weather up the Channel, it was sheer bad luck that prevented aircraft of Coastal Command, which had been watching the place as a cat watches a mouse, from detecting what was happening. The first person to see the ships proceeding up Channel was Group-Captain Victor Beamish, looking for trouble in a Spitfire off the French coast. As soon as he wirelessed back what was happening, wheels of action began to revolve along the South Coast. Bomber Command loaded up for maximum effort. At the same time little ships, Swordfishes and destroyers made attempts to torpedo from close range. They all returned safely and undamaged except for the six Swordfish which, led by

Lieutenant-Commander Esmonde,[1] pressed home their attack in the most gallant way and were all shot down. The trouble was that the Germans chose a day when the cloud was down to 200ft in places, while their fighters were swarming around the ships like bees around a honeycomb.

When our bombers made their attack, many of them found the ships, some made some gallant attacks, but the clouds were too low and often the bombs bounced off the armoured decks. Forty-two failed to return.

It looked as though the ships were going to get away. By now they were well past Den Helder and the Hook of Holland. But Air Marshal Pierse was up to the job. He gave an order. Armourers sweated blood; they immediately loaded up all aircraft again with magnetic mines, and that evening the greatest minefield ever was laid across the ships' paths which would lead them into the North German ports. Meanwhile, if they turned north to avoid the minefield, another force of the Royal Navy was waiting. They chose to go over the minefields, and this is what happened.

Both the *Scharnhorst* and the *Prinz Eugen* were damaged — to what degree has been hard to assess, but they at least each touched off a mine. To say that they had escaped scot-free is quite untrue, thanks to the work done by the minelayers. And to

---

[1] Awarded posthumous VC.

damage a ship the size of the *Gneisenau* was a major victory. The fact that she was later towed to Kiel, where she was again hit by a very heavy bomb, which blew a large hole immediately above her forward magazine, and the fact that she was later towed to Gdynia in Poland, where she was subsequently dismantled, are the answer to those critics who ignorantly attacked the Bomber Force.

However, the fact remained at the time that the two ships had sailed under our very noses — an unpalatable insult.

All could now watch the vast plan of the Axis, would-be world-conquerors, beginning to unfold itself. The ominous pattern of global warfare could be seen clearly on the map. Japan, unchecked, was driving west. Germany in the summer was to drive east both in Russia and in North Africa, to meet somewhere in the region of the Persian Gulf. First the Western World would go under, save perhaps Great Britain, which would be blockaded from all sides. Then South Africa, Australia and the rest of the islands. A short pause, consolidate, and then an attack on the New World from either side the Japs on the Pacific, the Germans in from northern Canada. It wouldn't take long, although the free peoples would fight to the last. Then the whole world could come under the Jackboot. England would collapse through starvation. The world would be conquered. What a prospect!

There is, when flying across the ocean, a point somewhere in the middle known as the "point of no return", when the range of the aircraft is such that it would only enable you to go on to your destination; if you turn back you are lost. I think the Allies had reached that point by March 1942. It was now a fight to a finish.

With the news bad and with the whole country clamouring for a second front, with Malta the only British port in the Axis-held Mediterranean, the one and only offensive being carried on against Germany itself was still that of Bomber Command. Air Marshal Harris, who had now taken over command, was launching his plan of action with heavy attacks against the more lightly defended military objectives, partly to give the crews confidence and partly to dissipate the enemy's defences. The first of these was a heavy one made against the Renault works in Paris. I saw these pictures in the Mess, and having had a hectic morning testing doubtful pilots in an old Blenheim with a spluttering port engine, I decided I would have to get back somehow to bombers.

Two telegrams tell the story:

"To S/Ldr G. P. Gibson, RAF
    Date: March 12th, 1942.
    Report pm today for interview C-in-C Bomber
    Command. Ends."

Two days later:

Copy: "To S/Ldr G. P. Gibson, RAF
      Date: March 14th, 1942.
      Time: 1215
      Post S/Ldr Gibson (39438) DFC to 106
      Squadron to
      command W/Cdr. Post. Ends."

I went.

It can be seen that the Air Marshal was certainly a fast mover.

My new squadron was in the North of England. Alick Worthington and Ginger Parkins flew me up there in a Dominie, after a farewell celebration with Group-Captain Fullergood. I was sorry to leave, in a way, because at least it was a happy place where everyone saw the fun in life. But although it may seem foolish to say so, it was nice to be going back to Ops.

When we landed, Nigger immediately found that the parting Wing-Commander's dog was a playful type, too, and I didn't see him for a couple of days. The Station was commanded by Group-Captain (Daddy) Rowe, DFC, a very pleasant, easy-going man. More the naval type than RAF was "Daddy". Stocky, pipe-smoking, he loved gardening, and especially his dahlias. His batman told me that his bathroom and sitting-room were so full of them you could hardly see him when he was changing.

In a few brief sentences he told me the facts. I was to take over 106 Squadron from W/Cdr Bob Allen, DSO, DFC and Bar, who had held it for over a year. It was a good squadron, well known for its fine record in Hampdens, but was now equipped with Manchesters. Soon it would have Lancasters. The other squadron in the Station was already equipped, and was very proud of the fact, as it was the second in the Group to have them. The CO of this outfit was W/Cdr Joe Collier, who used to be in 83 Squadron with me. After his crash in September 1940, he had come back to bombers again, and had done about sixty sorties to date. He went on talking for a while, and as I listened I realized that Daddy Rowe was commanding a happy station, even though there was a certain amount of rivalry between the two squadrons. But still, there always is.

As I walked up to the Mess, I think my chest was stuck out a little more than usual and I felt as though I was walking on air. This was my first command, my first squadron. I was the boss. I could put my own ideas into action at last, and I hoped I would be as good as dear old Ted of 29. I felt happy.

Nevertheless, it was rather lonely and strange walking into the Mess. I had been out of the Command for over a year and I couldn't say I expected to see anyone I knew. No one noticed me, no one said anything. Over in the corner was a fellow called Dunlop Mackenzie, who used to be in 83 Squadron. He had gone to his OTU in April, 1940, where he had been the only chap who dared to fly the 48-cylinder masterpiece, the Hereford, at night. For reasons of ill-health, however, he hadn't done many trips. When I told him that I had come to take over the squadron —

"God! you're a clot," he said, disrespectfully.

"Why?" I said, surprised.

"These Manchesters. They're awful. The actual kite's all right, but it's the engine. They're fine when they keep turning but they don't often do so. We have had an awful lot of prangs."

"I had heard the Manchester had had some teething troubles, but thought they had all been cured."

"No, they haven't," he said. "If you are hit in one engine you've had it."

"But surely they will fly on one engine?"

"Some will, some won't. A fellow called 'Kipper-Herring' from 61 Squadron brought one all the way from Berlin on one engine and got the DSO for it, but he's an exception."

"Have you had a prang in one?" I asked, thinking perhaps that he had had some trouble which prejudiced his statements.

"Not me, but I've been darn lucky. I have seen enough of them. Bill Whamond —"

"Who's he?"

"A boy in A Flight. He piled up after a daylight mine-laying do. He got away OK, though."

"I know — the CO told me. Just a belly landing."

"Maybe, but you should have seen W/Cdr Balston prang on his return from a daylight raid on Brest."

294

"What happened there?"

"Well, he was coming back pretty badly shot up and the weather was fairly heavy. All the rest of the boys had come in when he made his approach. It was then we saw that he had his elevators shot off, or most of them. Anyway, he came in, but was slightly high, about one hundred feet over the hedge. He opened his throttles to go round again, but the extra power forced the CG aft, and he began to climb with engines flat out. He went up to about 500ft until he was in a nearly vertical position. Apparently he couldn't do anything about it. Then the nose dropped slowly, oh! very slowly, and he went in vertically, dead in the middle of the aerodrome, a few hundred yards from the control tower, where everyone was watching. I believe his wife was there, too."

"Flames?"

"God! yes, nothing left."

"Must have been a horrible sight, especially as you could hear him on the RT."

"It certainly was. Thing was, he could have baled out, only his reargunner was badly wounded."

As we were talking there came the harsh roar of a Lancaster taking off.

"Now you watch this," said Dunlop. "This is a real aeroplane."

Bob Allen was standing outside and we watched, all three of us together.

The great tail came up, the engines screamed into full power, but she didn't leave the ground.

"He's going to prang," said Bob quietly.

"I think you're right," said I.

There was plenty of time to talk, no need to hurry. Quite slowly, at least it seemed so, the giant bomber rumbled across the aerodrome, at perhaps 120mph, but she wasn't getting airborne; something was wrong. Then, quite slowly, she struck one wing into the bomb dump and cartwheeled out of sight. A great cloud of dust arose, and seconds later there came a dull thud, as something finally hit something else.

"They've had it," said Bob unemotionally. We waited for the black smoke, none came. Then we went back into the Mess again.

"Who was the pilot?" someone asked.

"Tommy Boylan."

"Poor old Tommy!"

One of the navigators pressed the bell for the waiter, and there was a short silence.

Then in came Tommy. He was looking a little dirty and there was a lot of earth around his tunic; his hair was somewhat disordered, but otherwise he seemed none the worse for wear for his mishap. He was an Australian who had just left the squadron after doing sixty trips. He was a good type, and his hand was as steady as a rock as he grabbed the first can out of the waiter's tray.

"God! you're lucky," said Bob.

"Too right I am," said Tommy.

What had happened was simple, and certainly no structural failure. The leading edge of his port-wing hadn't been screwed down properly and had blown up on take-off, destroying most of the lift from that wing. It was just another of those thousand-and-one snags which are inevitable when re-equipping a bomber group; luckily Lancasters do not give so many. Nevertheless, I felt a bit doubtful about the future as I went down to the cookhouse to look for Nigger.

Later I met some of the boys. The circumstances were unusual for a new Wing-Commander. But on looking back I know of lots worse. We met at the bar of the WAAFs' Mess, where they were throwing a dance. I was sober as a judge, being careful not to put a foot wrong. But they were high, and in this state I heard all their moans, which might have taken weeks to get out of them in the ordinary way. There were moans about this, moans about that, but all of them showing some signs of proportion and most of them well deserved.

There was John Hopgood Hoppy they called him. He was a fair-haired chap about medium height, rather good-looking, except for one prominent tooth. The boys seemed to be always taking him off about this, but he took it very good-naturedly. He was a serious fellow at heart, though, even though he spent most of his time being with the boys. As soon as I saw him I thought, "What an ideal squadron type. I like that chap."

The rest were Rhodesians. All young, all keen, all pals. Bill Whamond, a Rhodes scholar, was learning to be a medico before he volunteered for flying. Bill

Picken, always happy except when he was going to
Hamburg; that was his moan tonight, there was too
much flak at Hamburg. Harry Stoffer, just engaged
to a WAAF officer, called Mary, on the Station.
There were others there, all drinking and talking,
whose names I just didn't pick up. But they were all
the same — they were the boys — they were
enjoying themselves.

Next day I saw the whole squadron on parade.
They seemed a good lot and I told them my rough
requirements. Then I had a word with the NCO air
crews. When I walked in, none of them stood up. I
suppose that they thought I looked a bit young, and
they could afford to take a few advantages. I am
afraid I was rather rude, but you have to be, so that
they can know what you think and you can know
what they think. Then I had a talk with the pilots,
some of whom I had been drinking with last night.
They were different now: standing stiffly to
attention, careful not to say one word out of place.
Tonight they were going to Lübeck, an important
port on the Baltic coast. No drink for them; that
was over until the next day; even in the Mess at
lunch-time I noticed a complete reversal from last
night. Now they were standing around in small
circles, talking quietly, drinking soft drinks, some
not drinking at all.

This, I might say, goes for all squadrons that I
have ever known. Unlike some last war pilots, the
boys will not touch a drop of alcohol before flying.
They know the danger and respect it. Even the wild

fighter boys were no exception. I have known them go all the way over to tell their host that they were "on" that night and refuse, with an iron will, any attempt on his part to make them have one, even for the road. To them it would mean at the most death, at the least a raspberry from the CO. But, worst of all, they might injure somebody else.

And so they sat there, being very polite, while I got to know them. Later I had a talk with the two flight commanders. Both had obviously been doing too much. They were excellent types, but tired out from an operational point of view. One had already done about sixty trips and had begun to feel the strain. Tonight he had put himself "on", and I could see at a glance what he was going through. He was jumpy, didn't listen to what was being said; his thoughts were miles away. Later, he got into his flight van and went off to see his wife, and I imagined the painful scene.

She had seen, for some time, the change that had come over him. All wives can. Now she knew he was going out. After the garden gate had slammed and after the noise of the van had died into the distance she would wait, first for the roar of them taking off, then the hours would pass slowly while she counted each one, until they came back later, faster and making an easier noise. Then she would know that they were landing at base, and that the weather was fit. Only one thing could stop him now, only one terrible thing. The minutes would seem like hours, and time would seem to stop until the noise of that van, the slam of the gate, and in he would walk. Then she would tick him off for not having his scarf on, in the cold of the morning. Something silly, anything to stop her going down on her knees and praying to God to stop him getting into the air any more.

I pictured all this because I, too, am married; but my wife was working in a war factory and didn't know whether I was flying or not.

As this fellow had done his bit, and done it well, I swore then and there that he would never have to do another trip after this one. I would also post the other fellow, and thus began life in my squadron with a new nucleus at the top, which is all-important for efficiency.

The raid on Lübeck was a success. The Flight-Commander got back all right with the rest of the boys. It had been a clear night with a full moon, each load had done its stuff, and the timing had been good. The whole raid was over in two hours; that meant 600 tons in two hours, nearly a record. The damage done was perhaps the most spectacular of the war, as the whole of the old town was burnt completely out.

Next night, while the GAF was bombing Exeter as a reprisal, we were giving young Harry Stoffer a bachelor party on the eve of his wedding to Mary. It was a good, almost sober party, and I thought at the time, as I watched this boy sitting there, laughing and joking, how young he was to be married. He had done a few trips and had got some experience, and I hoped that God would spare him his life — a life so young, so full and happy.

Next day he got married, with the blessings of all the boys. There were plenty of gags played on them as they went off on their honeymoon in his snorting old car. I think the jerry we tied on the back stayed there until they were well on their way.

Afterwards I went back to my office. These days there was plenty of paperwork to do. Such a thing was quite new to me. In Fighter Command they don't have half so much, but me found it pretty easy, the Adjutant and I, owing to the amazing knowledge of the Orderly Room Corporal who, as Bob Alien said, "practically runs the squadron". But one Command order caught my eye. It was from the C-in-C himself, and forbade in clear-cut language any wife living within 40 miles of her husband on a Bomber Base. Only those who were already living out were exempted, and a quick check-up with the Corporal revealed this as only four. This was the best news I had heard for a long time. You cannot fight a war and live at home, all at the same time. This order was to see that you didn't have to.

The Manchester was very heavy on the controls after the Beau. The take-off seemed to take hours and the turns were so slow that it felt almost unreal. But she was smooth enough at 180mph, so long as her engines kept running. We found this out together, Robbo and I. He had just arrived, the same day as I had. F/L Robertson was from New Zealand, a happy fellow, always smiling. Moreover, he had done about thirty trips, so I immediately promoted him to Squadron-Leader in charge of A Flight, with Bill Whamond as his deputy. He and I gave each other dual in the Manchester, and I think we shook each other equally much, I by handling it like a fighter and he by flying it like a bomber.

His promotion was a popular move, and Robbo began to shine as a leader, both in the air and on the ground.

After we had been in the squadron for a few days, we did our first trip together. It was a simple one, but I was being careful, as I hadn't seen real enemy flak for a year. All we had to do was to plant six mines in the water at the entrance of Kiel Harbour. There was no flak, there were no fighters, so we came away no more experienced than when we set out.

Two nights later we went back to Rostock. It was the third night of its blitz. The idea was that a force of bombers would attack the town and dock area, while we in No. 5 Group would bomb the factory which makes Heinkel 111s, about 10 miles away. The plan being that when the factory people, who had probably been bombed out, went off to do some work next day, they would find that their factory had been bombed out too.

On the first night there had been no flak over the factory at all, but then only twelve bombers were detailed; little damage was done. On the second night we went there was quite a lot of light flak and about sixty bombers attacked the factory, causing fires and doing some damage. And on the last night of the blitz, I believe the whole force was put on to the factory to hit the central hangar.

After the briefing, Hoppy and Bill came up. "Why the blazes," they asked, "didn't they put a large force on the factory the first night, when there was no flak? Then it would have been flattened first time!"

"I don't know," I replied. "It does seem rather stupid, though. I'll ring up Group."

There was no answer from Group; they just didn't know. All they wanted, they said, was photographs. By now all our aircraft were equipped with cameras, but these would not take good pictures below 4,000ft. I couldn't understand at the time why they wanted photographs which would mean bombing from above 4,000ft, and so not being as accurate, when they could have given the order for all aircraft to bomb lower and hit the hangar, even though the photographic results would be negligible. Anyway, I told my boys to go in at 2,000ft, hit the hangar and damn the photographs! A dawn reconnaissance showed that the factory was hit. But next night they went again to finish the job.

I sat up late in the Ops room waiting for them to return. A bomber Ops room is rather different from a fighter Ops room. The only things that hold your interest in it are, perhaps, the pretty girl behind the telephone and the large blackboard on the wall. On this board are written the various names of the captains who are undertaking operations that night. Much information is written against their name: bomb-load, time off, crew, etc. But the only important one was a space on top of which are the magic words, "time landed".

As I sat listening to the aircraft return, I watched the pretty girl mount the ladder and fill in those spaces. That pretty girl was Mary Stoffer.

Time passed.

One by one she would get up and fill in — X-X-ray landed 0520; Y-Yorker landed 0522 — until the whole board was complete except for that one small space. S-Sugar. Normally it is not very nice to sit there and watch that one space, waiting for it to be filled in. But tonight was even worse, for the name against that space was P/O Stoffer.

I sat there smoking cigarette after cigarette, until it became light and an orderly came in and drew the blackout curtains. It was hard to say anything. I wanted to go up to the crew room and talk to the boys, but I didn't like to leave her. She just sat there, staring at that space, a funny look — an incredible look. Someone came in with a cup of tea, but it had long since gone cold before she noticed it was there. Then there was a quick ray of hope, the 'phone rang. It was the Observer Corps to say that a Manchester had just crossed the coast coming in our direction. Could it be Harry? Her face lit up in a smile, hardly daring to say anything; then we heard it go over and pass on its way. Her face fell, her eyes began to glisten as she fought back her tears. An airman on the watch tower telephoned to say that it belonged to 50 Squadron. In the end I got up and took her by her arm and led her to my car. She wasn't crying, she was very brave. She insisted on stopping at the WAAF Officers' Mess to collect her shopping, which she had bought for their little home the morning before. Packed into the bag there was a cardboard packet of cornflakes, a 2lb jar of marmalade, some butter and some sugar, and a little bacon, their ration — simple things, little household things. She clutched them tightly as I dropped her at her house. There were nearly tears in my eyes as I drove home.

Despite the successful attacks on Warnemünde and Rostock, it was still obvious with the coming of spring that certain changes would have to take place in Bomber Command if we were to hit the target. One bad weather day in May a conference was called to discuss one thing, and one thing only: how to get more bombs into the target area. Air Vice-Marshal Coryton took the chair. He had sat in the Air Ministry for many years, and now was given his chance to command a Bomber Group. He was a keen, able, kind and inventive type, very popular with the whole Group. He was the sort, when driving round the aerodrome, who would look into an aircraft and discuss with an amazed electrician the full wiring diagram of an electrical revolution counter, much to the amazement of the man concerned. He knew everything. To me and the other Squadron-Commanders in the Group he was the most popular Group-Commander we had ever known and were ever likely to know. To all and sundry in the Group, which he looked upon as his own pet baby, he behaved like a father. As often as possible his little Proctor aircraft would touch down at least once a week on each Station to make sure that everything was running smoothly.

Now he began to talk:

"As you know, we have in the past few weeks been having some success, but the point is that these targets which we have been attacking are not really heavily defended. I know that Warnemünde cost us a serious percentage, but I think this was due to collisions. It seems to me that in order to hit precision targets, we must raid them in daylight, such as the Augsburg raid (where Nettleton was awarded the VC), but on this type of thing we must have absolute surprise and security, and this is very hard to have when so many people are involved in Bomber Command. The other way is to have better bombing at night. Now, how are we going to do this and at the same time get our losses down to a minimum, so that we can operate day after day in ever-increasing strength?"

He went on to talk, and he talked a lot.

The first thing he talked about was cameras. All squadrons must get photographic-minded. In order to do so a certain number of points would be given to the squadrons who got most bullseyes. There would be a photographic ladder in the Group and in Bomber Command. From these ladders it would be easy to see which was the top squadron and which was the top crew. Moreover, it would introduce a high degree of competitive spirit between the squadrons: thus doing a good job in trying to make each beat the other. From the results of the photographic plots the best crew could be detailed to carry flares to illuminate the targets. Sometimes the best squadrons could go in first (which is normally safer). There must be more practice bombing, not from 6,000ft but from 15,000ft, which is more like the height from which we bomb in the actual thing. There had been little done before he arrived. He now wanted to introduce a squadron bombing competition. He went on for a bit, saying much more, then asked for some questions.

One by one the Squadron-Commanders put their points forward. The AOC listened attentively, then a long discussion would arise; all this being taken down by a shorthand typist, for further reference.

One of the moans was the old subject of routeing. W/Cdr "Mary" Tudor of 83 Squadron was talking. "As you know, sir," he began in his rather high voice, "all our routes to the target are now being planned by Bomber Command men, some who haven't seen the flak in Germany for six months or so. Well, as you know, this is anything but static: they are always moving it from one place to another.

Even the searchlight belt has now disappeared within the last few weeks. They've put them all around the Ruhr towns, about two thousand of them."

"The Battle of the Ruhr has yet to start," said the AOC.

"I know, sir, we'll never be able to hit anything in the glare of all those lights. I think they're worse than the flak. But what I want is this. Let the routes and the general Flight Plan be decided by the squadrons themselves. After all, they're the chaps who have to do the job. About an hour before each briefing, I suggest we have a conference over tie-line telephones, which will decide the final plan. Everyone will be able to put forward suggestions. A route to the target will be taken which will not lead the boys over two other defended areas as well. The height for bombing will be correct and in dead proportion to the amount of flak. I think in this way we will get the boys happier, and thus far more bombs on the target." He sat down.

"Good idea," said the AOC. "We'll put this plan into action as soon as possible. But first, we must get the whole Group equipped with Lancasters. We can't do a thing until then. What shall we call your conference?"

"As it's about the Flight Plan, we may as well call it 'The Flight Planning Conference,'" suggested the SASO dryly.

"OK?" The AOC looked round: there was a murmur of assent, and he nodded to the typist.

Many problems peculiar to the difficulties of the time were discussed at length. First, training. We were equipping the Group with a large four-engine bomber; quite a change from the Hampden. How was this to be done? First of all, each squadron had been given a third flight, commanded by an operationally rested pilot, such as Tommy Boylan. As often as possible with his three Lancasters available, he would convert pilots into the new aircraft. But then the man-power problem was terrific. New flights meant more men. There were none available. We had to rob our own operational flights. The Hampden used to carry a crew of four. The Lancaster carries seven. These extra, highly skilled air crews had to be found from somewhere — where? The whole air-training programme stretching from the dusty offices of the Air Ministry to the far-off prairies of Canada had to be remodelled. And for one reason alone. Bomber Command was being reborn.

New navigational aids were coming along. These would enable us to find out where we were, above cloud, within a few seconds and to extraordinary accuracy. These, too, were very secret, and every aircraft had to be guarded day and night. This meant more men. Men from somewhere. But all the forces needed more men. It seemed a vicious circle.

Then they decided that a conversion flight was not good enough. This in itself was a waste of man-power. All flights would have to combine to form a conversion unit — which would supply every squadron with fully-trained crews. But would they? There was a shortage of trained flight engineers. Volunteers had been asked for, but it would take time. New airfields had to be taken over; larger runways to be built, for the longer landing run of the Lancaster.

Hundreds of problems confronted us, and I got up feeling quite dizzy after a four-hour session.

On my way back to the Mess a Lancaster roared overhead on its way to the sea. I noticed a couple of civilians who didn't even look up. They were used to the sight. But did they know even half the story? Of course not. Re-equipping a Bomber Group is a big job. But the whole of the Command was soon to be completely reequipped and reorganized. To tell the story of hard work would need a full-sized book. Mention must be made of everybody who worked flat out for a long time to do the job. The factories who turned out the new aircraft under conditions peculiar only to this country. The contractors who made the fields. The equipment officers — the new petrol installation experts — the list would run on for ever. Let it be to say that there is much work done behind the headlines. Work which, though not so glamorous as combat action, is carried out by quiet men with stout hearts. Funnily enough, it is only the air crews who really appreciate them.

Within the next few days we got Lancasters. They came, flown over by the ATA five at a time, all ready for action except for a few modifications. My own squadron did not have a conversion flight, and the conversion unit had not yet got going. We had to do our training ourselves. Moreover we were told to hurry because there might be a maximum effort at the end of the month, in two weeks' time.

Hoppy who had managed to pick up some training on an off day from the other squadron, had done more than other pilots, about ten hours. I asked him to show me how.

It was mostly a question of getting the cockpit drill dead right. The most important thing of all is this cockpit-drill business, when flying modern aircraft. All it means is getting to know the position of every tap so that you can fly the aircraft without having to look down for the controls. All movements have to be made automatically, as one does when driving a car. When flying a big bomber on a misty night, that split second when the pilot might turn his head away from the instruments might mean the difference between life and death.

As we climbed in I noticed the cockpit layout was much the same as that of a Manchester. Practically everything was in its usual place, only the four throttles and one or two refinements seemed to be the difference.

Hoppy climbed into the driving-seat while I stood behind him. Dave Shannon, a new chap who had just come, sat beside him in the second pilot's place to act as a Flight-Engineer. Hoppy explained the starting-up procedure in detail.

"Switches off," he said into his mike.

"Switches off," repeated Dave.

"Inner tanks on."

"Inner tanks on."

"Immersed pumps on."

"OK, on."

"OK, now read the list of checks," said Hoppy, and I listened in silence as Dave read out aloud a list which seemed very long.

"Check seat secure," said Dave.

"Checked, seat secure," doing so.

"Brakes on and pressure up."

"OK. Brakes on and pressure up."

"Undercarriage locked."

One by one, Hoppy answered until the list was finished, then Dave turned his attention to the crew. From the bomb-aimer to the rear-gunner each one was carefully checked in his equipment. All this took some time. When all was done, Hoppy turned round to me.

"Of course, that's the complete drill, sir. If I were you I'd do it for the first few flights, then you'll find you'll want to slack off. It'll all come absolutely automatic. The next thing is the starting-up, take-off and air drill, which never varies. Most pilots do this, no matter how experienced they are."

Then to the Flight-Engineer:

"Prepare to start up."

"OK. Ready to start up."

The ground crew had primed the engines and all was ready. Hoppy had his hand on the throttles. Dave was working the switches and booster coils.

"Contact-starboard outer," Hoppy yelled through his window.

Dave pressed the button and one by one the four great engines roared into life with that harsh crackling, spitting noise peculiar to Merlin engines.

"Chocks away."

"Chocks away."

As I glanced down out of the side window, I saw, 20ft below me, a small man dart in and out of the huge landing-wheels, pulling a long rope at the end of which was a chock. Funny things, chocks — everyone knows that they are there to prevent the aircraft running forward when its engines are running, but most people don't realize that, whereas aircraft have grown up in size since the last war, the good old chocks have still remained the same. This one had become wedged in the earth, and the little man was lying on his back underneath the huge propeller slicing through the air 4ft above his head, trying to kick it free.

At last another man came running in front with his thumbs stuck up, and Hoppy released the brakes.

There was a hiss of air, and we began to sway and rumble our way along the taxi-track. At the entrance to the runway, Hoppy stopped and ran up his engines to full power, one by one, each time checking the two-stage blower, the airscrew pitch control and the magnetos.

Meanwhile, Dave called up the control tower.

"Hullo, Control. Y-Yoke calling. May we take off, please? — over."

"OK. Take off. Listen out." This was a girl's voice, one of the many WAAFs who had taken over a man's job, thus releasing him for service elsewhere. A great crowd are the WAAFs.

Then came a string of orders from Hoppy.

"Flaps thirty."

"Radiators closed."

"Lock throttles."

"Prepare to take-off."

"OK behind, rear-gunner?"

"OK behind," came a voice.

He ran up the engines all together, evenly, until each one was showing Zero 600st., then released the brakes. The acceleration was terrific, and I had to grab the back of his armour-plated seat to hold myself upright.

"Full power."

"Full power," answered Dave, opening the throttles wide.

Soon the ASI was showing a speed of 110mph and the aircraft suddenly became steady. We were airborne.

"Climbing power."

"Climbing power."

"Wheels up."

"Wheels up."

"Flaps up."

"Flaps up."

"Cruising power."

As Dave adjusted the engines to their correct revolutions for cruising, I noticed our air-speed was about 120. Pretty fast for a big bomber. She was flying perfectly, hands-off. On the controls she was as light as could be. This ship was certainly a honey. Hoppy showed me how to stop (feather) an engine simply by pressing a button, how it would fly quite well on only one, losing height very gradually the whole time, but good enough to get you well away from the enemy coast. He showed how to "ditch" the aircraft, using slight flap and plenty of speed. The "drink" we used for the occasion was a stretch of smooth cloud at about 4,000ft.

After half an hour he had shown me everything, and he called up control and got permission to land.

"Now watch this carefully," he pointed out. "It's very important to get the landing drill wrapped up."

As we were going downwind around the circuit, keeping about a mile from the runway and about 1,000ft high, came some more orders.

"Flaps twenty."

Dave put down twenty degrees of flap. The ASI dropped to 160.

"Revs. up."

The constant-speed propeller controls were pushed forward and a loud whine came from all engines.

"Wheels down."

"Wheels down."

We were now turning into the runway.

"Radiators closed."

"OK. Closed."

Suddenly two green lights came on in front of the pilot.

"Wheels locked down," called Dave, seeing this.

By now we were pointing straight at the landing-strip, which looked about 6ft wide from my position.

"Full flap."

"Full flap." Dave put down the lever and immediately the nose came up, while Hoppy struggled with the trimming wheels, to balance her in the glide.

"Airspeed, Flight-Engineer?"

"Speed — 130 — 125 — 128 — 130," chanted Dave, as we dropped towards the ground.

"You want to keep the nose well up when landing these things," said Hoppy over his shoulder. Then:

"Height and speed, please," he called.

"300, 120."

"200, 120."

"100, 115."

"50, 115."

"OK," jerked Hoppy; "throttle back."

Dave snapped back all four throttles while Hoppy, with both hands on the wheel, pulled off a good landing to the accompaniment of crackling and popping exhaust stubs.

When we had run about 1,000 yards we came to a stop. He pulled his oxygen mask off his sweating face and grinned.

"There, now you have a try."

★ ★ ★

The next few days saw a lot of practice flying for my crew. There were only three regular members; the rest we used to beg, borrow or steal from other crews at the appropriate time. "Junior" Ruskell was the navigator. He was very young, hence his name, but a very fine navigator, especially in the use of electrical navigation boxes. Junior's one weakness was beer. He could take about one pint, then he became comically light. When we used to go out together, perhaps to Boston, he usually drank lemonade. Sometimes he got tight on that! Johnny the rear-gunner was older, and as conscientious as any I knew. Hutch was the wireless-operator, and had just got his commission. I must make mention of one more fellow who used to fly with us. His real trade was wireless-operator, but he could do practically everything except land the aircraft. They called him Jordy, and a very lovable character he was. A real London Cockney, he would go off on Ops as often as possible. He once did seven trips running in different crews, flying as a gunner one night, a flight-engineer the next and a wireless-operator the next. Jordy was amusing to see before a trip. His dress was always alarming and would not bear description here, but over his head he always wore a dirty silk stocking à la French-sailor style. He used to vow he would never do a trip without it, and so far as I know he never has.

In the end we got more or less proficient, and so one day we flew down to an airfield in

Cambridgeshire to collect Sir Archibald Sinclair, the Air Minister, and one or two brass hats. We were proud of this honour, but we were carrying, for our sins, a brand new flight-engineer. On the way home the Air Minister jabbed a finger in my back and told me to feather an engine. This was done, and he seemed very pleased. Then we feathered another one, and he seemed even more pleased.

After we had flown along like this for a few minutes, one of the brass hats came forward and told me to unfeather, as they were in a hurry. I gave the order, casually, to the flight-engineer. Suddenly, to the horror of both myself and the man with goggles on, looking over my shoulder, the two other engines began to feather themselves. Our new flight-engineer had pressed the wrong buttons. It was all right, though, because it didn't take a second to get all four going again. However, in that second I couldn't help thinking what stooges we'd look if we'd had to land in the middle of a field in England on a hot summer's day with nothing wrong with the aircraft at all, except finger trouble. All this with our Air Minister on board! However, he was testing the rear turret at the time, and I don't think he noticed anything amiss.

The two weeks which the AOC had hinted at came to an end. In that time, thanks to Hoppy, Bill and a few others, the whole squadron had been taught to fly Lancasters both by day and night. A flood of new flight-engineers had arrived, and we had no less than forty crews ready to operate.

On May 29th we were told what was happening. A major attack was to be made against Hamburg. All types of aircraft were to take part, including a few from Coastal and Training Commands. In all, about 1,300 aircraft would take off and drop something like 1,500 tons. It was to be the biggest air raid of all time.

However, the weather was kind to Hamburg and the show was put off until the next night, when the target was changed to Cologne.

Luck went all the way with the bombers and they did their job well. Towards the end of the attack the flak had been pulverized and the city resembled one mass of flames. Nearly 1,500 tons had been dropped in ninety minutes. An unheard-of concentration, so much so that Air Vice-Marshal Baldwin, who flew over the city, said he had never seen a sight like it before. We had sent thirty-eight aircraft from our squadron, and had dropped 88 tons of bombs on the target for no loss. This was a record, and great entries were made in the squadron history to this effect.

The plan of the raid was partly to destroy the industrial area of Cologne and partly to pep up the weary British people. However, it was successful because it was carried out on a night when the moon was full and the visibility good. The next night another force of nearly 1,000 bombers tried to do the same to Essen, but the complete opposite happened. There was cloud all the way, and bombs were scattered all over the Ruhr Valley. Nevertheless, those Germans who had country homes well away from the towns must have been considerably shaken.

There was only one more 1,000-bomber raid. This was on Bremen, towards the end of the month. It met with failure because of bad weather. They were abandoned mainly because of the great disruption to training they caused in Operational Training and Conversion Units. A smaller consideration must be given to the view that the proportion of bombs dropped on the target by the OTU crews could not justify the risk of the loss of an experienced instructor.

From now on we would get to war as often as possible with large forces varying between 400 and 600. I didn't do as much as the boys, but used to content myself with one trip every five nights. No Squadron-Commander can for that matter. Not only has he got to deal with the paper work, write long casualty letters and run the squadron generally, but has also to be up at nights. In fact, every night when the boys are out you will find him waiting in the Ops room for their return. But no lying in bed for him next day; after perhaps three hours' rest he must be up, ready to plan the next raid, arrange the bomb and petrol loads, organize the crews. But this applies to many others on a bomber station. Armament officers, navigation experts, intelligence officers, all of whom go about their work, looking very tired, but still keen to get more bombs on Germany.

Not many people realize in the outside world (and sometimes it does seem the *outside* world) that although the BBC will inform them that "Last night a strong force of bombers were out for the first time in seven days", hard work has been done on the bases. On each of those days the crews have most likely been briefed, bombs have been loaded on aircraft, then taken off again; sometimes they even taxi out to take-off when a red light shoots up from the control tower, telling them that it has been cancelled.

Imagine their feelings. Most people will agree with me when I say the worst part of any bombing raid is the start. I, for my part, hate the feeling of standing around in the crew rooms, waiting to get into the vans that will take you out to your aircraft. It's a horrible business. Your stomach feels as though it wants to hit your backbone. You can't stand still. You laugh at small jokes, loudly, stupidly. You smoke far too many cigarettes, usually only halfway through, then throw them away. Sometimes you feel sick and want to go to the lavatory. The smallest incidents annoy you and you flare up on the slightest provocation. When someone forgets his parachute you call him names that you would never use in the ordinary way. All this because you're frightened, scared stiff. I know — because I've done all those things. I have always felt bad until the door of the aircraft clangs shut; until the wireless-op.

(Hutch) says "Intercom. OK," and the engines burst into life. Then it's all right. Just another job.

But when that light goes up, then the spring is uncoiled. Some laugh. Others swear. A few get drunk.

"It's all very bad for them."

Tommy Lloyd and I were talking about this one day. He was the Senior Intelligence Officer. He had been recalled into the Service during the early stages of this war; he had served in the front line in the last, winning the DSO. We were in a little club in Skegness, having a quiet glass of beer with the boys. We were all tired out, having been on duty for the past fourteen days, during which there had been fourteen briefings but only four raids. A civilian had just come up and said something, about us having a rest. Something to do with Egypt. Perhaps?

I nearly exploded.

"It's all right," said Tommy; "they just don't understand."

"I know they don't — if they had to exist on three hours' sleep for a fortnight there would be a terrific row. Their Unions would object. Still, I suppose it was worse in the last war for you infantry boys."

"It was in a way — but we got our regular rests. But then, everybody knew about us — nobody seems to know what goes on in a bomber station today. Someone ought to tell them."

"Someone should. Perhaps one day I will," I replied.

Of parties: there weren't many these days, everyone was too busy. True we had a squadron party in the dance-hall in Boston, but it was nothing like the old days. The only incident of note was Bill Whamond lending his tunic to a roadsweeper in a local pub. This individual then made his way into the dance and I, thinking he was one of my new officers, told him to go and get a shave. Much to his surprise and indignation!

At this time there was a rumour that the whole of our Group might move to the Middle East. Things had not gone too well in the last few months, and this rumour seemed quite a possibility. However, nothing came of it. Nevertheless, air-power was definitely needed in that part of the world. After the heavy battles at Knightsbridge, when many of our tanks had been knocked out, we had been forced to fall back to El Alamein, the only natural barrier before Cairo. There did not seem much of a chance of holding them even there, and it was said that Mussolini himself had crossed to a safe part of Africa, bringing with him a gorgeous braided uniform for his state entry into Cairo. But, bringing up reserves and displaying incredible guts, our army held Rommel, whose Afrika Korps was already beginning to feel the pinch of a 1,500-miles supply line.

In Russia the Germans had attacked and were sweeping up the Don at an alarming rate. It looked as though the end there was in sight.

Submarine warfare in the Atlantic was cutting great hunks out of our life-line with America. It seemed almost impossible to get the answer to an enemy that fights at night, under the sea. In my squadron we had even detached a flight of Lancasters to Ireland to help look for U-boats in the bay, thus diminishing the scale of attack against Germany. Such was the gravity of the U-boat menace.

Only in the Far East had the aggressor been slowed down, and this because of the skill and foresight of the admirals of the US Navy. Both the battles of Coral Sea and Midway were fought on new lines. Carrier-borne aircraft were used in great numbers, with decisive results. The Japs' thrust at Australia had been parried. Perhaps their next move was a drive into India?

Only time would tell, but the people of this country and in Parliament were getting restive. The strain of waiting for good news was beginning to tell. In the House a heavy attack was made on Mr. Churchill and his conduct of the war. A vote of censure was taken, at the very time when he was planning with his Allies a vast enterprise which would be launched in the autumn.

But as the weeks passed and new crews came and went, the only permanent offensive was still that coming from a few score bomber squadrons.

The attacks on Hamburg and Düsseldorf on bright moonlight nights were partly successful, good concentrated bombing being achieved because the crews went in low to see the aiming points. But the full moon was beginning to be a danger. The German night-fighter force was growing every day. Soon it would become a serious menace, even worse than the flak. For protection some of us would fly in formation, but this had its difficulties when nearing the aiming point. One night Hoppy and I nearly collided over the docks at Hamburg when trying to fly in formation and look for the target at the same time.

But it had to be moonlight nights or nothing. The dark-night raids proved nearly useless and very dangerous. Crews, circling to find a pinpoint over a town, would run a serious risk of colliding. Sometimes as many as 400 aircraft would be over the target at the same time. When you consider that in England we think it dangerous for twenty aircraft to circle a base, with lights off, what could be worse than Bremen on a dark night with scores of aircraft about? But on all nights crews had to face the danger of staying over a target too long. In daylight it is easy to see what you are going to hit from a long way off. You can go over the target in a straight line, and in the shortest possible time, thus in the safest time. But at night they had to stooge up and down looking for what they wanted, always being fired at and undergoing the risk of collision the whole time. Aircraft would inevitably split up, and thus fall easy prey to night-fighters on the way home.

Something had to be done. We had got everything else. We could carry the loads for a long distance; 4,000lb and 8,000lb bombs were the order of the day. Tons of incendiaries could be dropped in a "stick" a mile long. We had the aircraft. We had the crews, who could bomb accurately with the new bomb-sights. Now we wanted the accuracy, so that we could "apply" the vast concentration of bombs straight on to the aiming point. Then we could begin to do some real damage.

How?

First the best crews in the best squadrons began to carry flares. These were carried in bundles of twelve, and when dropped would illuminate the ground well, but only for a few minutes. But sometimes these flares were more of a liability than an asset. Navigational errors on the part of the selected crews would cause the wrong city to be bombed, let alone the wrong target. Cloud would ruin everything and illuminate our bombers nicely for the nightfighters. But, nevertheless, they were a beginning. However, some targets, such as Krupps at Essen, which were surrounded by so many guns and searchlights that not even flares could pierce the glare, seemed quite immune from aerial attack.

One day we began to practice high-level formation in daylight. There were rumours immediately.

"We're going after the *Tirpitz* again."

"No, airfields in France to stop the Baedeker raids."

But I had an idea.

I spoke to Tommy Lloyd. Hoppy was there.

"What do you make of this high-level stuff?"

"I'm not quite sure — but I've got a good idea."

"Krupps?"

"Yes."

"I think so, too," I agreed. "The American boys have just started in their Fortresses. They're shooting the fighters down, too. I wouldn't be surprised if we were asked to go with them, protected by their guns."

"Wouldn't be very nice," said Hoppy. "Why don't we have guns like theirs?"

"We don't need them at night. The range is too short. But it would be nice to have the hitting power." This was Bill, who had just turned up.

"Well, how are we ever going to hit these heavily defended targets?" I asked.

"I can't ever see us getting Krupps. Day or night; it's just too heavily defended by flak."

"Nor I," said I.

But Tommy Lloyd had an idea.

"Well, I suggest," he began, "that a special squadron of Beaufighters or Mosquitos be formed out of crack crews. Their job would be to go in at dusk, just before the main force was due, and drop coloured incendiaries on the factory itself. These could be seen from high up, and the boys of the main force would be able to do steady bombing runs which would plaster the area with cookies."

"Seems a good idea — but the suicide squadron losses would be high."

"They probably would — but the target would be destroyed."

"Yeah; that's the main thing," said Hoppy.

It was lunch-time. I got up to go, when suddenly the telephone rang. Tommy picked it up.

"It's Group Ops," he said, quietly.

We waited, wondering what it was. We had been released tonight. There had been a small party fixed up.

"OK," said Tommy casually. 'I'll tell the Station-Commander." Then he looked at us, his eyes dancing. "You were right," he said. "Your squadron's on Krupps today. Take-off as soon as possible."

"What the hell!" I exploded.

"Oh, it's OK. It's only a cloud-cover raid."

We went. Six of us, within an hour. Within three, we were all back again.

On July 8th, a dark night, I took Dave Shannon as my second pilot to Wilhelmshaven. The winds were high and not as forecast. When we were 60 miles away flares began to go down. We immediately went over to have a look and saw nothing but open fields. More flares to the north; still open fields. In vain we looked around, hoping to find the target illuminated, but there was nothing doing. In the end we turned north, found the coastline and followed it along till we found the harbour. There wasn't even one fire burning there — twenty minutes after the attack was due to begin. Even Dave wasn't so sure whether we were over the right place ourselves.

The photographic plots for the night's work were disgusting. Bombs had been dropped all over north-western Germany. But worse than this, losses due to our lack of concentration had been high. The German News Agency said: "Last night enemy aircraft dropped bombs at random over North-West Germany. No damage was done."

From 106, P/O Broderick failed to return. I drove around to tell his wife after waiting until he was three hours overdue. As I approached the gate I saw a small white face looking out of the window. She opened the door before I even had time to press the bell. She knew what had happened. I could see that by her eyes. She just stood there as I told her, the world falling in a crumbled heap at her feet. Then she went upstairs without saying a word.

But as I went to my room I wasn't thinking of the painful scene which had just occurred. I was thinking of Bomber Command. This boy, like hundreds of others, had not come back, and I didn't suppose he had even seen the target. This would have to be altered. A new system like the scheme Tommy Lloyd mentioned. Perhaps even better.

CHAPTER
FOURTEEN

Turning of the Tide

If mere squadrons were giving plenty of thought to the matter of getting more bombs on the target, let us say something of the activities of the Commander-in-Chief. It was learned from reliable sources that he spent a lot, even the whole, of his time sitting at his desk interviewing pilots, cursing scientists and leaping on Group-Commanders from great heights in order to try to get some information out of them about the subject of bombs on the target. Why had the raid on Bremen gone wrong last night? Because the crews couldn't see the ground. Why couldn't they navigate blind? Because they couldn't get any idea of where they were within 20 miles. Why? Because the Germans were jamming our RT and navigational aids. Why weren't the flares dropped over Bremen? They might have been, but the smoke-screen was too good for them to see anything at all. Why did the few bombs that did fall anywhere near the area fall mostly south-west? Because the wind changed after take-off and there was no one to tell them anything about it.

330

And so it went on day after day. Everyone was interested; everyone was trying to see if there was any way in which it would be possible for a large bomber force to drop its bombs accurately on the target, without incurring any undue danger in doing so. And at last a plan was formed.

Meanwhile, in our squadron many of the faces which were there when I took over had gone, some for ever. But new ones had arrived. The conversion units had got into their stride and were turning out really good material: Bunny Grein, Wimpy Wellington, Johnny Coates, Taffy Williams and Ginger Crowfoot had all come within the last few weeks, and they will go down in history as the great men of 106 Squadron. Right from the start they began to get aiming point pictures of the target, and with the points gained by their photographs they brought our squadron up to the proud position of seventh in Bomber Command. Their keenness and skill were largely due to an excellent Flight-Commander who had just come to take the place of a vacancy in the other flight. Wooldridge was his surname, but he was rarely called that. He had been known as Dim ever since he learned to fly. He was a sort of "Algy" of the air, with a large moustache and a drawling voice. He had amazing habits, and at the time he joined he was engaged in the doubtful art of composing a concerto for piano and orchestra. I think it was a ruse on his part to keep him away from the boys. He had stomach trouble. He couldn't drink a lot, and his excuse always was that

331

he must sit down quietly in his sitting-room and write his concerto rather than go out and drink beer. Poetry was his line as well, but he was an excellent type, and, apart from all this, had done sixty-seven trips over the Third Reich. Dim was very good with the boys, but, I am afraid, rather unscrupulous with his Squadron-Commander, and even though I say so myself, he needed a lot of watching.

One day we were sent on a sudden daylight raid over North-West Germany. I strolled along to his office. "Can I have my O-Orange?" I asked.

"Awfully sorry, sir," he said, smugly; "she's blown an engine. She'll be unserviceable for a few days."

Cursing about maintenance, I went to Bill in A Flight (Robbo was missing from the previous week's Hamburg raid) and asked him for a reliable aircraft, but all the boys had had theirs and I was given a lousy job called B-Beer, dirty and oily inside and smelling strongly of disinfectant carried in the lavatory aft. Even junior was upset having to navigate in such a queer ship, especially after our own perfectly maintained "Queen of the Air".

When we got as far as Antwerp we were recalled. The cloud-cover we had depended on for protection had begun to break. It had become perfectly clear, and we could see as far and wide as we wished. Not a very pleasant sight when all alone. As soon as we got the recall we screamed round in a turn and dived low over Flushing on our way out to sea, hoping to bomb a 4,000-ton steamer which was steaming along on its own about 1 mile off shore. Doing exactly the same thing 1 mile ahead was another Lancaster, and knowing well the Luftwaffe was up after us, I quickly caught it up in order to get mutual protection with our twelve guns. (In actual fact we got three Huns that day, all FW 190s.) For a while we flew in formation with him, and at last reached some cloud, but Johnny was the first to see the aircraft lettering on the other ship.

"Why, that's O-Orange!" he said.

Looking hard through the window I could see Dim sitting at the controls, his great moustache sticking out of his helmet as his Flight-Engineer handed him a cigarette. Seeing us, he smiled. Then I think he saw who was alongside and promptly dived into the clouds.

"So that was O-Orange," I said to my boys. "She looked pretty unserviceable, didn't she?"

Not only that, on many occasions my car would vanish on the slightest provocation; mysterious faces would appear in the squadron, postings which Dim had engineered carefully without my knowledge — boys he wanted to have beside him. But, for all this, Dim was a good chap. He did a lot for our squadron. For too long we, including myself, probably more than anyone else, had thought too much in terms of tonnage and too little in terms of accuracy. But Dim had organized a lot of night bombing, and he got the boys up practically every night taking practice photographs.

All the time there was still the great problem of how to hit appointed objectives. The American Air Force had not yet begun to operate in force. We all knew they had a new bomb-sight, and we all knew that when they started bombing they would hit the target right on the nail, but at the moment it was up to Bomber Command. Meanwhile, the U-boat menace was still the big thing of the day. In Germany and their occupied ports they were building U-boats much faster than we could sink them.

Danzig was one of these ports.

Danzig lies in Poland, a long way from British shores, but in order to try to stem the tide of the Atlantic Battle, a daylight raid was planned on this place, where they were turning out at least twelve U-boats every month.

It was decided that Lancasters were to do the job. A long flight of some 1,500 miles over enemy territory in daylight was involved. If night-bombing had been accurate the job could have been done at night with the minimum amount of risk, but special orders had been given that we must avoid killing civilians at all costs. Thus extra risk had to be taken by flying unescorted over enemy territory in daylight. Such was the way of things.

Little need be said of that raid, the success of which as a precision bombing attack can best be gathered from a current newspaper report:

"Yesterday our Lancasters flew to Danzig in daylight to carry out a low-level attack on the submarine yards. Many searchlights were shot up by our gunners . . ."

There *were* flak and searchlights, because the timing had misfired. Most of us arrived over Danzig when it was pitch dark. In my aircraft, instead of bombing Danzig at night, where we couldn't even see the docks, let alone the streets, we had bombed a small ship in the outer harbour and missed it by 20 yards from 1,000ft. We had spared civilians, but we were still learning that raids must be planned carefully.

At that time there were rumours that a Pathfinder Squadron was to be formed, composed of the best bombing crews from all squadrons.

Dim said: "It seems a good idea to me, but I can see many snags."

"What are they going to do?" someone asked.

"Go in low and light up the targets for us with flares. We stay high and safe and bomb accurately," said Johnny.

"That's good."

"That's fine."

"Yes, but here are the snags," said Dim. "First it is hard to form a new squadron quickly, and if you form it quickly it is hard to form it well, and speed is what they want. I think it would be better to take the best squadron in the Command and call it the 'First Pathfinder Squadron'."

"That means us," said Taffy.

"No, we are about fifth now. I think 97 Squadron."

A short argument followed in which it was generally agreed that 97 Squadron should be chosen.

"The second snag," went on Dim, "is losses. If they are going to go in low, their casualties are going to be high — very high. How are they going to get away with it? New crews will take a long time to train."

"Squadrons will have to give up their best crews," suggested Wimpy, "on a strictly volunteer basis."

"Then the best squadrons will either be deprived of all their crack crews, or no one will volunteer and the Pathfinders will be starved."

"That's right. Keen squadrons will cough up their best crews and lose their place on the photographic ladder, while a lousy squadron will do nothing about it and go up to the top."

"*C'est la guerre*," said Dim. "It will be fair enough in the long run. But the third great snag, as far as I can see, is promotion in the squadron. If there are heavy losses, then it won't matter, but if there aren't, then good chaps who would become Flight-Commanders in an ordinary squadron would be kept down because they had volunteered to become Pathfinders. They would lose their promotion, and the old hands would stay on and keep their rank. It seems rather unfair."

"That goes for all special squadrons," I pointed out.

"I suppose so. Anyway, I wish they would hurry up and get cracking. Our bombing certainly needs a spot of accuracy."

Meanwhile, I am told, arguments, debates and discussions were taking place at length in Bomber Command. Some of the big noises were flat out for the day when Pathfinders would take the air. This included most of the Group-Commanders. Others, one or two of whom were in Bomber Command itself, were not so keen. It was a new idea. Why change three years' hard work? They argued and grumbled, grumbled and argued, hour after hour, day after day. Even the Prime Minister was consulted, and in the end it was he who did much to put the matter right.

Then came August 15, 1942, the day the Pathfinders came into being.

But let's go back just a few days. On the 9th and 10th we had all gone out to lay mines in the Baltic to try to stop the *Prinz Eugen* from slipping into the Atlantic. These were long trips in bad weather, both of seven or more hours' duration, and fifteen hours' flying in twenty-four was pretty tiring, to the average pilot. The weather was so bad when we took off from England that we were cloud-borne before we even got our wheels up, and coming back we had to land on the beam in daylight.

On the 11th we rested, but on the next night, my birthday, we made the last Pathfinderless attack on Germany and, queerly enough, it was a roaring success; 135 acres were destroyed. Every crew went below the clouds to find his objective; every crew bombed from 5,000ft. I couldn't help thinking at the time that I couldn't, myself and the boys, have given a better birthday present to the Nazis.

But after four trips in five days we were all pretty tired out and the whole squadron was given a night off. We went to our usual pub, the "Red Lion", and had a few beers.

Next day we heard which squadron had been selected to be the Pathfinder Squadron in No. 5 Group. There was a boy from this squadron with us at the time. He had landed at our place the night before with engine trouble, and he told us the gen.

"We are moving down south tomorrow," he said, "to a place in Huntingdonshire. Quite a good spot, I believe: the beer's good and the girls aren't bad. Anyway, it will be jolly nice to get out of Lincolnshire."

"Fine," said Dim dryly; "but what are the conditions of the Pathfinder Service?"

"As far as I know, we can do up to sixty trips without a rest, but have to give up when we get tired, and no one will call it lack of moral fibre. When we are qualified Pathfinders — which means ten trips as an illuminator — we are allowed to wear a special pair of gold wings underneath our medal ribbons." (He had the DFC.)

At this there was a chorus of sarcastic cheers.

"What is an illuminator?"

"Perhaps I had better explain the whole procedure. The new crews merely carry incendiary bombs and no flares at all, but they attack in front of the main force, so that the first incendiaries fall accurately on to the target. The next lot of crews carry a full load of flares. The job of these boys is to find the target, and so they are known as 'Finders'. They fly out on a course extremely accurately, keeping to dead reckoning, and when the ETA is up they begin to drop a flare every thirty seconds, and so a long line of country is illuminated for perhaps 10 miles. Meanwhile, the other Finders will spread out on either side, so that when zero hour arrives the whole German countryside for 10 miles square is illuminated. Not very well, but enough for the next crowd of boys to see."

"And the best crews?" I asked.

"They carry bundles of flares which they drop the moment they see the aiming point. In fact, they try to drop them on top of the aiming point. They fly right with the Finders, and they themselves are called the 'Illuminators'. When they see where the target is they drop a few flares in a certain pattern, and the rest of the Pathfinders immediately come along and dump hundreds of flares right over the target, which will illuminate it, we hope, like daylight."

"How about cloud?"

"We haven't got an answer to that yet, but the first thing we are going to do is to send a Mosquito out every night about an hour in front of us who will tell us exactly what the weather is like over the target. We may even send one out five hours before the raid is due to take off, so that we can be pretty sure that the weather will be OK when we get there."

"And fog?"

"Well, if there is any thick fog we will probably drop pink pansies. These are 250lb incendiary bombs which burn with a bright red glow on the ground and can be seen quite clearly through any fog."

"How long do they burn?"

"Oh, quite a long time — about fifteen minutes."

"That sounds good enough. At what height are you going to fly?"

"About the same as you. We may go in lower if the cloud is low, but we have had it impressed on us that the main thing is to be absolutely certain of our position."

"But how can you be certain of knowing where you are? The Germans are jamming our Nav. boxes so much that except for finding a position over the North Sea, we can't do a thing about it."

"Our idea is to keep to dead reckoning as much as possible. In fact, dead reckoning is our motto. We will get a wind — a good wind — early on, and then fly absolutely accurately, and if you work it out you can't be more than 10 miles out either way, after 300 miles, provided the pilot is good and compasses are right. Then, of course, the Finders will take care of the rest."

"It seems OK to me," said Hoppy. "But we still haven't got a point to aim at."

"Yes, that's right; bombing will be scattered."

"But it will be in the right place."

"Yes, it will be in the right place all right, which is something."

"I hope," said Dim, doubtfully.

The Pathfinders led the main force into action two days later, on a very small-scale raid on Emden. This is not a large port and is not defended by many guns, so nothing much could be gained from the success of this raid, but it gave the whole of the Pathfinder force a lot of confidence in their job. They had lit up the place well and bombs had fallen, causing destruction, which the Emdenites had never seen before.

We didn't take part in this and the following raids, because for a time we had been shifted on to special duties.

The story had begun a long time ago, when in our old Hampdens we used to make lonely dive-bombing attacks on the *Scharnhorst* in Kiel Harbour. Now the *Scharnhorst* was in Gdynia having certain new gadgets put on. The *Gneisenau* was there, too, being dismantled, together with a new aircraft carrier, the *Graf Zeppelin*, which was being fitted out for its first voyage. The admirals of the Royal Navy were fearful that these ships, together with the battleship *Tirpitz* and a few scattered cruisers, might set sail as a formidable task force towards mid-Atlantic, where their presence might be undesirable. Especially so, bearing in mind new operations of considerable magnitude which were being considered at that time.

Meanwhile, after the episode of the *Scharnhorst* and *Gneisenau* slipping through the Channel, certain scientists had gone into action. A new bomb had been designed. It was known simply as the "capital ship bomb". How it worked and what it was supposed to do were, and still are today, well-kept secrets. But the rough idea was that one hit took care of one battleship. It was very heavy, but like most new weapons it had its limitations. It was not a beautiful bomb; in fact, it was extremely ugly, and looked of all things rather like a turnip, and like most turnips its ballistics were not very good. When it was dropped at a high altitude, instead of following the path of a beautiful bomb it might easily swing out of its course. And so to hit a ship from 8,000ft would require a lot of luck, even though the bomb-aiming was extremely good. The other alternative, and the only alternative, was to go in low. Unfortunately, this bomb had to be dropped, if we went in low, from exactly 1,000ft if it was to do its stuff; and there is no future in flying straight and level over a battleship at 1,000ft. I think most naval gunners will agree with me that few Lancasters would reach the release point, let alone the aiming point.

Air Marshal Harris had given this "toy" to my squadron. We had been told to get on with a lot of practice in low- and high-level bombing. Two special bomb-sights had been acquired for the job. Now the Ministry of Aircraft Production, which works wonders in aircraft, can also always produce a good many other things when required, and they soon managed to get hold of two extremely accurate types. A high-level bomb-sight is very different from a low-level bomb-sight, but in any case we of the Royal Air Force have never made much of a song and dance of our bomb-sights, because night-bombing doesn't need a really accurate one. Anything within a quarter of a mile will do. However, the sight to which I am referring — the high-level sight — was really accurate, and soon we began to get, with practice, errors of only 60 yards from 10,000ft. This was good enough for what we wanted.

This training had gone on without a pause for two months, and six crews in the squadron had become fairly proficient. When clouds were low we had also carried out low-level practice, so that we could drop our bombs to the tune of an accuracy of about 15 yards. Should any German warship try to steal away under cover of low cloud we would still have been able to fix him, even though it wouldn't have been much fun. Every day for the last two months we always had three crews available, standing by in flying kit, who could take off immediately to do the job; sometimes I was one of them. But whoever we were and whatever we were like as pilots, I think they would all agree when I say that the boys owe their lives to the fact that no German admiral had the guts to put to sea.

"One thing," said Dim; "if we do go and attack those ships, one of us might possibly get a posthumous VC."

"Who wants that?" said Taffy.

"Not me," said one of the boys; "all I want is a Peace and Victory Medal."

Most of us agreed.

Then came the moon period of August. Special intelligence reports had said that the *Graf Zeppelin* was almost ready; the crew was supposed to be on board; the aircraft had been taken over; they were ready to set sail. Now, a German aircraft-carrier was a thing that hadn't been known before, and it was our idea that it wouldn't be known very long. We knew how to drop our bomb; and we were ready.

On the full-moon night of August 27th, while the rest of the boys were bombing Cassel, twelve of us set out for the 950-mile journey to Gdynia. We took off overloaded to the hitherto unprecedented weight of 67,000lb all up. In my crew we were carrying S/L Richardson as a bomb-aimer. He was a bombing instructor, and if anyone could drop a bomb accurately it was he, but he was making his first war flight since August 1918.

Our plan was to make accurate bombing runs from 6,000ft in the moon. It should have been easy; the docks in the brilliant light should have been clear-cut squares in the bomb-sight. Everything seemed to point in our favour. Out of twelve bombs, one would surely fall in the right place. But old man weather turned against us. When we arrived over the target the south-westerly wind had blown all the haze away from Berlin straight over Danzig and Gdynia. It reduced visibility to about 1 mile. Moreover, there was a lot of light flak and searchlights about.

Hoppy was nearest. He missed by about 50 yards, causing one of the largest craters they had ever seen in those parts. We spent an hour over the target, and made twelve bombing runs. We never saw the *Graf Zeppelin* — but the *Gneisenau* was there, and Dicky Richardson aimed at that. Each time he made his run he was completely oblivious of the fact that the flak was all round. I think he thought he was over the practice range on the East Coast. The first time he said "Dummy run" there was a silence; the tenth time he said it, a quick ejaculation came from Johnny Wickens in the rear turret. In the end, we saw our huge bomb fall into the water about 400 yards away from the *Gneisenau*. Dicky's remark was rather laconic, considering that by now we were alone over the target and the flak was giving us hell. He said:

"That's killed a few fish for the bastards," and added as an afterthought, "Blast it."

Combie in the mid-upper turret said he thought we had better be going. Junior said it would be daylight when we re-crossed the Danish coast. Hutch said he would send a message telling them we had just left the target, so that they wouldn't worry if we were a few hours late. Junior piped up again and said that he thought we should go a little north, so as to avoid Sylt on the way home — there were some fighters there. I said nothing, or very nearly nothing: just a few short words . . .

That's the worst of one big bomb: you go a long way to do your best; then you miss; then you have a five-hours bind on the way home. It is an infuriating business.

When we were circling base I looked at my clock. We had been in the air ten hours, and with no second pilot I felt pretty well all in. Ten hours' flying is a long time, but apart from our failure, the only worthwhile event was the Russians bombing Königsberg at the same time as we were bombing Gdynia. In the bright moonlight I saw over the target a funny-looking thing, rather like an elongated Heinkel. Next day some newspaper correspondent wrote of the "aerial arms shaking hands over Danzig". I am quite sure neither side knew the other was there.

A few days later we flew behind the Pathfinders to bomb Saarbrucken. We were carrying an 8,000lb bomb for the first time, and great excitement prevailed on board as we waited in anticipation to see what it would look like. We had never flown behind the Pathfinders before, and we arrived a little early to see what they would do. Sure enough the Finders laid their long strings of flares, the Illuminators hovered around and then dumped bunch after bunch of flares right over the town; the bombs, incendiaries first, began to fall thick and fast, about 1,000 tons of them. Soon the whole area was one mass of flames. Junior saw our cookie fall and said it caused "an expanding mushroom of blue-red flame which seemed to cover an area of about half a mile square for a full five seconds". Long words for junior, but I wouldn't have cared to have been in it.

Everything was fine. We all got back safely, although we ourselves had some of the biggest holes knocked in our wings and fuselage I have yet to see in a Lancaster, and we went to bed pleased. Our photographs had shown one mass of flames.

But next day we heard very bad news from the photo-reconnaissance unit. The Pathfinder Force had boobed. They had lit up Saarlouis, a small town — in fact, a tiny, town — 10 miles from Saarbrucken, and the Recco boys said that, judging from the photographs, there wasn't even a signpost left standing there. Those 1,000 tons had removed the place from the map. A few nights later the same thing happened at Frankfurt, when a small force had, through slight miscalculations on the part of the Pathfinders, bombed another small town nearby. But this time they destroyed by mistake a large and hitherto unknown factory making Opel trucks for the German Army.

But if some raids went wrong, others went right. The Pathfinders had already begun to pay good dividends under the command of Group-Captain Bennett, an ex-airline pilot. Devastation in industrial areas in many cities was on a scale hitherto unknown. The crews at last could see what they were aiming at, the area which they had set out for. The day had at last been reached when most of the bombs would fall in the right place, but unfortunately the right place was too big; bombing was still not concentrated. Marker bombs were still required to give the bomb-aimers a bullseye aiming point.

It soon became obvious that the pink pansies were no earthly use at all. The Germans hadn't been slow. They copied these pink pansies so quickly that soon they sprang up like poppies over all the open fields in Germany.

So it went on. A step had been taken in the right direction. Improvements were being made every day. Towns in the Third Reich were being raided every night, and reading from my logbook it can be seen that these were being raided with varying success:

On September 10th, Düsseldorf; target lit up well: many acres of industrial area were destroyed.

On the 13th, Bremen; a failure, we lost nineteen, including three from 106 — Taffy Williams, Dizzy Downer, S/L Howell — too much flak, target not illuminated, raids scattered.

On 19th, Ruhr area; cloud all the way; complete failure.

23rd, Flensburg; failure, due to haze, bombing not concentrated.

It was obvious that a snag had yet to be overcome. We had done everything else, but we hadn't beaten the weather. When it was good, a raid was successful; but when it was bad, the bombs were scattered far and wide.

On October 1st we moved to another airfield. As soon as we arrived we started training in mass low-level formation under the able command of Group-Captain Gus Walker of rugger fame, who had himself won the DSO and DFC. He used to lead us round the countryside, practising navigation at nought feet. There is no room in this book to say what a great man Gus is, but I know that all of 106 would like it to be said that he was one of the finest Station-masters they had ever served under.

We started off first in squadrons, then in wings, and finally in a sort of formation known as a group gaggle, meaning a flock of geese. We flew the length and breadth of England, never more than 300ft up; mighty dangerous it was, too. In the beginning there were no set positions, and we flew through the air, wing-tip to wing-tip, rather like a crowd of workers elbowing their way into a bus. The only snag was that if anyone touched it would be "curtains" to the two aircraft concerned. When we finally levelled out for the practice bombing run it was a question of closing our eyes and praying to God. Practice bombs whistled down all round, and one of my pilots, George Lace, flying on my left-hand side, once collected one in the mid-upper turret, but it merely fell through his gunner's legs without going off, much to his surprise.

On many occasions some of our Metropolitan Air Force fighters would carry out dummy attacks on us. Such was the nature of our formation that quite a few found it extremely difficult to get out of our slipstream once they had got in. More than one hit the deck making these dummy attacks.

All this culminated in one of the greatest low-level daylight raids of the war. It was carried out by ninety-four Lancasters flying in tight formation, and even though I say it myself, it was a fine raid, led, planned and executed by a fine group. My report next day, written while I was still in pyjamas in my bedroom, read:

For some days the squadron had been practising low-level formation flying — in threes, in sixes and with other squadrons in long cross-country flights. Quite obviously these exercises were leading up to something "big," something out of the ordinary — perhaps a mass formation raid in daylight. After several "flaps", during which aircraft were de-bombed almost as soon as they were bombed-up, the day finally arrived when all conditions were favourable for such an attack. The day was Saturday, October 14, 1942, and the target was the Schneider Armament Factory at Le Creusot, almost on the border of occupied and Vichy France.

The raid was exclusively 5 Group's — a grand force of ninety-four Lancasters assembling and forming up soon after midday. The squadron supplied ten aircraft and all of them took off without a hitch. The route was over Land's End, far out to the Bay of Biscay and then turning into the French Coast, crossing it just south of Ile d'Yeu and thence over some 200 miles of enemy-occupied territory, to the target. The formation flew the whole way between heights of 50 and 500ft, climbing up to 4,000ft as it neared the target.

The sun had set and it was getting dark when the objective was reached, soon after 6 o'clock, but the vast area of factories, workshops and warehouses was clearly seen. The attack lasted for nine minutes, during which time over 200 tons of high explosives and incendiaries were rained down with commendable precision. Huge fires broke out and terrific explosions were seen over a wide area and within a few minutes the whole town was blanketed with a thick pall of smoke.

In addition to the main target a formation of six aircraft were detailed to bomb the Montchanin Power Station — a vital target which if hit would cause widespread chaos and confusion. In this formation, No. 106 Squadron was represented by W/C G. P. Gibson, DFC, and F/L J. V. Hopgood, DFC. The attack was made from 500ft, each aircraft carrying 10 × 500lb bombs. Both crews claim that their bombs straddled the target — a claim which was justified by later reports which stated that the transformer house would take nearly two years to repair. Our two aircraft then circled the target and between them fired 1,000 rounds of ammunition into the transformers — a satisfactory and spectacular operation which brought forth vivid blue flashes each time a bullet hit a vital spot.

The attack completed, to the satisfaction of all concerned, the aircraft turned for home — independently since it was now dark, and by the shortest route. Weather, which had been favourable, was very bad over this country and the majority of aircraft were diverted to bases in the south.

Throughout the whole trip not a single enemy fighter offered combat (except to one aircraft limping home on three engines) and the opposition over the target itself was negligible.

All squadron aircraft returned safely and undamaged with the exception of W/C Gibson's (slightly holed) and F/L Hopgood's. This latter aircraft was damaged by the blast of its own bombs, F/L Hopgood (incidentally this was the last trip of his tour) being a little too enthusiastic and bombing from below safety height. All ten crews claim to have hit their target, so that from a squadron point of view the raid was 100 per cent successful.

Owing to the fading light, pictures of the actual bombing were not obtainable, but P/O Ruskell took several photographs of the outward journey from the Wing-Commander's aircraft, with an ordinary cine camera. Several of his pictures, the only ones taken on the raid, were subsequently published in the Press.

Captains of squadron aircraft taking part:

> W/C Gibson, DFC
> P/O Crowe
> Sergeant Lace, DFM
> P/O Shannon
> Sergeant Hamilton
> F/L Hopgood, DFC
> P/O Cassels
> P/O Healey, DFM
> Sergeant Phair
> P/O Wellington

Two days later we were briefed for Italy; this was to be the first raid here for some time. Because the Italians had no flak worth mentioning, and because the trip over France was similar to flying over England, Italy had always been popular with all bomber crews.

"Tonight it is Genoa," said Gus Walker. "I don't want to waste your time by making a speech, but it is the first time we have attacked Genoa for years. The targets, of course, are all in the dock area, where units of the Italian fleet are sheltering. You may wonder why we have been suddenly switched from Germany, and why you are going here tonight — I only wish I could come too. Well, all I can say is that you may, for all I know, be taking part in a large operation in the Mediterranean. For the first time in history you may be supporting land operations, hundreds of miles away. Anyway, off you go. Good luck."

We went and we all came back. It was a good prang. The Pathfinders lit the targets just like daylight. We all watched our incendiaries burn merrily away on the concrete roofs of the Genoa houses. We watched our block-busters disintegrate the buildings on the dockyards. And when we came back we all decided that Genoa was pretty cushy.

Next day the offensive in the Western Desert started. Mr Churchill had given his orders. Gus had been right.

This was a great week from the start, because the next day we went off to Italy again. This time it was a daylight raid. Apart from the damage we were going to do, I think the whole idea was to show the Italians that the British Air Force was all supreme on the Western Front. We were going to attack Milan in daylight at tea-time.

It is not being quite fair to the German fighters to say that we flew across France on the way to Italy completely unsupported. We crossed Selsey Bill at very low level mid flew towards that flat part of land between Cherbourg and Le Havre. A warm front had been reported lying across France which would give us cloud-cover when we approached. We were to climb up for this cloud as soon as possible. In actual fact the cloud had receded from the French coast, and we all stormed up over the cliffs in bright daylight, climbing flat out with the clouds in the distance. Most of us had gone a long way into France before the motherly safeness of the blanketing white mist had been reached. They fired at us a bit over the French coast, but I think they were all surprised to see a hundred bombers supported by Spitfires flying so low. Then we heard the Germans chattering away on the RT. We heard the controller say: "Hello, all German aircraft. The British bombers are too far south; you must land at the nearest bases."

On we flew, this bright, sunny day; it was getting warmer and warmer as we flew south, and junior helped me to take off my coat. We were carrying movie-cameras, and took many interesting pictures of little French villages, and some rather charming French people, who were all waving to us. One charming family group I remember stood in front of their white cottage — a young man, a little blonde daughter, about seven years old, and a sweet wife; at least she looked sweet from 100ft, with her blonde hair flying in the breeze; they were all waving like mad. Another time we saw a flock of what I thought at first were geese, clustered together in the middle of the field. When we had gone over them Johnny told me they were nuns.

After three hours we climbed up high over the Alps and gathered in a fighting formation over Lake Annecy; then stormed down on to Milan, another 60 miles further on, dropping our cookies from 3,000ft. The sun was still well up; in fact, we could see our shadows before us moving along the ground. The confusion in Milan was something to be seen. A few flak-guns fired spasmodically; private cars ran on to the pavements; people rushed to shelters; someone turned on a searchlight. But it was no use, the boys behaved like real gentlemen. They all went for military objectives, and they did a lot of military damage. As far as I know, not one civilian establishment was hit.

Then we turned around and came home again. The sun began to set over the Alps — a beautiful sight, a sight which perhaps we will never see again. An Italian fighter came in to have a look at us.

His was a biplane with only two guns; we had six. Johnny Wickens kept on saying in the back, "Come on, you beggar; come on, you beggar; come closer." But he never came. And then the sun went down, and we were flying safely over France again on the way home.

Later that night Halifaxes bombed the place again, and the panic in this second raid was said to beat all records, even for the Italians.

It was a good raid, this daylight on Milan, and must have shaken the Italians more than somewhat, especially as they relied on their great German partner to protect them from the Northern Approaches. But a few days later Genoa had it two nights running, and we all began to wonder what was happening. Were we trying to give the Pathfinders a break, or were we trying to give them confidence in illuminating weakly defended targets? Or was it to try to bomb Italy out of the war? The rumours had it that things were going pretty badly inside Italy. When the King visited Genoa, people were said to have gone down on their knees and prayed for peace. Some even said that most of the statesmen were entertaining the idea of making a separate peace. But why were we bombing Genoa the whole time? Why not Turin? We knew the Fleet was at Genoa, but Turin was the better target. There is not so much concrete there. Why bomb the Italian fleet the whole time? — it never put to sea, anyway.

But on November 8th we got our answer. North Africa had been invaded.

We had been trying to prevent the Itie fleet from interfering.

From now on Italy began to get it whenever the weather was suitable for the occasion. Not only the fogs in England often stopped a raid, but the big cloud-banks over the Alps themselves made the trip almost impossible. We were briefed practically every night, but each time the Met. man would walk in with his "cloud board", which showed the heights of cloud all the way to the target. Icing cloud was marked in deep red and the non-icing variety in blue. When he walked in, as he usually did, with his board looking as if it had been dipped in red paint, nervous howls of laughter would go up from all the crews. Then the target would be changed to somewhere else, possibly in Germany. This meant last-minute flaps — a new briefing, a new flight-planning conference, new maps and bad tempers all round. We were briefed many times, but the weather often held us back.

But despite the fact that Lancasters from our Group were the only ones capable of "doing" Italy, we flew in the month of November no fewer than 1,336 sorties to that fair country for the loss of only two aircraft. If we should cast our minds back and say, for a matter of example, that an airline flew three flights a day to Italy for three years running and lost only two aircraft, they would consider themselves one of the safest airlines in the world.

Moreover, we had to contend with what little flak there was; but whatever damage our bombs did, it was certainly a good portent of the future of civil aviation and the complete reliability of British aircraft.

By now the Italians were getting jumpy; these raids were doing their stuff. We were, as they say, on a good wicket. It is a well-known fact that bombing accuracy and effect increase indirectly with the weakness of flak and morale. Italian flak, though bolstered up by certain Nazi flak regiments, was still bad. We would often bomb at very low level, picking out targets at will, and nothing could be worse for the people below than to see those great Lancasters flying around, making a tremendous noise, and dropping their cookies out one after another, on exactly the right spot.

On November 29th my crew and I dropped the first 8,000lb bomb of the war on Italy. Turin received it with displeasure, and I took a movie picture to show it bursting, and also to show the boys what it was like when we got home.

After this "Woe-Woe" Ansaldo reached a new high in moans about the war. He said that the whole thing was unfair, that there should be no such thing as aerial attack. Perhaps he had forgotten Abyssinia and gas.

"Darned good show, too," said Johnny Searby, one of the new Flight-Commanders. He had taken the place of Dim, who had wangled a posting to a "secret" place in London, probably the Savoy. Johnny was a little older than the average, rather taciturn — sometimes severe — but a very good-hearted fellow. He was married and had a baby. He had done a lot of work in Ferry Command. Now he wanted to fly on Ops badly, and was doing trips as often as possible.

"Yes, the Ities are getting absolute hell." This was Charles Martin, the Adjutant. He was about forty-five years old and had won the Military Medal in the last war, and for his sins had done about twenty trips at the rear turret of a Wimpy in this one. Why they had never given him a gong, if only for the magnificent example he had shown, I cannot think.

We were sitting in the dining-room of the "Black Boy Hotel" at Nottingham. The food had been good, the wine even better. Now we were smoking cigars and drinking a modest brandy. Often we would treat ourselves like this, just to get away from the drab routine of station life. All the rest of the boys — Hoppy, Bill, Brian Oliver, my new gunnery officer, Gray Healey, Mike Lumley, his wireless-operator, Don Curtin, from Long Island, USA — were upstairs in the American bar, cracking jokes with the two barmaids and drinking a terrible potion known as the "106 Special", which I think consisted of every drink under the sun mixed into one glass. We had driven them in. They were having a noisy evening. We were having a quiet one.

"You know," said Charles, "it is amazing how this war has changed. Last year about this time things looked pretty grim. Last summer I think they looked even worse, and now everything seems fine; that is, at least, we don't look like losing it."

"I wonder when it will be all over," I said to myself, more than to the others.

"A long time yet," said Charles.

"I agree," said John, "but when you mentioned just now that things had changed a lot since the summer, I think you can almost say that the turning point of the war was reached in the month between October 22nd, and when was it that the Russians started their Stalingrad offensive?"

"November 22nd."

"Yes, that's right, between October 22nd and November 22nd the course of this way changed completely. Last summer the Axis came to the limit of their advance; they had come as far as they could. Then they were held; their initiative died away at Stalingrad, at El Alamein and in the Solomons."

"Go on."

John took a sip at his brandy. Charles lit his cigar and I listened, watching his smoke curl into the air.

"Well, you know the rest," he continued. "On October 22nd we attacked at El Alamein, and after a week broke through and turned the whole German line there into a complete rout. On the 8th they invaded North Africa, and although I am not quite sure of that man, Admiral Darlan, things seem to be going pretty well. On the 22nd Timoshenko counter-attacked at Stalingrad under Stalin's orders. And now what has happened? A vast German army is trapped, and the loss of men on the Eastern Front might make all the difference to the fighting. In North Africa both sides are going forward well. They look like meeting in a couple of months' time. Then another German army might be annihilated, or what is left of it. After all, we have complete sea-power in the Med. now."

"Yes, we have certainly got sea superiority," said Charles. "Then perhaps we will invade the fortress of Europe."

"Perhaps next autumn."

"Depends on how things go. The Russians are yelling for a Second Front, but we can't do a thing until we have beaten the submarine menace. Besides that, we've got to get air superiority on all fronts first. It is pretty easy for the Germans; they are tucked up inside their fortress, and they can meet anyone on the outside rim by moving all their forces to that point. Our job is to get complete and utter air superiority everywhere."

"Don't the Russians think the African campaign a Second Front?"

"No. It isn't killing enough Germans."

"They like our bombing, though," I said. "It has quite an effect on German morale at home."

"But surely you don't think bombing could win the war alone?" asked Charles.

"I don't know, Charles; that is what we are taught, as you know; but we are dealing with the mass psychology of a nation — and a bad nation at that. It is run, organized and controlled by Gestapo and SS police. They might crack, if they can break out of the iron ring, or they might not. No one can say."

"And if our bombing gets heavier?"

"You are asking the impossible. The German people are extraordinary; they have never faced devastation on their home front before. But the fact still remains that if they were to give in, they would have everything to lose and nothing to gain. I think myself they will fight till the end. A lot of people go around talking so much bull about the crack appearing and once the crack has appeared the foundation will weaken, etc, etc. In fact, so much so that the British public is getting very much 'win-the-war-by-the-easiest-method' minded. The Yankee boys have already started going farther and farther into France — Rouen had it the other day. No one can tell where they will stop. Not, perhaps, until they reach Berlin. At the same time we shall obviously be increasing our effort. The whole

Bomber Command is getting Lancasters and improved Halifaxes, but even then, who knows?"

"It's funny they're not making any real attempt at reprisals for all that," put in John. "That Canterbury raid was just a hate sortie. From what I am told by eyewitnesses, they came in at teatime at low level in the middle of the busiest shopping hour. Casualties were pretty heavy."

Charles offered me a cigarette.

"That was a hate raid all right," he said; "but I think I agree with the wingco in what he has just said. The Germans may get their cities devastated, they may even get their cities wiped out, but they will never understand war until an army marches in as it has never done before, as far as we know, in our history. This army must not be made up of cissies, but an army which will just show these bastards exactly what we mean by telling them that war doesn't pay. Hitler, Goering and the rest of them must be dealt with in the appropriate manner — though God knows what that is."

"Let's hope the Russians get there first," said John, feelingly; "but if they don't, then let's hope we do a really good job."

There was a short silence. Then I changed the subject.

"I think Goering's a complete clot. He started off thinking the Luftwaffe was all-powerful and prepared it for a short war with a minimum of reserves. Now he is finding that his ambitious programme is not so good. All his boys have to fly

363

old types with no guns on board which don't fly very well, anyway. He is backing a real loser."

"Don't you let him hear you say that," said Charles, laughing.

And so we sat there, talking over our cigars and brandy, mostly about the war, for there was little else to talk about. We went on to the Jap war: how the little yellow bellies themselves had been halted, and how the balance of sea-power had swung back in the Allies' favour; how once again the Japs were being beaten back; about the U-boat war; how aeroplanes were now being equipped with certain devices which would be able to attack the U-boat when they least expected it; the aerial war — we all had stories to tell, ideas to put forward. The liqueurs were doing their work well. Conversation flowed easily.

Up to now it had been a long road of defeat and failure; a long uphill road which had taken a lot of climbing. Now at last we were over the hump. It was pleasant to sit there and rest awhile and think that the worst was behind. Perhaps the Hun would now retire right into his European fortress. In fact, we knew that he had already begun to do so. The German leaders in their speeches were tacitly acknowledging this governing factor in their policy. They were now going to organize all Europe as an impregnable fortress, capable of resisting a definite siege until war weariness, or internal dissension, should cause the Allies to abandon any attempt to try to crack an impossible nut. Exploitation of conquered territories had become so ruthless as almost to shake the quislings. Italians, Hungarians, Rumanians and other vassal nationalities had been herded by their thousands to the death-pit of the Russian front. By cold-blooded murder and an unexampled campaign of cruelty a strong attempt had been made to obliterate the entire Jewish race. France had been made to enter into full collaboration with the Axis. Adolf Hitler had proclaimed himself above the law.

But we would attack that Festung Europa, and we were going to get inside for the first time. And this time we would be able to dictate to the German people in the language of the sword — their own language, and the only language they will be able to understand until we alter their entire educational ideas. After this would come the Japs. It would take a long time, but they, too, would earn the penalty meted out for aggression.

"It really does seem," said John, yawning, "that once we invade the end is in sight."

"The executive word is 'once'; in fact, a big word is 'once'," said Charles.

We got up to go. The evening had been pleasant and we had practically "won" the war. But we shouldn't have been so pleased if we had known of the long battles that were to be fought, the heavy casualties to be borne, and the fact that the war was to be so prolonged. The tide had turned, but had a long way to go back.

CHAPTER
FIFTEEN

The Shape of Things

The raids on Italy ended as suddenly as they began — that is, for our Group. We began once more to bomb the Ruhr valley. On the other hand, a few Halifaxes and Stirlings would wend their lonely way down to the south over the Alps and drop a few tons on the industrial areas of Turin and Genoa, but these were more spasmodic than usual. In our Group we even made one heavy raid on Milan in which my 106 Squadron topped all previous records by obtaining six aiming-point pictures of the target, a feat which brought us up from third to the proud position of top of Bomber Command.

But taking things by and large, Italy was off, the battle of Germany was on.

While little had been done to Germany in the past few months, when most of the bomber force had been engaged elsewhere, the scientists had not been idle. "Boffins", we call them, why I don't know. They are not longhaired, spectacled old men, as you might imagine. They are just ordinary types, some young, some middle-aged, who have not had the chance to fly but are doing the next best thing.

They were out to beat the weather. For months they had slaved with short-wave radio trying to work out a system. Now, at last, they had got it.

One day towards the end of December the Group Bombing Leader, F/L Bob Hay, explained exactly how it was to be done. He was speaking to us in our briefing-room in front of a large blackboard on which were drawn many complex diagrams. "Now so far in this war," he began, "you have always bombed something on the ground." I looked across at John Searby and smiled. Of course we had always bombed something on the ground; what else could we bomb? "If you can see your target easily, you have always done your best to hit it; but when your target has been covered by cloud you know what happens — you just drop your bombs on ETA, or on a timed run from the nearest landmark, and this means that your bombs are scattered over the countryside."

There was an expectant hush, everybody was listening.

"Now we've got something new. We're going to bomb through cloud, we're going to bomb completely 'blind'. You're going to aim at something in the air. This something will take the form of a coloured flare which will be dropped by the Pathfinders in a certain position right over the aiming point."

Bomb a flare! Somebody laughed.

"It is nothing to laugh about," Bob went on; "wait till you hear the rest. These flares are going to be dropped by certain aircraft of the Pathfinder force who have been practising over England for some time, and I can't tell you how they do it. It's all a question of a super instrument. For the benefit of the bomb-aimers I might tell you that you use your sight in the normal way, except that you set up the following data."

He went on for a while in his cut-and-dried manner expounding technical stuff about wind velocities, terminal velocities, trail angles and the rest of the thousand things that make up the information fed into the modern bomb-sight. Gone were the days when the Royal Air Force bombers had to use sights produced in 1932. Now the Mark XIV had come along. It did practically everything. You could fly at any angle, you could dive at any speed, but minute little gyros revolving at many thousands of revs per minute took care of everything except the wind, and the bombs were sure to fall near the target. Such was the character of our new bomb-sight that it became known as the all-singing, all-talking, all-dancing weapon.

One of the most enthusiastic persons about this new technique was Gus Walker. He, too, had had his fair-share of bombing Germany when conditions were bad, hence his DSO and DFC, and he knew the game inside out. But, unfortunately, for a while Gus was not going to see this new system put into operation.

It all happened on one of the worst nights I can ever remember. We were sending a lot of aircraft off and it was dusk, just at the time when you cannot see very well. About thirty aircraft were taxiing around the perimeter track waiting for each other to take off. Gus and I were watching from the control tower. Suddenly, right on the far side of the aerodrome, we saw that a few incendiaries had dropped out of the gaping bomb-doors of one of the Lancasters. Gus, thinking that this aircraft had a "cookie" on board, immediately rushed over to warn the crew to get out. I saw his car go speeding straight across the aerodrome, over the runways in front of aircraft taking off, to carry out his plan. But we knew it was a reserve aircraft, and I had to stay in the watch-tower, anyway, now that he had gone.

Watching him through fieldglasses, I saw him get out of his car. I saw him run towards the aircraft, his arms waving against the lurid light cast up by the incendiaries. He was within 20 yards of the cookie when it went off.

There was one of those great slow explosions which shot straight into the air for about 2,000ft and the great Lancaster just disappeared.

We turned away, trying not to think of the horrible sight; we thought that Gus had surely been blown sky high. But he was too tough for that. He had been bowled over backwards for about 200 yards; he had seen a great chunk of metal swipe off his right arm just below the elbow, but he had picked himself up and walked into the ambulance.

Ten other men, belonging to the fire-tender crew, were also injured, and now that I was acting

Station-Commander, I arranged for the sick quarters to work at top speed in order to try to save their lives. The Station Medical Officer was away, but Doc. Arnold, our own doctor, worked wonders, and soon all the limbless men were tourniqueted up and, with lots of morphia in them, were fairly comfortable.

Gus's wife came over, having seen the explosion. I think she knew something had happened, and her face was a picture which cannot bear description, a picture of rapture, when she found out that Gus was not dead.

Before he was taken off to a base hospital he said two things. He asked me if I would look for his arm, which had a brand-new glove on it, and he told me to ring up the AOC and ask him if he would take a one-armed Station-Commander in two months' time. And Gus came back in that time to the day.

Towards the end of the year came the night when we started our sky-marking technique raids on the Ruhr Valley. Essen was the target, Krupps the objective. Although this little city had had, up to date, hundreds of air-raid alerts, very few bombs had actually fallen in its built-up area: now we were going to try to do it "blind".

Twenty-five of us were going there, bombing from 23,000ft. It was not a large number, in fact it was dangerously small, but this was because timing played such a big part in this new method of bombing.

The other Squadron-Commander did the briefing. "You take off," he said, "and in the first hour and a half climb as high as possible. Then you set course at the exact second for Ijmuiden. From there you alter course and fly straight to point X, where two yellow flares will burn in the sky straight in front of you. These flares will be 25 miles from the target. You go straight on, taking no avoiding action until you come to point Y, when two red flares should be on either side of your wing-tips. A few minutes later, straight in front of you, you will see a cluster of green flares. You are to aim your bombs at these on a correct heading of 170 degrees magnetic. It doesn't matter a lot if you are two minutes late in bombing them, because the wind can only carry them a mile or two. But it is very important to bomb on that exact heading; if you are 10 degrees off either way, your bombs will go about 10 miles from the target."

We set off, we saw our flares and we bombed them, and we came back, having been through the worst flak of all time.

There were too many troubles, many aircraft had turned back. We were not used to flying as high as this. And by these early returns the aircraft which did press on found that some 1,500 guns gave them their undivided attention for nearly half an hour. Not very pleasant.

There were oxygen failures, icing troubles, engines had overheated, guns had frozen up in a temperature of minus 60 degrees. Only ten out of twenty-five claimed to have bombed the target, but next day the German radio, for the first time in history, said that "last night enemy bombers raided the town of Essen".

It was a beginning, and from that day on the whole Group went on persevering, trying to solve our various difficulties. The plan itself was all right; the only failures were those due to the extreme conditions in which we were flying. The AOC quickly invented a special type of radiator flap which prevented the engines overheating. An instrument-maker fitted a gadget which prevented the oxygen failing. Guns were wiped quite free of oil so that there would be no friction at the highest altitudes; electrical flying kit was introduced so that the crews, especially the gunners in the turrets, would not suffer from cold.

But, for all this, the losses were extremely high. Although twenty-five aircraft would bomb the target within thirty seconds or so, there were so many guns in Essen that each aircraft was subjected to a veritable curtain of steel. One night we lost three from my squadron, and three very good fellows at that.

But the bombs were falling on Essen from above cloud, and the Germans were beginning to get worried. They even introduced a new kind of flak, which we called "V" for Victory flak, because when bursting it looked like the Prime Minister's favourite sign, but they had a long time to wait if they thought that flak was going to stop what was now becoming a definite possibility.

A few weeks later the scientists introduced yet another innovation. This was the marker bomb. It took the form of a light-case 250lb missile which burst at about 3,000ft above the ground and cascaded on to the target hundreds of small red balls which burned for about five minutes. Moreover, the colours of these balls could be changed at will, and it was well-nigh impossible for the dummy target men in Germany to simulate anything like it on the ground. We called these bombs "target indicating markers", or TI bombs for short. These were the bombs that put night bombing on the map.

From now on our plan began to shape itself. The jigsaw puzzle which had taken three and a half years to put together was almost complete. With the new year a new series of raids began which marked the end of German cities. Numbers were increased; bombloads were stepped up. Extreme concentration and timing to seconds began to be their keynote of success.

On January 13th the target was Essen. The TI markers were seen clearly by all crews from a great height. An unknown concentration of bombs dropped on and around the doomed city. On the 16th and 17th Berlin was raided; here, once again, a limitation had crept into our weapons, in that they could not be used for a very long distance, and these markers fell this time about 6 miles south of the centre of the city, but, needless to say, great damage was done in the suburbs.

So it went on. We were just at the stage of transferring from the wrong to the right. It took about a month to get the new technique absolutely wrapped up by all crews. Now and then the effort was dispersed to Lorient, the centre of a vast system of U-boat pens. These raids were extremely devastating, and the whole dock area and town itself were wiped off the face of the earth. These Lorient raids, carried out under conditions of not too much flak, resulted in all crews getting to know the sky-marking and target-indicating method of attack so well that they would be able to do a good job when the time came to bomb Germany again.

With this technique at last buttoned up, the bomber boys once more turned their attention to the Ruhr.

Then came the real battle of Essen, and after three really heavy concentrated raids the famous Krupps works were almost wiped out. One after another, Nuremburg, Cologne, Düsseldorf and the rest of them began to get the real attack. At last the answer had been found, and whenever a German fire-watcher saw one of the deadly TIs come down on the right spot, he must have realized that the best place for him was below ground.

Meanwhile, with the increased bombing of those cities, to the German Herrenvolk came news on their radios, if they dared to listen, which must have made them apprehensive. The Russians were driving forward everywhere. On January 31st, the German Sixth Army, under General von Paulus, surrendered before Stalingrad. Black flags were hung out in Berlin.

In Tunisia, the British and American armies had begun to squeeze the nut-cracker. It looked as though the Axis would be driven into the sea, and they just did not have the sea superiority to take them off safely, as we had had at Dunkirk.

The Casablanca conference was in session. It was decided that only unconditional surrender was acceptable to the Allies. Also at Casablanca something else was being prepared for the Germans. General Eaker had flown there to plead the cause of the American daylight bomber, the Flying Fortress. He won, and the future of the Luftwaffe was sealed. All that the Germans knew was that a few days later a successful daylight raid was made by American bombers on Wilhelmshaven. The German people no doubt thought that Goering would soon drive them off. They did not know how wrong they were. No one had told them that by March their U-boat had been beaten at sea, that the Allies, thanks to the combined use of secret weapons, air and sea power, had at last settled accounts with their one and only successful weapon beneath the seas, and that our ships were now sailing to England and to North Africa practically without loss. All they did know, in fact, was that the systematic destruction of their country had begun. They could not help knowing that, no matter what their propaganda said. Soon even Goebbels had to change his tune and, instead of minimizing the damage, had begun to multiply it so that the whole world would look on the bomber as a murder weapon. This sort of article would appear from time to time in German newspapers:

"We know from experience gained in the towns afflicted by the air terror that civilian losses are heavy, and often very heavy! We cannot comply with the wishes of the population, however greatly interested they may be, by publishing any figures, since even now the enemy must not be able to estimate the results of his activities. The figures are high, but it must be stressed again that they are by no means as high as is stated by nervous and over-excited rumour-mongers in the Reich and even in Central Germany . . .

"Many towns which have now been partly destroyed by the enemy terror once believed that it would never be their turn because fog or their concealed position or other equally unfounded factors hampered the enemy's observation and prevented him from finding his way there. But the enemy found and hit some of these towns and some of these people."

Yes, we found and hit those towns in fog and often from above the clouds. Old man weather, the last obstacle of all, had been overcome. Now it was the Germans' turn to moan. In fact, they were now squealing and wailing and appealing to the Pope to stop the bombing. But did they remember Warsaw, Rotterdam, Belgrade, Coventry, Bristol, Plymouth, Glasgow, Swansea and London? Did they remember Hitler's threat to raze every British city to the ground, to destroy Great Britain's population? If they did not, they had short memories — but that is typical of the Hun.

For year after year they had waged war on defenceless European countries, bleeding them, starving them, murdering them. They had done this for 150 years, and the German had never known what it was to have his own home destroyed. Wars had always been glorious, far from the fat Fräulein's doorstep. But now it was just starting. First the nearest German cities to our bomber bases began to get the new bombing; soon there would be new devices which would enable them to drop their TIs just as accurately as far as the long arm of the Lancasters could reach. Towns in the Ruhr Valley had already begun to disappear. The usual thick haze which hung over the river had dispersed, factories were beginning to close down, absenteeism by panic-stricken workers began to make itself felt on production.

But to destroy a big industrial area was a big job to tackle even for the bomber; nevertheless, it had been begun. Meanwhile, another raid which would help bring production in the Ruhr Valley to a standstill was being planned. Only a few men knew that the scientists had already begun their work.

Orders had been given, special trials were to begin soon, but it was all very secret.

The Nazis spent most of their time attacking the British "air pirates", calling them rude names and issuing dire threats of reprisal. But despite all their boloney, from travellers and other sources the news leaked out from Germany into the neutral Press that our bombing was doing serious damage now. Some of it was hard to believe; probably the correspondents let themselves go when writing their stories. They, too, probably had friends in Poland, Greece and Yugoslavia.

This was the sort of thing written about the fate of a certain town as seen by one neutral correspondent:

"The British bombardments have transformed the population with a high standard of living into troglodytes. Over two million people live in holes, cellars, in ruins or rough wooden hutments. Apart from a few tens of thousands who are anxiously awaiting the moment when they too will lose the roof over their heads, these two million people are about all that is left of the population of five million. The rest are scattered in all directions. Half a million are in Poland, hundreds of thousands are in Pomerania and Southern Germany, while still more hundreds of thousands are in Thuringia and Czechoslovakia. They are all living, squeezed close together, a prey to growing despair, increasingly attacked by the virus of nihilism because they are only pariahs, and for a long time now they have abandoned their belief in the wonderful promises of propaganda that would like to make them believe that with victory they would regain their possessions.

"There is also the question of looting. Clothes and furniture from bombed houses disappear magically from the pavements where they have been temporarily placed. Sometimes whole suites, grand pianos, sideboards complete with their silver, disappear without anyone knowing how. The authorities do not try to contest the facts, but for reasons of national pride they attribute them to foreign workers. There probably are black sheep among the latter, but it may be asked, how do they manage to conceal sideboards, wardrobes and pianos in the barracks where most of them have to live?

"The population of this city lives in perpetual terror, terror of the police, terror of bombs, terror of looting and terror of foreign workers. All misdeeds that cannot be otherwise explained are imputed to the last named. For example, recently there were bands of saboteurs wandering through the blacked-out streets removing sewer gratings. The results of the 'jokes' can be imagined. The hurrying bombed-out people, rescue columns, even policemen on their beat fall through the openings into the sewers which swallow them up. The coin boxes in automatic telephone booths are mysteriously emptied of their contents. Water mains for fire fighting are blocked with cement."

How was all this done? How was it organized? Who did all the work, and what were the aims of Bomber Command, anyway, if it was doing all this damage?

We never thought we could win the war by bombing alone. We were out to destroy German industry, to cut their transport system, to stop them building U-boats and ships and to make their channels unnavigable by mines. We were out to bomb them until they found themselves weak and punch-drunk from our blows, so that they would fall back before our invading armies. This in turn would save the lives of our own men — the young men of the Allies on whom the future of this world depends.

This was March 1943, the year when the grand Allied strategy went over to the offensive. This was the year that sealed the doom of the Nazi master race. The Americans, with their prodigious capacity for production, had begun to turn out a bomber force which soon would exceed our own. They had staked their own claim on daylight bombing. We would stick to the night, and so it would go on, day and night, city by city, until there was nothing much left, until the Luftwaffe was destroyed. This was the aim of Bomber Command. The formidable shape of

4,000 aircraft over Berlin — it would come to that — one day.

How was it being done?

Picture Bomber Command, a few brick buildings and a few trees. Inside sits Air Chief Marshal Harris, surrounded by his advisory staff, who have all done their fair share of duty over Germany. He has a conference with his staff, he gets the weather forecasts from meteorological experts, he decides that the target to-night will be Berlin, aiming point X. He picks up his telephone and asks to be put on to all Group-Commanders on a broadcast. He is a grim man, is Air Chief Marshal Harris, and looks even more grim as he sits at his desk, crouched over the telephone, his glasses perched on the end of his nose, his finger pointing to a place on the map of Berlin in front of him. He is speaking into the telephone: "Hullo! Are you all there? Is that you, Alec? OK. Target tonight aiming point X."

And he gives a code word over the telephone which means Berlin. "All aircraft are to operate, maximum effort. Full instructions will follow in an hour's time. That is all. Goodbye."

In the Group-Commander's office this curt message is given to Group Operations Officers, then down to stations, thence to squadrons. The Squadron-Commander is a young man with plenty of responsibility. He sits there quite calmly as he receives the message and presses the bell for his two Flight-Commanders. They come in, hats on the backs of their heads, smoking cigarettes, looking inquisitive. "Berlin tonight, chaps," says the Squadron-Commander. "Maximum effort; get cracking."

On the airfield a few minutes later there is a roar of engines as Lancaster after Lancaster takes off to be given its air test. These air tests take about half an hour each, and are very thoroughly done. Everything is tested — wireless, guns, navigational instruments, bomb doors. Sometimes even a few bombs are dropped for practice to make sure that the bomb-aimer will be on his target tonight.

Then comes lunch. A short, absent-minded meal taken in the minimum of time. Not much is said, most minds are preoccupied, often the Squadron-Commander does not have time for lunch at all. The 'phone bell is ringing incessantly.

After this comes briefing. Here all the information is transmitted to the crews who are going to take part in tonight's big effort. The room is packed, many of the boys, in their roll-necked pullovers, are standing crowded up against the back of the room. In the corner there may be one or two war correspondents and perhaps a visiting army officer.

The Squadron-Commander comes in, followed by the navigation officer, and the crews get up and stop talking. The babble of conversation dies away and he begins his briefing. "OK, chaps; sit down. Berlin tonight, aiming point X. This is the centre of a cluster of factories making Daimler-Benz engines. You can see it quite clearly here on the map." He points to a position somewhere in Berlin. "Tonight a total of 700 bombers are going. They are all four-engined types, so if you see anything twin-engined you can shoot at it. The bomb-load will be one 4,000-pounder and sixteen cans of incendiaries, so the total load will be about 2,000 tons. It ought to be a pretty good prang. The met. man says the weather will be clear all the way, which is pretty phenomenal. Let's hope he's right. The Pathfinders are going to attack from zero hour minus one to zero hour plus 35; it is going to be a quick concentrated attack. Your bombing height will be 21,000ft. Don't get out of this height band or you will run into other aircraft. As it is, we are very lucky not to be the bottom squadron; they will probably see a few bombs whistling past them on the way down. The route is the usual one marked on the board here. The Pathfinder procedure will be detailed by the navigation officer." He cocks his head over to the corner of the room and calls, "Nav."

The navigation officer, a big round man with the DFC and bar, gets up and begins talking. "Zero hour is 1945 hours. At zero hour minus three and a third minutes the Pathfinders will sky-mark the lane to the target with red flares which will change to green after 120 seconds. At this time, too, they will mark a point on the ground exactly 15 miles short of the aiming point. With the ground speed of 240mph this should give three and three-quarter minutes to go to the target. The timing has got to be done in seconds. If anybody is late, he will probably get a packet, so pilots must keep their air-speeds dead right. The target-indicating marker will go down at exactly zero minus one, and should be right on the factory roof. The sky above will also be marked by green flares in case the TIs are obscured by fog or smoke. I will see all navigators after the briefing to give them the tracks and distances."

He turns round to the Squadron-Commander, who gets up again and gives his final orders. "Now don't forget, chaps," he begins; "once you have reached the preliminary target indicator you turn on to a course of 135 degrees magnetic and hold it for four minutes. You are to take no evasive action, but to keep straight on past the target. Once you have dropped your bombs you may weave about slightly and gain speed by going down in a gentle dive. The Pathfinders will drop a cluster of green and red flares 30 miles beyond Berlin, and you are to concentrate on these, and return home in a gaggle. Now don't forget, no straggling. We've had pretty low losses so far and we don't want any tonight; and don't forget to twist your tails a bit so that you can see those fighters, which come up from below. I think that's about all. Don't forget your landing discipline when you come to base. I will see you down in the crew room before take-off. OK."

The boys go out noisily. Some are on their first trip and look a bit worried. The veterans look as if they are just going to a teaparty, but inside they feel differently. After the briefing a war correspondent comes up and asks the Squadron-Commander a few questions.

"Why all this concentration?" he asks. "What is the exact idea?"

The Squadron-Commander is a busy man, but he gives him the whole answer. How there are so many guns in Germany, all depending on short-wave electricity for their prediction, so that if one aircraft were to go over every five minutes, each gun would have that aircraft all to itself. Similarly with the night-fighters. But if all the aircraft go over more or less simultaneously then the guns cannot pick out and fire at any one aircraft nor can the night-fighters be vectored on to any one aircraft. With the result that losses are kept down. Moreover, the bombing takes a more concentrated form when all aircraft bomb together.

"How about collisions?" the war correspondent asks.

"There won't be any," says the Squadron-Leader, "provided they all keep straight, and if the Pathfinders are on time. Sometimes this doesn't happen. One night at Stuttgart the Pathfinders were fifteen minutes late and there were some 400 bombers circling the target waiting for them; eighteen didn't come back. Some of those were collisions, I think."

The time after the briefing is not very pleasant. No one knows what to do. Some sit in the Mess, listening to the radio, and wishing they were far away from all this. A few play billiards. But most of them just sit in chairs picking up papers and throwing them down, staring into space and waiting for the clock on the wall to show the time when they must go down to get on their flying-clothes.

The time passes slowly, minutes seem like hours, but it is a busy time for the Squadron-Commander and his Flight-Commanders. First Group telephones to confirm that there is the full number of aircraft on from the squadron. Then the maintenance officer to say that C Charlie has blown an engine, shall he put on the reserve? Yes, put on reserve.

A call from the armament officer — a cookie has dropped off Z Zebra.

"Is everyone all right?"

"Yes, everyone's all right."

"Well, put it on again, then."

The oxygen has leaked from G George — get on to the maintenance flight to have new oxygen bottles put in. And so it goes on, the 'phone ringing the whole time. He does not have time to think, and presently everyone is in the crew rooms dressing for the big raid, putting on their multiple underwear and electrically heated suits before going out to the aircraft.

All the boys are chattering happily, but this is only to cover up their true feelings. But they all know that they will be quite all right once they get into their aircraft.

"Prang it good, boys," says an Australian who isn't coming tonight; one of his crew is sick.

Then comes the take-off. A thrilling sight to the

layman. Exactly at the right time they taxi out, led by the Squadron-Commander in his own aircraft with a gaudy design painted on the nose. They come out one after another, like a long string of ducks, and line up on the runway waiting to take off. There is a cheery wave of goodbyes from the well-wishers on the first flare. Then the pilot slams his windows shut and pushes open the throttles. The ground underneath the well-wishers shivers and shakes, sending a funny feeling up their spine, and the Lancasters lumber off one after another down the mile-long flare-path. And off they go into the dusk.

Over to a farm labourer sitting on his tractor in a field . . . He has just done his ploughing and is about to go home. He is looking forward to his evening meal. Looking up, he can see hundreds of specks in the sky, black specks, all getting smaller and smaller as they climb higher and higher into the night air. He turns to his tractor and says, "They be going out again tonight. I 'ope they give 'em bastards hell. May they all come back again, God bless 'em. Good boys they be." Then he begins to trudge home.

Over to a girl typist about to get out of a bus in the nearby city. She hears the roar of the aircraft and says to her companion, "Oh, there they go again. I do hope they will come back early; otherwise they will wake me up . . ."

Over to one of our aircraft flying high . . . They have just reached their operational height. The engines are throttled back to cruising revolutions.

"Hullo, navigator. Skipper calling. What time must I set course for the rendezvous point?"

The navigator gets a quick fix. "We are about 60 miles away. If you circle here for five minutes, then set course at 240mph, you will be there dead on time."

"OK," says the skipper. "You all right, rear-gunner?"

"Yes," comes the voice from the back.

In five minutes' time he sets course and the blunt nose of the Lancaster points towards the east. At that moment nearly all the bombers have done the same thing and, with navigation lights on at their various heights, they all converge on to the rendezvous spot at exactly zero minus two hours. They reach it more or less together, then all navigation lights go out simultaneously and they straighten up on their course for Berlin. The captain yells to his crew to check that all lights are out on board. The bomb-aimer fuses the bombs, the gunners cock their guns and they are on their way.

To describe this big bomber force flying out in this formation is not easy. But imagine a glass brick 2 miles across, 20 miles long and 8,000ft thick, filled with hundreds of Lancasters, and move it slowly towards the Dutch coast, and there you have a concentrated wave on its way. The Dutch coast looms up incredibly soon, rather too soon . . .

It is now 5 o'clock. At this hour in Germany operational messages have come in from Gruppen and Staffeln of night-fighters scattered throughout

German territory. Messerschmitt, Focke Wulf and other types of fighters are fully loaded with fuel and ammunition, ready for take-off from the operational bases. Aircraft and personnel are ready, mechanics, engineers, armourers are on duty on many airfields ready to supply suddenly arriving aircraft with fresh fuel and more ammunition. Everything has been done to ensure the quickest possible employment of the night-fighter arm.

At this hour it is quiet at the German searchlight and flak batteries. Ammunition stocks have been made up again since the last raid. The enormous power-plants of the searchlights need only be switched on by the young Luftwaffe helpers to convert the electric current, enough to supply a medium-sized town, into shimmering light and send it up into the night sky. The sentries on the large 8.8cm guns pace up and down and watch the approaching night. It will soon be pitch dark, as the sky is covered with heavy rain-clouds, and the crescent moon will not rise until later. Even then its light will scarcely pierce the dark clouds. The British prefer nights such as this.

1740 hours. A message comes into the centre near Berlin from the Channel coast. An alarm bell rings. Strong British bomber units are crossing the Dutch coast. A telephone call warns the air-defence forces of the Continent. The night-fighter units in Holland have already taken off and are on the look-out for the enemy on his eastern course, attach themselves to his units, and while the first night engagements between the German night-fighters and the British bombers are setting the stage for the great night battle, the ground crews of countless other Geschwader in the region of Central Germany are putting the final touches to the aircraft as they stand ready to take off.

Behind the great glass map stand female signals auxiliaries wearing headphones and laryngophones, with a thick stick of charcoal in their right hands with which they draw in the positions of the enemy units. From the control room only their shadows moving behind the glass plate can be seen. Ceaselessly the strokes and arrows on the great map give place to new markings.

Every officer and man takes up his position. Each knows exactly what he has to do, and all work together without friction.

The glass map shows that the enemy is advancing along several different directions, but it is clear that the main force is continuing eastwards. The enemy bombers have crossed the frontier of Western Germany. Suddenly they swing round towards the southeast. A few weaker formations are flying southwards up the Rhine. Cascades are dropped over two West German towns; it may be that the main attack is to be directed against these towns, but it may also be that this is a feint movement designed to lure the German night-fighters into the wrong areas. The enemy hopes that a wrong German order will gain him valuable minutes to get his main attacking force into the prescribed target area, where he would then find weaker German night-fighter forces.

The control officer, who is fully acquainted with the many different problems and questions, the possibilities of attack and defence, makes his decision after conscientiously checking the situation and a brief talk with the OC. The British force is still on its way towards Central Germany. The main force of the bombers has made another turn and is again flying east. The last message reads: "Front of enemy formation in Dora — Heinrich area, course east."

1830 hours. At this moment fighter unit X, whose aircraft are ready at the end of the runway with their engines roaring, receives the order "Unit X — village take off by visual beacon Y."

A few minutes later the aircraft are racing over the ground, climbing rapidly, flying towards the flashing light of visual beacon Y. In Berlin the Underground is still running, and traffic goes on as usual. Then the population gets its first warning; the Deutschlandsender goes off the air. The bright lights at the marshalling yards are switched off. The great city sinks into darkness.

The enemy has meanwhile flown past to the north of the first large central German town. In a bare hour he may be over Berlin. At a height of 6,500m the four-engine bombers are roaring on their way eastwards.

1845 hours. A message in the headphones: the

enemy has already lost seven aircraft before reaching Osnabrück.

Other night-fighter units are ready to take off to protect the capital. The meteorologist is describing the weather situation. Cloudless sky over South Germany, where night-fighters can land after the battle.

Meanwhile the night-fighter units, which have assembled in certain areas, are guided closer to the enemy. The German fighters have already made contact everywhere with the enemy bomber formations. Now the sirens are sounded in Berlin.

Important decisions are taken relating to the activity of the searchlight batteries, taking into consideration the weather situation. Orders are issued to the batteries of the Berlin flak division.

1916 hours. The enemy is 100 kilometres from Berlin. A large number of night-fighters are accompanying the British bombers.

The OC sits next to the 1A (Intelligence) officer. In order to clear up a question quickly he asks to speak to the OC in another Luftgau; command priority call to X town. In a matter of seconds a female signals auxiliary has made the desired telephone connection.

On the great glass map the arrows draw closer and closer to Berlin. The positions of the night-fighter units are exactly known.

1941 hours. Is the enemy going straight for Berlin? At 1943 hours fire is opened by a heavy flak battery in the west. It is still impossible to say whether the mass of the enemy bombers will not again make a sharp turn short of Berlin and perhaps attack Leipzig.

Above the inner part of the town the enemy drops streams and cascades of flares. Strong forces are reported over various suburbs. A hail of HE shells from the heavy flak rushes up to the heights of the approaching bombers.

In spite of the difficulties of the weather the night-fighters hunt out the enemy. In the brilliant beams of the searchlights the British aircraft are clearly recognizable. The enemy drops his bombs on the city's industrial areas and then tries to get away as quickly as possible. At top speed other German night-fighters chase after him to shoot up as many of his forces as possible.

Over to the leading Pathfinder aircraft.

"How far are we from the target, Nav.?"

"About 25 miles."

"OK. Stand by to drop preliminary target marker."

"Standing by."

A voice from the mid-upper turret. "Flak coming up port behind, skipper."

The guns are just beginning to open up down below. Ahead lies Berlin, still and silent. Berlin seems to be lying down there like a gigantic mouse, frightened to move, petrified. Suddenly it is galvanized into life; hundreds of gun-flashes come up from its roofs, its parks and its railway flak.

"Don't weave, for Christ's sake, skipper; only another minute." This from the navigator.

Again the captain's voice, "OK."

He is not saying much. Both hands are on the wheel, his eyes are darting everywhere, looking for trouble and hoping not to find it. His aircraft seems huge, it appears to be the only one in the sky, every gun down below seems to be aiming at him, the gun-flashes are vicious, short and cruel.

Down below, to the Germans, he is the first of many hundreds of small spots on cathode-ray tubes. The civilians have long since gone to their shelters, but those of the ARP, police and firewatching services are beginning to hear the loud, angry roar of the invading force.

"Coming up now, skipper. Steady — coming up — coming up now! OK. TI gone."

A few seconds later it bursts and cascades on to the ground; a mass of green bells, shining brightly, for all the world like a lit-up merry-go-round, an unmistakable spot of light.

Over to one of the main-force aircraft.

"There she is, skip.; straight ahead." This from the bomb-aimer.

"Fine; the Pathfinders are dead on time."

The navigator looks at his watch and makes a note to that effect. The bomb-aimer starts his stop-watch. Three minutes and twenty seconds to go. On all sides other bomb-aimers are doing the same, beginning their straight 15-mile run through a curtain of steel. Flak is coming up all round, leaving black balloons which float by at an alarming speed. Searchlights are weaving, trying to pick up a straggler. The bomb-aimer begins to count.

"Three minutes to go, skipper."

Like a fleet of battleships the force sails in. Above are hundreds of fighter flares, lighting up the long lane of bombers like daylight. Now and then Junkers 88s and Me 110s come darting in and out like black moths trying to deliver their attack. The sky is full of tracer bullets, some going up, some going down. Others hosepipe out horizontally as one of our rear-gunners gets in a good squirt.

Two minutes to go.

More flares have gone down. It seems even lighter than day. Searchlights, usually so bright themselves, can hardly pierce the dazzling glow of flares up above. Now the tracers are coming up in all colours as combats take place left, right and centre. On all sides bombers are blowing up, as they get direct hits — great, slow flashes in the sky, leaving a vast trail of black smoke as they disintegrate earthwards. Someone bales out.

One minute to go — bomb-doors open.

The bomb-aimer is still counting.

"Fifty seconds."

"Forty seconds."

There is flak all round now. The leading wave of bombers has not been broken up, a few have been shot down, but the rest have held their course. But the short time they held that course seemed like a lifetime.

There comes the bomb-aimer's voice again. "Red TIs straight ahead."

"Good show; there's the sky marker too."

"Thirty seconds."

Still dead level. Someone in front has already started a fire. Great sticks of incendiaries are beginning to criss-cross across the target-indicating marker. These sticks are a mile long, but from this height they look about the length of a matchstick.

"Twenty seconds."

"Steady — hold it" — and then the bomb-aimer shouts: "Bombs gone." There is a note of relief in his voice.

The Lancaster leaps forward, relieved of its burden, diving, slithering. But it keeps straight on over the burning city. Throttles are slammed wide open, the engines are in fine pitch; they make a noise of an aircraft in pain.

A volcano is now raging down below, great sticks of incendiaries are still slapping across the point where the target-markers had first gone in. Now black smoke is beginning to rise, but as these target-markers burst and drop slowly into the flaming mass, the later bomb-aimers have a good chance of aiming at the middle. Cookies are exploding one after another with their slow, red flashes, photoflashes are bursting at all heights as each aircraft takes its photographs. This is a galaxy of light, a living nightmare.

As the last wave of bombers roar over, the fires started by the first are beginning to take hold.

Against their vivid light can be seen the bottom squadrons, flying steadily on, over the battered city.

The flak is beginning to die, the searchlights have gone out. Once again the ground defences have been beaten.

A few leaflets drift down through the bluish glare, only to be burnt in the flames of the burning houses.

Soon the area is one mass of flames and the last bomber has dropped its bombs. At last the rendezvous is reached and the surviving bombers turn for home.

That is how it is done, by young men with guts, by science and by skill. The Germans do everything in their power to stop it, but in vain. There are too many variations; feint attacks can be made, or the bombers can attack in waves. They can come in at hourly intervals; they might come over on a night when the German fighters cannot get up. And on every raid new devices are carried, made by scientists, to help defeat the German defences.

This was the beginning, the end of three years' hard experiment. The real answer had been found, and the bomber could at last hit hard. It could choose tactical or strategical targets. Both were allergic to bombs.

CHAPTER
SIXTEEN

Squadron X

It was the middle of March. The flak over France wasn't bad. It was coming up all around in spasmodic flashes as some straggler got off his course and struggled through a defended area. Otherwise the night was lovely. There was a three-quarter moon which shone brightly into my Lancaster, lighting the cockpit up almost as if it were day. Down below us the grey features of France were partially hidden by a thin layer of white cloud.

It was getting hot inside. I yelled to my wireless operator, "Hey, Hutch. Turn off the heat."

He said: "Thank God for that."

The heat in a Lancaster comes out somewhere round the wireless-operator's backside; hence the relief expressed by the long-suffering Hutch.

Around me, above, below and on every quarter, I could see the Lancasters moving forward towards their target, flying straight and flying fast, with their great chins thrust forward and looking to me more powerful than anything I had ever seen before.

I was feeling pleased because this was going to be my last raid before going on a few days' leave; for now I had done 173 sorties without having had much rest. It seemed almost too good to be true that after this raid on Stuttgart I should be able to go down to Cornwall with my wife and relax. Once again I should be able to walk down to St Ives with my pipe in my mouth and my dog, Nigger, running along by my side. Once again I should be able to stand and watch the sea when it became angry and fought with the north-west wind. In the evenings, instead of sitting up here with an oxygen mask over my face, I should be leaning back in my armchair looking at the ceiling and scratching the back of my dog. There would be no bomber raids to organize, no bomb-loads to think about.

As I was thinking these things, my Flight-Engineer yelled, "Port outboard's going, sir!"

Sure enough, the port outboard-engine was packing up. I could feel it in the throttle control. There was no power coming from this engine. Rapidly, my heavy-laden Lancaster had to lose height.

This was bad. If I turned back now I should have to go out again tomorrow night. Maybe there would be no tomorrow night. Maybe the weather would be bad. Maybe I should have to wait four days; I should have to wait four days for my leave. Maybe it would be better to go on.

Scriv, my navigator, was standing at his station scratching his head and watching the air-speed needle drop rapidly.

I said, "What shall we do, Scriv?"

"It's up to you, sir,"

"OK, Scriv; we are going on at low level. We will try to climb up to bomb when we get there."

The Lancaster slid quietly out of formation, and like a wounded bird, dropped towards the earth. On all sides of me the flak was coming up from Mannheim, Frankfurt and Mainz. From where I was I had a grandstand view of the boys above getting shot at. But the Huns did not shoot at me. They did not even fire machine-guns at me. Perhaps they thought that I was a night-fighter. Now and again I caught sight of a Lancaster far above, 4 miles above, as it got into the beam of a searchlight and as a light flashed on its wings; and I almost thought I could distinguish the separate aircraft as they flew over, merely from the light of the flames which danced through the streets of Stuttgart. The town was on fire.

An 8,000-pounder came whistling past my wing-tip on its way down, and a few seconds later a great, slow, heavy flash came up from the ground where it had landed, and my aircraft was bounced and tossed about as though it were a leaf. I remember that once I distinctly saw a shower of incendiaries not 200 yards in front of me. It is indeed curious to be underneath a heavy bombing raid in an aeroplane.

We dropped our load, and my poor Lancaster on its three engines jumped into the air as the bombs fell out of its belly and I banked around and dived for the deck.

During these moments there had been little talk, but once we were clear of the target area all the boys on board started talking.

"Leave tomorrow."

"Tomorrow we go on leave."

"I'm going fishing."

"I'm going to sleep."

"Tomorrow we go on leave."

My wife had been sweating it out in a factory near London for a long time without any rest, and now I should be able to take her home and let her breathe for a moment the fresh and pleasant air of Cornwall.

Soon, after dodging the night-fighters, we were back over England, and a few minutes later I was in my room, hurriedly packing my clothes before jumping into bed. As I dozed off, I thought of the morrow and of leave, and of the sound of the waves on the rocks down in Cornwall.

Next day I woke up late. My ears were still singing, my eyes felt red and sore as if I had rolled them through a gravel pit. I wanted to keep lying there in my warm bed, where it was quiet and peaceful. I wanted to think, and I wanted to be alone. After a year of this sort of thing I was getting a bit weary. It seems that no matter how hard you try, the human body can take just so much and no more.

Charles, the adjutant, came in. "Is it important, Adj?" I said sleepily.

"It's your posting, sir." He sounded rather sad, or else was a very good actor.

"My — my — posting? What on earth — where?"

"To 5 Group."

I had heard that I was about due to be rested. The AOC had mentioned that I had done enough for a bit, but this was a bit of a surprise and a great shock. Posted to a headquarters, of all places.

I picked up the 'phone beside my bed and asked to speak to Group. Charles sat down in the corner, watching Nigger chewing one of my slippers on the mat in front of the fire.

A few words with the SASO and I found out the truth. John Searby was taking the squadron over and I had to be at Group, the next afternoon. The reason, he said, was the AOC. He wanted me to help write a book for the benefit of the would-be bomber pilot.

"Write a book!" I had never done such a thing in my life; and what a time to begin, just when the real bomber offensive was starting.

At the most I had wanted a station, and at least thought that I would be given some job that would deal with operations exclusively. Worst of all, my leave was cancelled.

I asked Charles to send a wire to Eve and told him that the rest of the crew could go. When I had finished giving my orders, Charles quietly picked up the 'phone and booked a large private room at the Bridge Hotel, our local pub.

That night there was a party. Wine was drunk, many kind words were spoken. I staggered to my feet and made a rotten speech, looking nervously into my glass while the other boys sat around rather self-consciously.

I said I had been in the squadron over a year and I was sorry to go. I wished them good luck in whatever operations they would undertake after I had gone. They were still top squadron of Bomber Command and I thought they were the best. It is hard to say anything at a time like this, and when I sat down there were a few kind remarks of approval.

Then we got down to some solid drinking.

Next day I went to Grantham. Now Group Headquarters in particular, or any headquarters in general, are funny places. There is an air of quiet, cold efficiency about the whole place. WAAFs keep running in and out with cups of tea. Tired men walk through the corridors with red files under their arms. The yellow lights over the AOC and SASO's doors are almost always on, showing that they are engaged. Great decisions are being taken the whole time. There is not much time off and I found it quite difficult to settle down.

I had been there one or two days and had tried to get down to the factual business of writing, when the AOC sent for me. Air Vice-Marshal Coryton had gone, to the deep regret of everyone in the

Group, and the new Air Vice-Marshal was the Honourable Ralph Cochrane, a man with a lot of brain and organizing ability. In one breath he congratulated me on my bar to the DSO, in the next he suddenly said: "How would you like the idea of doing one more trip?"

I gulped. More flak, more fighters; but said aloud: "What kind of a trip, sir?"

"A pretty important one, perhaps one of the most devastating of all time. I can't tell you any more now. Do you want to do it?"

I said I thought I did, trying to remember where I had left my flying kit. He seemed to be in such a hurry that I got the idea it was a case of take-off tonight.

But two days went by and nothing happened.

On the third he sent for me again. In his office was another man, one of the youngest Base commanders in the Group, Air-Commodore Charles Whitworth. The Air Vice-Marshal was very amiable. He told me to sit down, offered me a Chesterfield and began to talk.

"I asked you the other day if you would care to do another raid. You said you would, but I have to warn you that this is no ordinary sortie. In fact it can't be done for at least two months."

(I thought, hell, it's the *Tirpitz*. What on earth did I say "Yes" for?)

"Moreover," he went on, "the training for the raid is of such importance that the Commander-in-Chief has decided that a special squadron is to be formed for the job. I want you to form that squadron. As you know, I believe in efficiency, so I want you to do it well. I think you had better use Whitworth's main base at Scampton. As far as air crews are concerned, I want the best — you choose them. W/C Smith, the SOA, will help you pick ground crews. Each squadron will be forced to cough up men to build your unit up to strength.

"Now there's a lot of urgency in this, because you haven't got long to train. Training will be the important thing, so get going right away. Remember you are working to a strict timetable, and I want to see your aircraft flying in four days' time. Now up you go upstairs to hand in the names of your crews to Cartwright; he will give you all the help you want."

"But what sort of training, sir? And the target? I can't do a thing —"

"I am afraid I can't tell you any more just for the moment. All you have to do is to pick your crews, get them ready to fly, then I will come and see you and tell you more."

"How about aircraft and equipment?"

"S/L May, the Group Equipment Officer, will do all that. All right, Gibson."

He bent down to his work abruptly. This was a signal for me to go. There was a big raid to be organized that night. As I was closing the door, he looked up again. "Let me know when you are ready; and remember, not a word to anyone. This is just an ordinary new squadron. Secrecy is vital."

As we closed the door, "See you at Scampton," said Charles. "If you come over in a couple of days I'll get everything fixed up for you. How many chaps are you going to bring?"

"About seven hundred."

I was left standing alone feeling very bewildered. Charles went back to Scampton and I went upstairs to see various men who, though unknown to the general public, are the very life-blood of the Royal Air Force. These men, most of them too old to fly, themselves, deal in such things as equipment, bodies, erks, air crews.

The first man I saw was a fellow with a red moustache sitting behind a huge desk. This was Cartwright. His sales were air crews. It took me an hour to pick my pilots. I wrote all the names down on a piece of paper and handed them over to him. I had picked them all myself because from my own personal knowledge I believed them to be the best bomber pilots available. I knew that each one of them had already done his full tour of duty, and should really now be having a well-earned rest; and I knew also that there was nothing any of them would want less than this rest when they heard that there was an exciting operation on hand. Cartwright helped me a lot with the crews because I didn't know these so well, but we chose carefully and we chose well. I think he was a bit puzzled either at the urgency in the matter or my desire to have the very best, perhaps both.

Then into another office to see the equipment officer. We would require ten aircraft to begin with, with all their gear. Later we would need more. This was a big job; there were trestles, trolleys, spare wheels and bumble motors. There were many other things, but I won't put them all down here. Enough to say that Cartwright knew his job inside out. He promised that they would be delivered at Scampton tomorrow.

Afterwards, back to another huge desk; here tools were arranged for, kit, motor transport, beds, blankets, kites, typewriters, tents, towels and beer. Also a few spare engines. All this took a long time, in fact the whole day.

Next morning to the personnel officer, to fix up the ground staff. We were taking a few ground crews from each squadron, but in the case of the NCOs it would be necessary to have the very best men available. I asked for them and got them. Then along to the WAAF officer to see that we got our fair share of MT drivers and cooks; very important.

By now things were beginning to get beyond me. I went to the stationery department and got a little book and wrote down everything to be done in a long column. Every time anything got fixed up I would tick it off, but by the end of the day there weren't many ticks to be seen. Then would come the visit to the SASO, the AOC's deputy. This was Air-Commodore Harry Satterly, a big, blunt man who had the habit of getting things done quickly and well. His help was invaluable — in fact, I don't know what could have happened without him.

And so by the end of two days the squadron was formed. It had no name and no number. We had worked too fast for that branch of the Air Ministry which gives squadrons new numbers and identification letters, and we decided to call it simply Squadron X.

All personnel were to be at Scampton by the next morning. Training would begin that afternoon. The AOC had said that we had not got much time. We had certainly started off pretty well, but it had been hard work.

But somewhere else in London the other men were working even harder. They were in a hurry, too. They didn't wear uniforms or medals. They were working on graphs, explosives and metal, and on reinforced concrete. Out in the open, away in the Welsh hills during those blowy March days, they stood with the wind whistling round them as if to howl down their experiments. But they went on, slaving, watching, waiting, praying, hoping . . .

Next night I arrived in the Mess at Scampton with Nigger sniffing his way along happily at my heels. I think he smelt a party. He was right. In the hall were the boys. I knew them all — that is, all the pilots, navigators and bomb-aimers — but there were a few strange gunners and wireless-operators knocking around.

Within a second a whisky was shoved into my hand and a beer put on the floor for Nigger, who seemed thirsty. Then there was a babbling of conversation and the hum of shop being happily exchanged: of old faces; old names; targets; bases; and of bombs. This was the conversation that only fliers can talk, and by that I don't mean movie fliers. These were real living chaps who had all done their stuff. By their eyes you could see that. But they were ready for more. These were the aces of Bomber Command.

All in all they probably knew more about the art of bombing than any other squadron in the world.

From all over the world they had come: from Australia, America, Canada, New Zealand and Great Britain. All of their own free will. All with one idea: to get to grips with the enemy. As I stood there talking to them and drinking beer with them I felt very proud; surely these were the best boys in the world. If there could come any better I should like to see them.

From 106 Squadron had come three crews. Hoppy, of course, and Dave Shannon from Australia. A Canadian Flight-Sergeant, Burpee, was the third. He had just married a young English girl and was busy trying to find her a house not too far away. He was telling me that he had found it a very difficult job. The rest, I am told, would have liked to have come, but it was the hard case of having the best and only the best.

From the Middle East came the senior Flight-Commander, "Dinghy" Melvyn Young. Cambridge — California and sixty-five trips. "Dinghy" because he had ditched twice in Mare Nostrum. A big man, Melvyn, and a very efficient organizer. I was to find out later that he could drink a pint of beer faster than any other man I know, with his elbow in the traditionally almost vertical position.

From New Zealand came Les Munro, ex-97 Squadron. Like all New Zealanders, he was a most charming fellow, with an excellent operational record. He was one of those types who can always be relied on to do the right thing at the right moment. There he was, standing quietly and drinking slowly and thinking a lot. Then there was David Maltby, large and thoughtful; a fine pilot.

Brooklyn gave us Joe McCarthy. He was one of the Americans who had volunteered to fly in the Royal Air Force before America was at war with the Axis. He had been given the chance to rejoin the United States forces, but had preferred to stay with the boys. He had just come from the same squadron as Les, and both were great pals. He had tried to get in my squadron once before, but despite all the strings we tried to pull between us it did not work. Now he was happy. We all were, standing there at midnight with our glasses in our hands initiating the historic walls of Scampton Mess with Squadron X spirit. The portraits of Babe Learoyd and Sergeant John Hannah stood looking down on us, as though wanting to join us. They were the two VCs that Scampton had already won during World War II, apart from many other decorations.

Eton gave us Henry Maudslay, the other Flight-Commander. A champion runner at school, he was one of the best pilots from 50 Squadron. He was standing there quiet and suave, and not drinking too much. Later on Henry became one of the mainstays of the squadron in supervising our training.

Then there were the others. Micky Martin from Australia with his fellow diggers — Jack Leggo, crack navigator; Bob Hay, Group Bombing Leader. Toby Foxley, Les Knight, Len Chambers. All from Australia, all with the DFC, all feeling very pleased with themselves.

Playing with Nigger and trying to get him tight were some of my own crew. Terry, Spam, Trevor and Hutch had long since gone to bed with the rest. Nigger knocked back about four full cans, made a long, lazy, zigzag trail of water down the corridor, then went to bed himself with his tail between his legs. The party went on till late, and Charles Whitworth joined in with Briggy, his second-in-command, to make us feel welcome, and in this they succeeded very well.

Soon it became obvious, even to the casual observer, that this was no ordinary squadron. The mess waiters had already begun eyeing us curiously. They had never seen a bunch of boys like this before, all in one squadron. Many of them had two

DFCs, and most of them wore one, some had the DSO. No doubt while they were fetching the rounds they began to wonder what was happening. One of them told me that we had not been there three hours before the canteen buzzed with rumours:

"Heard about the new gen squadron?"

"They're going to Russia!"

"They've come from North Africa."

"Something special?"

"Yeah, something special."

The boys noticed it all. They felt curious and wondered. They also felt very proud to all be in the same crack unit, but they wanted to know why. They thought they had a right to know why. At last Coles, a Canadian navigator, wandered up and asked the inevitable question. It was late, but I remember my reply: "I know less than you, old boy, but I'll see all air crews at 9.30 tomorrow and give you some gen."

Next day I got them all together. There were twenty-one crews, comprising 147 men: pilots, navigators, wireless-operators, bomb-aimers, flight-engineers. Nearly all of them twenty-three years old or under, and nearly all of them veterans. I saw them in the same old crew room, which brought back many memories of 1939–40 days. Now it was packed full of young, carefree-looking boys, mostly blue-eyed, keen and eager to hear the gen. I felt quite old among them.

My speech to them was short. I said, "You're here to do a special job, you're here as a crack squadron, you're here to carry out a raid on Germany which, I am told, will have startling results. Some say it may even cut short the duration of the war. What the target is I can't tell you. Nor can I tell you where it is. All I can tell you is that you will have to practise low flying all day and all night until you know how to do it with your eyes shut. If I tell you to fly to a tree in the middle of England, then I will want you to bomb that tree. If I tell you to fly through a hangar, then you will have to go through that hangar, even though your wing-tips might hit either side. Discipline is absolutely essential.

"I needn't tell you that we are going to be talked about. It is very unusual to have such a crack crowd of boys in one squadron. There are going to be a lot of rumours — I have heard a few already. We've got to stop these rumours. We've got to say nothing. When you go into pubs at night you've got to keep your mouths shut. When the other boys ask you what you're doing, just tell them to mind their own business, because of all things in this game, security is the greatest factor.

"It will take a couple of days to get things organized, and I shall want you all to help. Most of you have been in squadrons some time, so you will know what is required. First thing I want done is to get our new aircraft tested, then you, Bill" (this was to Bill Astell, Englishman from Derbyshire, deputy Flight-Commander to Dinghy Young), "I want you to take your crew and to fly over every lake you can see in England, Scotland and Wales and take

413

photographs of them. Let me have the photographs in thirty-six hours."

The AOC had told me to get this done by telephone earlier in the morning. What for I could not think, and I could see the boys were wondering why, too, so I went on:

"It's OK, chaps, don't go jumping to conclusions. The AOC wants this for his Conversion Units for cross-country practices; we're the only squadron with enough time to do it."

This was the first of many white lies. Then I went on to say a lot more. I have forgotten what it was, but it was all on the same lines. About discipline — flying discipline — about working hours, about leave. There was to be no leave.

Then I handed over to Melvyn, the American, who with Henry began to divide the crews into flights, choosing those they knew best, allotting them flying lockers and crew rooms, sorting out the offices. And I went upstairs.

In my bare office were one chair, one telephone and one table; nothing more. It was cold and damp, as the hangar heating had not been turned on, but there was a lot of work to be done.

At Syerston there was a young man by the name of Humphreys who was doing an assistant adjutant's job. He had been in business in peacetime and everything from orderly room clerk upwards in war. He was mad on flying, but his eyes had stopped him. Moreover, he was young and keen. Such men are the right type for this job, and a quick call by Charles to Group had him posted within forty-eight hours. But for the next few days we had to work without an adjutant, and the job of forming the entire squadron fell on the broad shoulders of three people of whom I must make special mention.

First there was F/Sgt Powell. He was the squadron disciplinarian, and he sat interviewing our new members, 700 of them, all day long, allotting them beds and bunks, getting their sections organized, supervising the unloading of the equipment. Chiefy Powell was small and dapper, not at all the bull-necked disciplinarian of the old days. He was something of a psycho-analyst and interviewed his men kindly, getting the best out of them. He did not know it, but he was laying down the foundation of the spirit which was to serve this squadron in such good stead later on. A great little man, and a king in his own way.

The second was Sergeant Hevron, boss of the orderly room. Group had been very efficient, and had given us everything in the way of equipment and air crews, but they had omitted to give us certain essential tools: typewriters and stationery and people to work them. So Hevron had to beg, borrow and sometimes steal from every imaginable source the much-required bumph so that he could start some form of filing system. Letters were already beginning to pour in. He was the only one who could type, and for a while he put in eighteen hours a day, filling in arrival reports, checking personnel documents and in the intervals pleading with me to get some help from somewhere.

The third was a WAAF. I don't know her name, but I think they called her Mary. She was plump and fair and the type that would make someone a very good wife some day. She had heard that we were in trouble, and so she had come over from one of the satellite airfields to give a hand with the typing. If she had been a civilian she could have put in a very reasonable claim for overtime.

And so they worked, those three, moulding the new squadron, while I sat in my bare office, slightly amazed at the way it was forming around me.

During those first two days Jack Leggo and Bob Hay were busy collecting the maps, setting up the bomb-sights, checking the bomb-stocks. They already knew that bombing was going to be one of our favourite occupations in the next two months. The Flight-Commanders were busy supervising their flights. There were many snags, too numerous to be detailed. There were no parachutes, there were no Mae Wests, there were no compass keys. But you cannot hope for everything when you form a squadron in two days.

The WAAF was still typing, Chiefy was still interviewing, ground crews were streaming like ants around our new aircraft. Air Ministry had at last woken up to the fact that a new squadron had been formed, and had given us a number — No. 617 Squadron. Our squadron marking letters were A.J. Now they were being painted on in big red letters.

Upstairs I sat meeting all the new operational crews. The captains would come in and introduce their boys to me. In the short conversation that followed I had a chance to get hold of some of their ideas. Then out they would go, and in would come another crew. So it went on. There were a few unlucky ones whom, for no discredit to them, I could not accept.

There were other troubles, too. Personal ones for me. Some of the squadrons which had been told by the SASO to supply us with tip-top men had taken the opportunity to get rid of some of their duds. From 106, the squadron which I commanded a week ago, came two men whom I myself had tried to get rid of. It was a rather plaintive voice that rang up Charles, the adjutant of 106, to tell him what I thought of him. The two men went back to 106. Then another squadron supplied me, rather unkindly, with two pregnant WAAFs. They were both married, of course, but they weren't any use to me because they had to leave the service anyway. There were other little games played on us which I won't mention.

By the third day everything was ready. We were all set to begin training, and I was not sorry. Nor, I am sure, were the rest of the boys.

In one of the big hangars Chiefy Powell got all the ground crews together, and I stood on top of my Humber brake and spoke to them. I said much the same as I said to the air crews, stressing that security was the most important thing of all. There was to be no talking.

417

Then Charles Whitworth got up and welcomed 617 Squadron officially to Scampton Base. He made a good speech, and I remember thinking that it would be a good idea if I could remember it, so as to copy him on some future occasion, but now I have forgotten what he said, except for one thing.

He said, "Many of you will have seen Noël Coward's film, *In Which We Serve*. In one scene Coward, as commander of a destroyer, asks one of the seamen what is the secret of an efficient ship. The seaman answers, 'A happy ship, sir.' And that is what I want you to be here. You in the Air Force use a well-known verb in practically every sentence; that verb is to bind. I can promise you that if you don't bind me, I won't bind you!"

That afternoon Humphreys turned up and together we wrote out our first training report. It was very short, because little had been done. It read: "Although the squadron was formed on 20.3.43 full facilities for training were not available until 25.3.43. Between these two days limited low-level cross-country flying was carried out. The squadron was organized into two flights on 22.3.43, but general deficiencies such as starter batteries and tool kits did not arrive until 26.3.43. No parachutes are available, but some have been borrowed from 57 Squadron. There are still no Mae Wests, but our crews don't seem to mind flying over the sea without them. Most of them feel that they are flying so low that they could not do anything about it, anyway. The aircraft are all serviceable, and training is expected to begin at maximum effort tomorrow.

"The following crews have finally been selected" [overleaf].

Next we started training in earnest. First there was a conference in my office, which by now wasn't so bare. Someone had put a carpet on the floor. Dinghy, Henry, Jack Leggo and Bob Hay sat around in chairs.

"The AOC has told me to get on with this low-level flying nonsense," I began. "We'd better limit the height at first to 150ft because we don't want the chaps going round the countryside hitting trees. We had better lay down ten standard routes so that the Observer Corps won't have too much of a job. I'll let you know what sort of country we want to practise flying over later. Any routes will do at first, but none over three hours — it's going to be pretty hard work these bumpy days. We'll want to be able to fly day or night, so flying can go on into dusk, to give the boys practice in moonlight flying. After all, it's much the same. All navigators had better have a chart with the practices kept against their name so that we can see how they're getting along."

I asked Jack if he had any problems, and Jack, the navigator, had some. The four of us discussed them. First there was the map problem. When flying at low level the ground goes by very quickly, and as you want large-scale maps, the navigator would have continually to keep changing them. The answer was roller maps.

PILOT	F/ENG.	NAVIGATOR	W/OPTR	B/AIMER	MID-UPPER	REAR-GUNNER
Leader						
W/C GIBSON, DSO, DFC	Sgt Pulford	P/O Taerum	F/L Hutchison, DFC	P/O Spafford, DFM	F/L Trevor-Roper, DFM	F/S Deering
"A" Flight						
S/L YOUNG DFC	Sgt Horsfall	Sgt Roberts	Sgt Nichols	F/O MacCausland	Sgt Yeo	Sgt Ibbotson
F/L ASTELL, DFC	Sgt Kinnear	P/O Wile	Sgt Garshowitz	F/O Hopkinson	Sgt Garbas	Sgt Bolitho
F/L MALTBY, DFC	Sgt Hatton	Sgt Nicholson	Sgt Stone	P/O Fort	Sgt Hill	Sgt Simmonds
F/L SHANNON, DFC	Sgt Henderson	P/O Walker, DFC	F/O Goodale, DFC	F/S Sumpter	Sgt Jagger	P/O Buckley
F/L BARLOW	Sgt Whillis	P/O Burgess	F/O Williams	Sgt Gillespie	F/O Glinz	Sgt Liddell
P/O RICE	Sgt Smith	F/O MacFarlane	Sgt Gowrie	F/S Thrasher	Sgt Maynard	Sgt Burns
P/O OTTLEY	Sgt Marsden	F/O Barrett	Sgt Guterman	F/S Johnson	Sgt Tees	Sgt Strange
P/O DIVALL	Sgt Blake	F/O Warwick	Sgt Simpson	Sgt McArthur	Sgt Allatson	Sgt Murray
F/S BROWN	Sgt Feneron	Sgt Heal	Sgt Hewstone	Sgt Oancia	Sgt Buntaine	F/S McDonald
Sgt BYERS	Sgt Taylor	P/O Warner	Sgt Wilkinson	Sgt Whitaker	Sgt Jarvie	Sgt McDowell

Flight Bombing Leader: P/O Fort   Flight Gunnery Leader: F/O Glinz   Flight Navigation Officer: F/O MacFarlane

PILOT	F/ENG.	NAVIGATOR	W/OPTR	B/AIMER	MID-UPPER	REAR-GUNNER
"B" Flight						
S/L MAUDSLAY, DFC	Sgt Marriott	F/O Urquhart	Sgt Cottam	F/S Fuller	F/O Tytherleigh	Sgt Burrows
F/L HOPGOOD, DFC	Sgt Brennan	F/O Earnshaw	Sgt Minchin	F/S Fraser	P/O Gregory, DFM	P/O Burcher, DFM
F/L MARTIN, DFC	P/O Whittaker	F/L Leggo, DFC	F/O Chambers	F/L Hay, DFC	P/O Foxlee, DFM	F/S Simpson
F/L MUNRO	Sgt Appleby	F/O Rumbles	Sgt Pigeon	Sgt Clay	Sgt Howarth	F/S Weeks
F/L McCARTHY	Sgt Ratcliffe	F/S MacLean	Sgt Eaton	Sgt Johnson	Sgt Barson	F/O Rodger
F/L WILSON	Sgt Johnson	F/O Rodger	Sgt Mieyette	P/O Coles	Sgt Payne	Sgt Hornby
P/O BURPEE	Sgt Pegler	Sgt Jaye	P/O Weller	Sgt Arthur	Sgt Long	F/S Brady
P/O KNIGHT	Sgt Grayston	F/O Hobday	Sgt Kellow	F/O Johnson	Sgt Sutherland	Sgt O'Brien
F/S TOWNSEND	Sgt Powell	P/O Howard	Sgt Chalmers	Sgt Franklin	Sgt Webb	Sgt Wilkinson
F/S ANDERSON	Sgt Paterson	Sgt Nugent	Sgt Bickle	Sgt Green	Sgt Ewan	Sgt Buck

Flight Bombing Leader: F/O Johnson   Flight Gunnery Leader: F/O Tytherleigh   Flight Navigation Officer: F/O Urquhart

These were to be home-made. Jack said that he would get all navigators making their own. Then we got down to the refinements of low-level navigation. Jack said, "As we're going to fly low, presumably far into Germany or somewhere, we won't get much navigational help from wireless. So I guess it will be all map-reading. I suggest that the bomb-aimer be the key map-reader, the navigator sticks to his chart, and both flight engineer and mid-upper gunners lend a hand in looking out when the time comes. In this way about eight pairs of eyes will be watching for landmarks, and everything should run pretty smoothly."

I agreed to this and many other suggestions he put forward connected with his own job. Then I handed over to Dinghy to supervise further training while I took myself on a journey south.

We stopped, the driver and I, at Grantham, on the way, and I saw the SASO. He said, "I'm sending you on a journey down south to meet a scientist who is working on your project. He's going to show you nearly everything, but remember only the AOC and myself and five others know anything about these matters, and you'll be the seventh. I can't stress too much the need for secrecy. It's absolutely vital."

We went on, down the winding Great North Road, meeting very little traffic except vast army convoys going north: past London into the southern country and up to an old country railway station. There I caught a train. My destination was so secret that not even my driver was allowed to have any idea of where I was going. Half an hour later I was met by a tall man whom I shall call Mutt. He was the senior test pilot for a very well-known aircraft firm, and had himself been responsible for testing the prototypes of more than one of our most successful bombers. We drove in his little Fiat car quite a way, without saying a word. I don't think he expected to see such a young fellow, and I didn't expect to see a civilian, and I think we were both wondering what we were doing there, anyway. At last he pulled up at an old country house. Here our passes were checked and re-checked and I had to pull out my special buff-coloured pass (numbered seven) which the SASO had given me earlier in the day. Then a couple of tough policemen gave us both the once over and we entered this queer place. We went down a long, dimly lit corridor, down dark stairs, farther and farther into the earth. Mutt seemed to know the way, and at last we came to a large iron door. There were two more guards here, and once more we went through the same procedure. They were certainly being careful. Then one of them opened the iron door and we went in to a sort of laboratory. It was bright inside, much brighter than the dim corridors, and I blinked to try and get accustomed to the light.

Then I met a man whom I'm not going to try to describe in detail, for I know he wouldn't like it. But I'm going to call him Jeff, which of course is not his real name. He was a scientist, and very clever aircraft designer as well. Jeff was neither young nor old, but just a quiet, earnest man who worked very hard. He was one of the real back-room boys of whom little can be told until after the war, and even then I'm not sure their full story will be told. He looked around carefully before saying anything, then abruptly, but benignly, over his thick spectacles, "I'm glad you've come; I don't suppose you know what for."

"No idea, I'm afraid. SASO said you would tell me nearly everything, whatever that means."

He raised his eyebrows. "Do you mean to say you don't know the target?" he asked.

"Not the faintest idea."

"That makes it awkward, very awkward."

"But SASO said —"

"I know, but only very few people know, and no one can be told unless his name is on this list." He waved a list in front of me. I could see there weren't many names on it.

"This is damned silly," said Mutt.

"I know, but it can't be helped — but I'll tell you as much as I dare. I hope the AOC will tell you the rest when you get back."

I said that I thought this would be all right and waited, very curiously, for him to go on. Then he said:

"There are certain objectives in enemy territory which are very vulnerable to air attack, and which are themselves important military objectives. However, these need a vast amount of explosive placed very

423

accurately to shift them or blow them out — you know what I mean, viaducts, submarine pens, big ships and so on. I have had my eye on such things for a long time, but always the problem has been too great — much too great. First of all, there wasn't an aeroplane with a high enough performance to carry the required load at the required speed. Then along came the Lancaster bomber, and this problem was solved. The next one was the explosive itself. It would have to take the form of either a very large bomb or a very large mine. But if it was to be dropped accurately enough to do its job it would have to be placed within a few yards of the right spot. There are three snags to this. If bombing is to be as accurate as that, then the attack will have to be at low level, which means below 300ft. But with these great big bombs there's always the danger that they may explode on impact from this height, and you know what that means. And if they're dropped above that height, then accuracy diminishes and the job can't be done. It's a sort of vicious circle. The other two snags are, of course, the danger of flak at that level and balloons, and the difficulty of flying over water at low level."

"Over water?" I said.

"Yes, over water at night or early morning, when the water will be as flat as a mill-pond backed up with a lot of haze or fog all round."

I began thinking of possible targets. *Tirpitz*, U-boat pens? No future in this — but Jeff was still talking.

"For a month or two now we have had the go-ahead order from the War Cabinet to try and overcome these difficulties. So we've been working hard, Mutt and I, on a certain theory of mine. I discovered the idea quite simply, but you won't want to know about that. Come, I'll show you."

The lights went out in the lab. and a small screen lit up with a flickering motion picture. The title was simple, "Most Secret Trial Number One." Then an aeroplane came into view, diving very fast towards the sea in a sort of estuary. When it got to about 200ft it levelled out and a huge cylindrical object fell from it rather slowly towards the water. I was amazed; I expected to see the aircraft blown sky high. But when it hit the water there was a great splash, and then — it worked. That's all I can say to describe it — just that it worked, while the aeroplane flew over serenely on its way. Then came pictures of many more trials. Now and then Mutt or Jeff would explain a point, but it seemed to me that everything was behaving perfectly each time. And, what's more, it was hitting its target with amazing accuracy. Then the screen became white and the lights went up. "You see," said Jeff. "That's my special mine to overcome our difficulties, and it does work. But I'm afraid it's only one quarter the size of the real thing which is required to do the job. When we get to the big fellows, I think we're going to run into a lot of difficulties."

"Has any been made yet?" I interrupted.

"No, not yet; the first will be ready in about a week's time with a modified Lancaster to carry it. Avro's are doing a great rush job to get the special fittings put on; I believe they're working twenty-four hours a day. Now what I want to know from you is this. Can you fly to the limits I want? These are roughly a speed of 240mph at 150ft above smooth water, having pulled out of a dive from 2,000ft, and then be able to drop a bomb accurately within a few yards."

I said I thought it was a bit difficult but worth trying. I would let him know as soon as possible. Then I was on my way. Out of this strange house and into the open air again. Mutt drove me to the station, and four hours later I was back at Scampton.

There the boys were all flying, so I took Nigger for a long walk to think things over. It's always the best way to think things out, and as we walked the more the problem seemed to be insoluble. Nigger was the only happy one. He was catching rabbits.

Next day we had another conference. I told the boys what I knew about the accuracy required and the height at which we must attack, but nothing about the weapon I had seen. Then came the problem. Dinghy began speaking. "The first big snag will be to get practice in moonlight. I suppose it will be moonlight or dusk, won't it?"

I said I thought it would be.

"Well, you know the difficulties in this country; there's not much moon, anyway, and if there is, the weather's sure to be bad, so we won't get much practice. We'll have to try and get some form of synthetic night-flying training."

"Didn't the SASO tell us to fly around with dark glasses on?" This was Henry.

"Yes, I've tried that. It's no good. You can't see your instruments. But I've heard that the AAF have brought out a special form of synthetic night-flying. All the windows of the aircraft are painted blue, and the crews wear yellow goggles inside. These are complementary colours or something, and apparently you get the effect of soft moonlight with all the high lights outside on a bright, sunny day."

"Well, that sounds fine to me. Go and find out from SASO where we can get hold of this stuff, will you?"

He came back with the information a few minutes later.

"I've been on to the SASO. The stuff's at Ford. He says we've got immediate priority, and we can have three aircraft fitted up right away if the maintenance unit can find the men. He's going to ring us back as soon as he has found out."

Then Jack Leggo came back on his nagivation problems again. There were routes to be considered. Would the routes take us over canals and lakes, so as to make it easier? Could slow bomb-aimers be put in crews as eighth men so as to get extra practice? They were already beginning to put in eight hours' flying a day, which is a lot.

Then Bob Hay got up. There were no bomb-carriers, and he understood we had to do a lot of bombing. There were no flamefloats, which are essential for oversea navigation. What sort of targets were required on the bombing range? And could we have priority on the use of the range from dawn to dusk? All these problems were solved by the ever-reliable SASO, who seemed to eat, sleep and live at his office desk. He fixed them all.

Trevor had his troubles, too. He wanted to get his gunners cracking. If we were to attack at low level, he wanted his gunners to be able to hit back. And for this he wanted maximum range tracer, so that although we were only firing .303 bullets, they would look like cannon-shells to the flak gunners on the ground. The tracer he wanted was hard to get, but we got it — from the SASO.

Hutch was rather in a haze about the whole thing. He didn't quite know where his wireless-operators came in. I said to him: "It's OK, Hutch. Just you concentrate on getting your wireless-operators on the top line, and your turn will come later. Now for a few general points, chaps. I've been speaking to the maintenance people, and they tell me that already a few aircraft have come back with leaves and tree-branches stuck in their radiators. This means the boys are flying too low. You've got to stop this, or else someone will kill himself, and I might also tell you that the Provost Marshals have already been up to see me about reported dangerous low flying. We all know we've got to fly low, and we've got to get some practice in, but for God's sake tell your boys to try and avoid going over towns and aerodromes and not to beat up policemen or lovers in a field, because they'll get a rocket if they do. Now, if you'll excuse me, I've got to do some trials on a certain reservoir, to find out if we can do the thing at all."

Half an hour later we were on our way in my faithful G for George towards the reservoir called Derwent Water near Sheffield.

This lake is in the Pennines, surrounded by high ground with just enough industrial haze blowing over it to make it ideal for the job; moreover, the water was always calm because there was no wind in that valley. Remembering what Jeff had said, we came screaming down at the right air-speed to pull out as near 150ft as we could judge (Hoppy was sitting beside me), and released a missile. It fell short. Then we were twisting and turning our way through the valley, with high hills on either side. We climbed up again for several more tries, and in the end found it more or less fairly easy.

That night at dusk, with the fog already beginning to fill up in the valley, cutting visibility down to about a mile or so, we tried again. This time it wasn't so good. The water, which had been blue by day, was now black — we nearly hit that black water. Even Spam said, "Christ! this is bloody dangerous," which meant it was. Not only that. I said to Dinghy there and then, that unless we could find some way of judging our height above water, this type of attack would be completely impossible. "But why must we fly at this dead height?" asked Hoppy.

"I'm afraid that's the snag. The scientist I met told me that in order to make his weapon work we would have to fly within a few miles an hour at the right air-speed and within a very few feet of the right height. That's our problem."

The next day the AOC sent for me, and as I entered his office I noticed three large packing-cases on the floor; he handed me a screwdriver. "There are models of your targets," he said. "Now I'm not going to tell you where they are, nor am I going to tell you what they are, although, of course, you will probably realize as soon as you see them. Jeff has rung me up and told me that you won't be able to train your squadron unless you know, and so I am leaving it to him to tell you all the details. However, don't forget that you have got to be the only man in the squadron who can possibly know the target until the day before the attack is made. Now let's have a crack at opening those cases."

All of them were scaled up and marked "Very Fragile". Not being a carpenter by trade, I went to work gingerly, and at last had all the screws undone. Then, between us, we lifted off the heavy lids. The three models were perfect in every detail down to the smallest tree, and my first feeling was — thank God it's not the *Tirpitz*. This was something I did not expect. There were models of three dams, and very large dams at that. Then the AOC was talking.

"Now you've seen what you've got to attack, take an aeroplane and fly down and see our man right away, and report to me when you come back."

Professor Jeff was in his office. He seemed pleased to see me.

"How did you get on with the trials?" he asked.

I told him that it was easy by day, but harder by night, and that flying level over water at 150ft was very nearly impossible.

"But you could see the end all right?"

"Yes."

"Good. Now to work. Mutt, will you get out my file on Downwood?"

"What's that?" I asked.

"It's the code name for the operation you're going to do. The AOC has told me that I can tell you the target."

It was hard to analyse my feelings, because I wasn't sure where these dams were. The AOC had talked of haze and industrial smoke, which put them into a built-up area, and that wouldn't be too hot. Mutt gave me a cigarette, Jeff opened his file and began: "The dams which you saw in model form in the AOC's office are great barrage dams in the Ruhr Valley. The weapon you saw in my laboratory the other day is known as Downwood, and it's my idea that by really accurate use of this weapon we shall be able to knock down the concrete walls of these dams."

"But surely a smaller bomb would do that easily?"

"No." Jeff laughed. "A lot of people think that; they think dams are just curved structures that hold back water by their shape, much the same as the arch of a bridge. There are dams like that, but they are known as vault dams. These barrage dams are known as gravity dams, and hold back the water by their weight. As these are 140ft thick of solid concrete and masonry and 150ft high, you can see that there is a colossal amount of masonry to shift. But let me begin at the beginning."

I was listening intently.

"As you know," Jeff said, "the Ruhr Valley is the most highly industrialized area in the whole of Germany, mainly because of the coal and heavy steel industries situated there. I know that a lot of Germany's factories are now dispersed, but as yet they have not moved many of their heavy industries, so the Ruhr Valley is still a very important target, even though you boys have done your best to knock it flat. However, there is one great snag to the Ruhr Valley itself, and this is the water supply. The Ruhr River itself is too small to supply much water, and the Rhine is a long way off for such big towns as Essen and Dortmund and the rest. So in 1911 the Germans, realizing this, built a mighty barrage dam blocking the Möhne Valley through which the River Ruhr flowed. The main idea of this dam was to create a storage of the surplus winter rainfall of the Ruhr catchment area — thus providing a reserve which could be released gradually during the summer months, to maintain a fairly constant level in the river and protect the underground water-table which provided supplies for industrial and household purposes. This table had been gravely in peril prior to the dam's construction. The dam also provides improved navigability of the lower Ruhr, controls winter flooding and maintains a constant flow of water for electrical power. Needless to say," he went on, "the Germans are very proud of this dam. In fact, it is rather beautifully built, Gothic and all that. It is some 850 yards long and 140ft thick, and as high as it is thick, and the lake it holds back is about 12 miles long, holding 140 million tons of water. At the same time they built another dam near by, called the Sorpe. This is very much smaller and is of earthen construction, which, if you know what I mean, consists of a sloping bank of earth 600ft long on either side holding up a water-tight concrete core. Between them they hold back about 76 per cent of the total water available in the Ruhr Valley. If they were to be breached, the consequent shortage of water for both drinking and industrial purposes might be disastrous. Of course, the damage done by floods if they were breached quickly would result in more damage to everything than has ever happened in this war.

"There is a third dam I must tell you about, and this is the Eder. This dam is some 60 miles away. It was built in 1914 primarily to prevent winter flooding of acricultural land and to assist in improving navigability of the lower Weser River. The dam also provides some water for the Mittelland

Canal, which, as you know, is one of the main canals in Germany, running as it does on the main route from the Ruhr to Berlin. But, unlike the Möhne Dam, the Eder has no water-supply functions. However, it supplies a lot of hydro-electric power. This one's a little larger than the Möhne Dam and lies in a valley 40 miles from Kassel. And it holds back 202 million tons of water. But to breach these things is an entirely different matter. You can imagine that many attempts have been made," he went on, "to devise some method of breaking down dam walls. But it's not so easy as it looks. When you consider that we in England here have ourselves been saved from an ordinary explosive bomb when we were behind 3ft of concrete, you will begin to realize what I mean when I talk about shifting about 150ft of the stuff."

I said, "Yes, I think I do."

"Well, we have been making experiments and trying out the effects of explosives on such walls for some time. Now, let me show you something."

He opened a book containing pictures of a small dam, some 6ft across, which had been breached by a certain charge of explosive. "You can see what we were after," he said. "Our next experiment was to try out our theories on a larger dam. We built out in the garden a dam some 200ft across. This dam, I might tell you, was brick for brick in strength the same as the Möhne dam. The lake was filled with water, and by manipulation of certain charges, we intended to try out there the theories we had evolved from the smaller models."

This, I thought, must have been fun. I could remember the time when I was a kid, when we used to go down to the beaches in Cornwall and shovel the sand across the little streams which ran down the granite cliffs. I could remember how we dammed up the water until it made a big pool behind the sand, and I could remember how, when it was time to go home for supper, I used to smash the whole thing with one sweep of my spade, letting the water rush out down the beach. I could also remember how angry my brother used to get when I did this.

"And what happened?" I asked.

"Well," went on Jeff, "after a lot of trouble we got a charge in the right place which we worked out a Lancaster on the same scale could carry, and the dam wall cracked. It cracked round about its base, and after a few more charges had been detonated the wall moved over backwards and water ran down into the garden. But this was not enough, we had to still make tests on a full-size model. At that time we heard that a certain County Council in the Midlands had just built a new dam to supply their town with water. We heard about it and wrote to them and asked them if we could knock down their old dam, so that the water would run into their newly built one. After a lot of quibbling they agreed to let us do this, and once more after much trouble, we succeeded in knocking it down. Here are the pictures."

I bent over his shoulder and studied them carefully. The dam had been breached right down to its foundations, a breach about 3ft across. There was a dead frog lying on the mud bank.

"Well, after that experiment," he went on, "we knew more or less where we were. The next thing was to find the suitable weapon. Well, you've seen that. But we've not finished," he added. "Not nearly finished." He paused and then went on quietly: "My smaller-scale weapons have worked, but we haven't had a chance to try the big ones yet — they aren't ready. But I think they will be in a few days' time, and so the trials are set for the 16th. If the big ones work, Avro's will have to modify twenty-five Lancasters to carry them. This is quite a big job, because these mines weigh a lot and are about 11ft in diameter. Then there's the time factor. The ordnance factory will have to construct the weapons, you'll have to plan a special method of attack, and all this will have to take place inside a month."

"Why the urgency?" I asked.

"Because dams can only be attacked when they are full of water. Every day photo planes are going out to take pictures of these dams, and we are watching the water rising. At the moment it is 12ft from the top, but we can only attack them when the water is 4ft. This ensures that the maximum amount of water is in the dam and at the same time makes certain that there is 4ft of free board on the lip against which you have to throw your mines. That is why you have to be so accurate. I have calculated that the water level will be suitable during the week 13th-19th May — that is, in about six weeks' time. This, as it happens, is a moon period — I think you will have to do it at night or dawn: you couldn't get into the Ruhr by day, could you?"

"God, no."

"Then the moon will be useful, but if you want more light you'll have to do it at dawn — but that's up to you. But to get back to our side of things let me tell you more about these dams. Your projectiles will have to fall so that they sink into the water actually touching the dam wall itself about 40ft down; if they are not touching, it'll be useless. Then, when the mine explodes by a hydrostatic fuse, I have calculated that crack will appear just as it did in the models. By placing more mines in exactly the same spot you will be able to shift this wall backwards until it rolls over, helped, of course, by the water pressure. The Sorpe Dam requires rather a different technique, but we will go into that later."

"So those are our three objectives?"

"Yes."

"However did you arrive at this theory how to crack these things?"

"Mutt, you tell him; I'm hoarse."

"Well," said Mutt, reaching for the file. "Jeff's always been playing about with things, large or small, since he was a small boy, and it came to him just like that one day when playing with his children in the garden."

"And you think that this will have disastrous results?"

"I know it will. The Prime Minister is terribly keen on it."

"You mentioned a special type of attack?"

"Yes; well, the first thing you've got to do is to get there. These mines are very heavy and you'll have to carry a lot of petrol because the operation may take some time. So you won't be able to fly very high. But again, that's up to you. The attack will have to be carried out at a dead height within a foot or so of 150ft, and that's going to be hard. At the same time your air-speed's got to be bang on; remember that you've got to dive down into the valley and you may get up a hell of a speed and your aiming has got to be perfect."

"That's going to be mighty difficult."

"Over black water at a constant height when you can't see the thing in bad visibility."

"Oh Christ!"

"And remember this, you'll have to drop your mines slightly before you reach the wall, so an ordinary bomb-sight won't do. If you under-shoot, nothing will happen; if you over-shoot, the mine will go over the top. But it's best to be accurate, because if you make a mistake the mine might hit the parapet and explode underneath your tail. That'll be pretty uncomfortable."

"Where will it go off in the ordinary way?"

"About 100 yards behind. You'll be OK. There's not much blast from an underwater explosion. Besides, the parapet will protect you."

"I see," I said slowly.

I didn't see. I was completely and utterly bewildered. The limitations seemed almost impossible. But all we could do was to try. Jeff told me to come down for the trials on the 16th, and in the meantime I would be free to get on with training for the next two weeks. Half an hour later a puzzled Wing-Commander and a thirsty dog were flying their way back to Grantham in the communications aircraft. Perhaps baffled is a better word than puzzled.

The next few days passed quickly. The synthetic night-flying aircraft had arrived; we all had a crack, and found it perfect. It was funny, though, flying along at night in daytime. It makes you quite sleepy. The boys had begun to get good at their flying, and now I knew where and what the targets were we could plan a route similar to the one which would actually be used over Germany. This meant flying a lot over lakes, but the excuse for these was always the same: they were good landmarks and a good check on navigation. As we would have to fly to Germany at tree-level height, keeping to track was most important, and it meant navigation to the yard. There hadn't been any accidents — yet, but birds were already beginning to get in our way, coming into windscreens and getting stuck in the radiators; trees were being hit, and sometimes even water. Many times out at sea the boys were getting fired on by His Majesty's ships, who have notoriously light fingers, but they took it all in good stead because, as Micky Martin put it, "It's good practice. It makes us flak happy."

I pitied my own crew because I was busy all day and we could only do our practice in the late part of the evening and at night. Many times we would take off about 6 o'clock and fly up the west coast of England to the northern tip of Scotland. It's a funny thing about England and Scotland; many people think it's a small place and that we're overcrowded in our little island, but it's amazing how unpopulated the country really is. In the Western Isles, for instance, you can fly for miles without seeing any sign of habitation.

And so these long, lonely trips took place every night, because if we were to lead the show we would have to be trained. Funnily enough, the boys thought it was a good thing. I once heard Trevor say, "It's a good thing flying with the Wingco; it keeps us off the booze."

One fine day in April a Wing-Commander from MAP came up to see me. I was sitting alone in my office when he came in. He began at once to tell me of our sighting difficulties on the Eder and Möhne Dams. The latest anti-submarine bomb-sight, he explained, would be no use when carrying out our special form of attack. I was horrified.

"How the hell do you know all this?" I asked, rudely.

He went on to explain. He was the sighting expert and had been let into the secret so that he could help us. No one else knew. I calmed down. Between us we worked out a plan, although it was his original idea. He took out a piece of paper and by drawing queer lines he explained what he meant — it took the form of a very simple bomb-sight using the age-old range-finding principles. From aerial photographs we had noticed that there were two towers on the dam, and when we measured these we found they were 600ft apart. Our mines had to be dropped exactly a certain number of yards short of a certain position along the dam wall. He worked it all out. He was a mathematician. Then we handed it to a corporal with glasses, and within half an hour the instrument section had knocked up the prototype of the bomb-sight. It cost a little less than the price of a postage stamp.

That afternoon we went up, he and I, to try it over our dam in Sheffield. It worked. He was very pleased that he had been able to help, and took himself back to London. Just another back-room boy. His name? Dann.

Well pleased, I told Bob Hay to get cracking with all our bomb-aimers to teach them to make their own sights based on the prototype. From then on our bombing range at Wainfleet echoed to the thud of bursting practice bombs. Soon extraordinary accuracy was being achieved. F/Sgt Clifford sent

441

down eight practice bombs from 150ft — error 4 yards. He had free beer that night. Next day Les Knight managed to get this down to 3 yards. He was the pilot — the drinks were on him — but he didn't.

Soon we went on to night training, and again I found it very much harder, because although we could see the targets clearly enough, we couldn't see the water. It was practically impossible to fly at exactly 150ft. A few went too low and rubbed their bellies along the water; others went too high and under-shot by miles. After the second night's bombing Dinghy landed, sweating. "It's no use. I can't see how we're going to do it."

I had to agree.

"Can't we get electric altimeters? Ours don't give the height to 50ft. But personally I can't see the necessity, anyway, of flying to a few feet. It's easy enough to fly within 10ft of the height, why 2ft?"

Melvyn, like all the boys, didn't know the target. I had hinted at U-boat pens or the *Tirpitz*. But an electrical altimeter would only have worked over open sea or in a harbour. I knew it wouldn't work in a valley. There were too many hills around.

"I'll try," I said, and left it at that. But this height question was to be one of our greatest difficulties for some days to come. In the end, however, it was to be solved as simply as the problem was complex, but more of this later.

By the end of the third week all crews had done about twenty cross-countries by night, and could now find the "tree" which I had asked them to find. Their navigation was really expert. We had dropped about 1,500 practice bombs on our range, and the average error for all these was as low as 25 yards. With this basic training behind us we felt that the time had now come to plan our route to the target, so that we could imitate it as much as possible over this country. This would give the boys a chance to get there when it came to the real job — and getting there was the main thing.

We went down to see Charles Pickard of F for Freddie fame, who probably knew more about the light flak defences in the coastal areas of Holland and Belgium than any other man living. From his safe he pulled out a map on which all the defended areas along the coast were shown in red. There was a lot of red. But there were gaps. He showed me how to get through these by means of a winding route in which nowhere did we get closer than one mile to the guns. Then Charles Whitworth and I, with the help of the SASO, sat down to imitate this winding journey, if possible, over England. This was easier than we expected. The flight out across the North Sea was simulated by a flight across the North Sea, but out in the middle our route turned round and came back towards England again. It crossed the coast inland over the Wash, which is similar to the Dutch islands. From then on it led from canal junction to river-rail crossings; from railway crossings over canals to road bridges, because all these show up well in moonlight and at

443

dawn. But each turning point we selected because it looked exactly the same as the real thing. If we were to turn on a certain shaped bridge in Holland, then we turned on a similar bridge in Norfolk. For the River Rhine we had the River Trent, for the Ruhr Hills we had the Cotswolds, for the Möhne Lake we had Uppingham Reservoir, which was much the same shape though, of course, much smaller. Colchester Lake gave us a good idea of the calm waters of the Eder Reservoir. In fact, everything was much the same. On the way home our dummy route left England at the sand dunes near a point on the Norfolk coast, which corresponded exactly to our "gap" near Egmond on the Hook of Holland. There was even a windmill nearby which was much the same as another windmill over there, and a wireless mast. Moreover, the total distance was nearly the same as the real thing, which was ideal. We knew all this because we took the trouble to fly around it and find out. And so the great imitation route was planned. I gave it to Jack Leggo and told him to get all crews so used to it that they could go around blindfold.

"But why the lakes? We're not going to pinpoint on lakes?"

"That's all right. I've told you — those are the checks." Another white lie.

Meanwhile, it may well be imagined that the Germans would have liked to have known all about this. If they had known they would have improved their dam defences. But we knew that the defences were the same as at the beginning of the war. Even the double torpedo net was getting rusty from old age. The security measures were evidently efficient. All our telephone wires were tapped, all conversation was checked. One boy rang up his girlfriend and told her that he could not come out that night because he was flying on special training. Next day, in front of the whole squadron, I told him that a lapse of this kind would end in a court-martial. There was no more loose talk. Guards were stationed all round the vicinity; lectures were given on security to every man and woman on the station. All our letters were censored, and if anything which might give the game away was written, the letters found their way back to me. Special policemen in plain clothes were stationed in the vicinity. Their job was to eavesdrop. They did it well. Some say that even the local barmaid in the nearby pub was given three months' holiday. Everywhere in the factories and on the testing grounds, in the Air Ministry — the same measures were in force. Taking things all round, I think every serviceman and every civilian co-operated very well. They knew that they had 125 lives on their hands. They did not talk.

And so, after three weeks, things were going pretty well. Operational training and security marched forward side-by-side. The weather had been kind — the aeroplanes were behaving themselves. The crews had begun to settle down to the dangerous art of low flying, and no one had killed himself yet. The pilots had begun to practise formation flying at night at low level to get used to their fighting formations. Bombing was generally very accurate and the speed of bombing was both high and constant. In fact, the only two great questions now remaining were, of course, the weapon itself, and the height problem. A high esprit de corps had already begun to creep into the squadron. The adjutant in his squadron diary wrote on April 14th: "The whole of 617 has by now a feeling of solidity. The officers and NCO air-crew had shown remarkable enthusiasm for their job not only in flying alone, but in cleaning and painting the hangars and offices. We seem to have got tradition already."

On the 15th, with one month to go, the SASO rang up. Bob Hay and I were to fly down to Parkstone, a place on the South Coast not very far from France, to witness the first trials of the new weapon. The first of the problems was about to be dealt with.

CHAPTER
SEVENTEEN

By Trial and Error

Down at Parkstone, Bob and I sat in the sun and waited. We had been told that things weren't quite ready, so we drove round the town of Margate to see what it looked like in time of war. It was pretty hard to realize, as we lounged on the beach, that this was the same old sunshine resort of peacetime; the hotels were all closed, "Dreamland" was an army barracks, barbed wire was everywhere and the place was full of soldiers. The only thing that had remained was the fish. We had just stuffed ourselves full of Dover soles and now felt pleasantly lazy in the early afternoon, listening to the screaming of the gulls as they glided over the harbour.

Suddenly there was a noise like the release of compressed air, then the chattering of cannon guns, followed by the full crump of bombs. Like a flash, glinting in the sun at "nought" feet, four FW 190s rocketed over our heads going flat out towards France, followed closely by four Typhoons. The many Bofors parked along the front chattered after them, sending up red balls one after another in a gentle curve towards the whole ensemble, enemy

447

and friend. This was the well-known up-and-run raid. Bob said a rude four-letter word with emphasis. Then the sirens went. Later in the evening we heard that all four had been smacked down by the "Tiffies".

We also heard that the tide would be just right for the trials at 7 o'clock next morning. We were told that after each mine had been dropped the scientists wanted to examine them to see how they had stood up to the shock of hitting the water at that very high speed. The idea was to drop one when the tide was on the ebb so that, when it went out, we could walk down the beach and examine it thoroughly at our leisure without the difficulty of recovering it from the sea.

Early next morning we stood together, Bob, Professor Jeff and I, on the range facing the sea, waiting. It was one of those white mornings with the cloud spread evenly over the whole sky; there was hardly a tipple on the water; it was cold and rather grim and our collars were turned up. Jeff looked at his watch and said, "Shorty should be here any minute now." Shorty was one of Mutt's test pilots — he was 5ft 6in high and rejoiced in the name of Longbottom.

Behind us, round the barbed wire which surrounded the range, special policemen patrolled, their job to keep away strangers. No one else was meant to see these trials. Near us, a slow-motion movie camera sat angularly on its tripod with an operator panning its lens towards the east. Out at sea 100 yards away two white buoys bobbed up and down. These were the aiming markers. A small dinghy lay on the beach with a naval lieutenant asleep in it; he was the proud captain of this craft, whose job was to see to the repair of buoys if they got damaged.

Then out of the sun came the two Lancasters. They were both in fine pitch and making a very hearty noise for that time of the morning. They flew in formation; one the motion-picture aircraft, the other with one of our mines slung underneath. Inside the gaping bomb doors we could see it quite clearly painted black and white, looking large enough even against the massive black Lancaster itself. Down came the Lanc. with Shorty Longbottom at the controls to about 150ft, travelling at something like 270. We saw him level out for his run, then climb a bit to get his exact height over the calm water. We saw him tense at the controls, getting his horizon level on the cliffs further on. Jeff stood beside Bob, crouching like a cat. The movie camera began turning. I picked up a pair of binoculars. Then the mine fell out quite slowly. It seemed to hang in the air for a long time before it hit the water with a terrific splash and a dull thud. In a minute we would know whether or not Jeff's calculations had been right or wrong, but for the moment there was nothing except that mighty wall of water which reached up to the aircraft's tail as if to grab it. Then it all subsided and we knew. The great mine could be seen taking its last dive smashed into six different fragments.

"Broken," said Jeff, and looked at the ground. I said nothing. I knew the work he had put in, the hours of sitting at the desk with slide rule and calculator. Now it had failed. Would the mine have to be altered? Would the whole project fail? What next?

"They all said it wouldn't work," Jeff was saying. "They all said it was too big and too heavy, but I'll show them. We have got another in the hangars up there, and we'll strengthen it this afternoon and have some more trials this evening."

In our secret hangar that afternoon there was feverish activity as the mine was strengthened by steel plates so that it wouldn't break when it hit the water. Small men with glasses toiled side-by-side with sweating airmen, none of whom knew the use for which the thing was intended. They had no meals, and worked through an alert without pause. At 5 o'clock that afternoon they straightened their backs. It was ready.

In the late afternoon we again stood waiting. Jeff was hopeful; the extra plating should do the trick. We had just had a look at the broken weapon, and it seemed it had hit so hard that the impact had broken the outer skin. By strengthening this outer skin with half-inch steel plate it seemed that we had got the answer.

Then over they came again; once more the suspense and once more the mighty splash. Then

Mutt, who was flying it this time, banked steeply away to have a look. But we weren't looking at him, only at the bits of our smashed-up weapon which were hurtling round the sea like flying-fish. Then the foaming water settled down again and there was a long silence.

Jeff suddenly said, "Oh, my God," and I thought he was going to have a fit. But he soon calmed down, for he was not temperamental, and as we trudged along the shingle to the car park he began planning his next move. Here was a man who would not be beaten.

To make things worse, Bob and I took up a single-engine aircraft to fly back to Scampton. When we were about 300ft over Margate the engine stopped. When an engine stops in a four-engine aircraft you do not have to worry much about it — you have always got three others, but when it happens in a single-engine aircraft, then the long finger of gravity points towards mother earth; and so we began coming down. In ordinary parts of the world this is quite easy, but at Hell's Corner they made quite certain that aircraft do not land safely in fields. There were abundant wires and other devices because German glider-borne troops were not very welcome. So we fell into the trap . . .

After the aircraft had rolled itself into a ball and we had stepped out of the dust, a man came running over to see if we were hurt. His words were memorable.

"I think they teach you young fellows to fly too early," he said.

Then a policeman panted up and took a statement. "I'm glad to see our anti-aircraft landing devices work," he said without sympathy. We stumped back to the aerodrome.

Back at the squadron our great problem was the height. By now we had realized that we would have to get some method of flying accurately at 150ft or the whole project would have to be called off. Many methods were tried; one of them consisted of a long wire which we trailed behind the aircraft with a heavy weight on it.

The idea was that this weight would hang down exactly 150ft at a certain speed and so, as the aircraft approached the water and the weight hit, there would be a jerk and the pilot would then know what height he was at. However, this method proved unsatisfactory because the weight has a nasty habit of trailing up straight behind the aircraft.

Then we tried to get practice by judging height. To do this we put a couple of men on the side of a hill overlooking a lake with a special instrument to measure aircraft height. One by one we dived over the water and were told afterwards whether we had been right or wrong. This was all right for daylight, but proved impossible at night. Then one day the problem was solved. Mr. Lockspeiser of MAP paid the SASO a visit. He said, "I think I can help you." His idea was an old one; actually it was used in the last war. He suggested that two spotlights should be placed on either wing of the aircraft, pointing towards the water where they would converge at 150ft. The pilot could see these spots, and when they merged into one he would then know the exact height. It all seemed too simple, and I came back to tell the boys. Spam's first words were: "I could have told you that. Last night Terry and I went to see the show at the Theatre Royal, and when the girl there was doing her strip-tease act there were two spotlights shining on her. The idea crossed my mind then."

I said, "Never mind about strip-tease. You, Henry, take an aircraft down to Farnborough — I know it's a weekend; that doesn't count — and get two Aldis lights fitted up, one in the nose and one in the tail. Fly it back here as soon as it is ready and we will do some dummy runs across the aerodrome."

Farnborough worked hard, and Henry was back within twenty-four hours. He took the aircraft up, and I stood out on the aerodrome to watch him. It was dusk when he came whistling across the aerodrome with his two thin beams of light shining down on the ground. He looked so low in his great aircraft that if he turned on to his side one wing would rip along the ground. It all looked very frightening, but when he landed he said it was quite easy and suggested that the navigator should get the height calculations and leave the pilot to concentrate on his instrument-flying.

Then a party of men descended on our workshops and all the aircraft were fitted within a matter of days. Night after night, dawn after dawn, the boys flew around the Wash and the nearby lakes and over the aerodrome itself at about 150ft, while others with theodolites stood on the ground and measured their heights. Within a week everyone had got so good that they could fly to within 2ft with amazing consistency. But as I stood there and watched them with their lights on, I knew that whatever losses there might have been before, we were certainly going to make it easier for the German gunners flying around with lights on.

Down in the South work was still going on. Every day dramatic experiments took place. One cold morning after another Shorty and Mutt flew over the range and dropped their missiles while this great little man, Jeff, stood in the shingle beside the water with his shoulders hunched and his hands in the pockets of his overcoat watching to see what would happen. One after another the experiments failed. The mines were not working. I can remember clearly the sight of that cold, quiet figure standing sometimes alone, sometimes with two or three others, on the brink of the water, looking up at the great Lancasters. There was a tenseness about the way in which he stood, with his legs apart and his chin thrust out and a fearful expectancy about everything. There was sometimes frost on the ground during these early mornings, which made things sharp and bright and real.

For many days they worked and flew while he modified and experimented and the boys trained and trained and I watched and watched. But every time it ended in the same thing — failure.

One day Shorty came up to collect me in a Mosquito. "I have got to take you to Brooklands," he said. "Jeff's there, and he wants to have an urgent conference with you."

I needn't say how much Shorty shook me going through the balloon cables at Brooklands, nor need I say how tired Jeff seemed when I came in. He said to me, "The whole thing is going to be a failure unless we jiggle around with our heights and speed."

"What do you mean?"

"Simply this. From the slow-motion movie cameras which have taken pictures of these things dropping, I have found out a few facts. I have drawn this graph here to illustrate what I mean. It's all a combination of speed and height. You see here that they will work and won't break up if we drop them from 150ft at a certain speed. On the other hand, if we drop them from 40ft at this speed they will also work. The best height to suit your aircraft is here at the 60ft level at 232mph. But that is very low, and that's why I have asked you to come down. Can you fly at 60ft above the water? If you can't the whole thing will have to be called off."

I thought for a second and wondered if it could be done. If 150ft was low, 60ft was very low. At that height you would only have to hiccough and you would be in the drink. But I said aloud, "We will have a crack tonight."

All this time we had reconnaissance aircraft flying out over Germany watching the dams as a cat watches a mouse. They never flew straight to them because then the Germans would know what they were looking for, but always took a roundabout route, crossing the dams as if by accident. They were looking for two things; the first and more important was the height of the water level. It was slowly rising. The second was the state of the defences. If they were being intensified, the Germans must know we were coming.

It was very thrilling in those cold spring evenings, watching the water rise. By April 17th it was some 15ft from the top of the dam wall. By the beginning of May it was only 10ft, and so it went up and up. We would have to be ready when it was 4ft, and it looked as though we were behind schedule.

When I got back to Scampton we immediately altered the spotlights so that they converged at 60ft and made our first trials over the Wash. I think David Maltby was the first to take up the aircraft to experiment at this height. He found it all right, but said that it seemed very low. We checked with our theodolites and found it was exactly right. Then I went up with Terry and flew along the calm waters of Uppingham Lake, and it seemed to me that we were a little higher than the height of the trees; it certainly was low, but there was no real danger because the spots were very accurate. When we were coming down Terry would say, "Go down, go down," very slowly, whereas if we were below 60ft he would yell, "Go up," and a quick pull on the stick would shoot the Lanc. up into the air.

We heard that these spotlights would work satisfactorily over water with a slight chop, but over glass calm the spots would shine through the water and converge underneath, so that there was very great danger of flying straight into the drink without knowing the danger.

Many a lonely bargee was frightened at the dead of night as we experimented like this along the still canals of Lincolnshire, and we found that the theorists were wrong. The spots did, in fact, keep on the surface. Within a few days all crews had tried it, and all crews were satisfied.

By May 1st I had rung up Jeff and told him that we could do it. He asked me to come down for the trials again.

Then one morning early in May, Mutt flew over and dropped one which worked. The man on the ground danced and waved his hands in the air and took out his handkerchief and waved it madly. I threw my hat in the air. I could see Mutt in his cockpit grinning as he banked around after his run, and I waved back at him and shouted into the noise of the engines. I believe, although I do not remember very well, that Jeff threw his hat into the air. This was a wonderful moment.

Then there were urgent telephone calls and many signals written in cipher, and messengers rushing to and fro, and factories receiving priority orders, so that men and women should work day and night making these things which we were to carry with us over to Germany to be dropped on the Möhne Dam. There was great excitement. One of the boys flew back to the squadron with the good news and there were smiles on all faces; we even persuaded Jeff to take a glass of beer afterwards. As he was sipping it one of the high officers of Bomber Command went up to him. I heard him say, "It's OK. You seem to have got your weapons to work, but you will never knock down that rubble; it's completely impossible." And Jeff smiled and I scowled and thought this officer was a bum, because he should have remembered that the barman was listening.

Meanwhile, Avro's began to churn out the new aircraft. Soon they were delivered by special pilots on to our aerodrome. The Engineer-Officer, F/L Capel — we always called him Capable Capel — began to delve into them; they were very different. There was no mid-upper turret; this had been taken off because of the weight. A lot of armour had been taken out; there were new gadgets everywhere so that we could carry out our mission successfully. One by one they were allotted to crews who took great care of them, and I once heard a pilot swear lustily and go red in the face when his bomb-aimer got inside with muddy boots on! And at the same time in the early morning long eight-wheeled trucks arrived on our station covered with tarpaulins. These were our mines arriving. They were glistening new and still warm because they had just been filled with their very special explosive. Our armament officer, Doc Watson, had to deal with these, and it meant a lot of trouble because each one had to be treated like a diamond — they were very delicate and very hard to fuse and prepare. He and his armourers worked day and night getting them ready for our next trials.

Meanwhile, the whole squadron was beginning to get a bit tired. They had had nearly two months of continuous training, getting up at dawn and dusk so that they could fly in conditions which were nearly like moonlight. They had flown about a hundred hours of training, and because of the uncertainty of the whole thing the strain was beginning to get them down. For this reason I sent them off on three days' leave so that they could recover, but told them not to say a word to anyone outside. And I began to get ill too, and irritable and bad-tempered, and, of all things, there began to grow on my face a large carbuncle. I went to the doctor. He was very kind and he said: "This just means you are over-worked. You will have to take two weeks off." I just laughed in his face. Poor man! These medicos sometimes do not realize that there is a war on and when a job's got to be done personal health doesn't enter into the question. Nevertheless, I took part of his advice and began taking some tonic.

A few days later we went down to Parkstone again to watch the final handing-over trial. This was to see that our mines would actually explode in water. I flew in the camera aeroplane and Shorty flew the aeroplane which would drop it. It was a tense and dramatic moment watching the mine fall out, hit the water and not break up. And then, when Shorty had passed over it by about 100 yards, the whole surface of the sea shook as if by a mighty earthquake, and about five seconds afterwards a great column of snow-white water slowly rose into the air, beautiful to watch. It rose to a full 1,500ft and stayed there for perhaps fifteen seconds, then slowly melted away in the spring sunshine. Our mines were ready.

On May 6th we held our last training conference. Both Capable Capel and Doc Watson were there because they were very much concerned. All the captains came too. I think they were now beginning to guess about targets, although none of them, of course knew for certain. They sat in chairs round my office, smoking and talking — while Nigger sat in my place giving them the once over. I sat on the window-sill and began to talk.

"Well, chaps, you know as well as I do it has been absolute hell getting this right in the last few weeks, but now I think we are more or less set; that is, we are set to begin co-ordinating our training in the one tactical operation. When we began, navigation was the main problem. Now I am satisfied you can fly to a target in the moonlight at low level. I am satisfied you can reach it and identify it. As you may have realized, the actual attack will be no ordinary one, and it will have to be closely controlled by RT and WT so that everything runs smoothly.

"The purpose of this conference is to discuss this special attack so that I can get out some form of operational plan when the time comes."

"When will that be?" asked Dinghy.

"Within the next fortnight; but don't tell anyone, for God's sake, because I can only repeat that if the Huns knew we were coming they would take steps to see that we would never get away with it. Photo aircraft have been over every day and have not yet reported any increase in the defences. So far security must have been pretty good. But to go on.

"After our navigational problem we had three others:

(1) how to fly over water at night;
(2) how to bomb accurately in the special way that is required;
(3) to find a suitable weapon for the job.

"Well, you boys between you solved the first two, and a crowd of test pilots and scientists, whom I hope you will meet one day, solved the other, and the time has now come when our very high standard of training can be fitted in to carry out our special operation. SASO has given permission for us to use the reservoirs at Uppingham and Colchester to practise on. He has fixed up with a film studio or something to rig up a special framework on the water barrage which will make them look very much like our own objectives — that is U-boat pens, or whatever they are.

"From now on we are going to carry out attacks against these places using nine aircraft at a time. These attacks will begin tonight. The sort of thing I visualize is three flights of three aircraft flying in formation at night along our special route. We will reach the first lake; we will then attack singly, according to my instructions on the RT, from exactly 60ft and at exactly 232mph. I needn't tell you again how necessary it will be to keep to these limits. If you don't, the whole thing will be a failure. When we have destroyed the first objective, we will fly down to the next and repeat the tactics. Then we will fly home out along the special route as if we were actually leaving Germany.

"In the meantime, other crews are to keep their hands in with bombing and spotlight flying over the Wash. Six other special crews will be sent to another lake to carry out a special form of attack there."

"Then you will need practically all serviceable aircraft?" asked Capable.

"Yes, we will want maximum serviceability. From now on your ground crews will have to work twenty-four hours a day, I'm afraid, to do it, but tell 'em it will be worth it in the end. And you, Doc. — stop chewing gum — you will have to get your mines organized by the 12th because we will want to drop these on a final practice."

"It will be a bit of a job, sir," put in Doc. "They haven't all arrived yet; that is, the modified ones, and they take twenty-four hours to prepare. You know how short of armourers we are, and my boys have been sweating blood as it is."

"OK. I will ask the SASO to lend us a few more men; they can give us a hand during the last week. But don't forget that they can't leave the Station once they know that there is something special on.

"Now, another point. We want to practise flying at our proper all-up weight, so that I want the petrol load worked out. Don't forget some of the armour has been taken out. You can do that, Melvyn; get Pulford to work out the full load, and get another Flight-Engineer to cheek it. Don't exceed 63,000lb all up, because we won't get off otherwise."

"OK," said Dinghy. "I believe you want the front gunner to remain in his turret the whole time so that he can deal with any flak guns we may meet. The snag about this is that his feet dangle in front of the bomb-aimer's face. It would be a good idea to fix up some stirrups for his legs, because he would be more comfortable himself and the wretched bomb-aimer wouldn't have to put up with the smell of his feet."

This was a good idea, and the long-suffering Capel was asked to fix up these things right away.

"Another point," said someone. "How about fixing a second altimeter in front of the pilot's face attached to the windscreen so that he can see it easily? It will save him looking down into the cockpit when he's near the drink."

Another good idea, and the instrument boys again were asked to fit up all aircraft by the afternoon.

One by one the boys put forward their suggestions, and most of them were adopted because they were good ideas from chaps who knew their job. What they exactly were cannot be written here because they were and still are secret. Enough to say that many civilian workmen were moving around the hangars working on air-position indicators and other things which all helped navigation and bombing.

"How about radio telephony?" asked Dave Shannon. "I am pretty hazy about this, not ever having been a fighter boy."

"Well, as far as I can see, this is the procedure," I replied. I took from my drawer something I had been working on the night before. "The idea is that we use plain language, backed up by simple code words. If the radio should fail we will have to use WT as well. We won't use Air Force code because wars have been lost in the past by the waste of time when decoding. We will invent our own simple code; it must be very simple and self-explanatory. Here's a slip of paper, giving the full gen."

On this piece of paper were a few short code words which we were to use. For instance, the word "Dinghy" would mean that the second objective had been destroyed. The word "Nigger" would mean that the first objective had been destroyed. Words like "Artichoke" and "Beer" indicated that we would change frequency from Button A or B. There were many other words, and I told the boys to learn them off by heart.

"Now, the next thing is the procedure," I went on. "Hutch here has fitted up in the crew room twenty dummy aircraft headsets. In a minute we will go down there and run through the drill until we know it by heart. I will be the leader, Hoppy, will be deputy-leader and Mickey Martin will be the second deputy-leader. It is important to have two deputies because, you never know, one of us may get shot down. We will do this half an hour a day, and I think it will get us fully into the technique."

For the next week we started by having our dress rehearsals, and at the same time practising our attack on the ground in the radio room. All this time the water was getting higher on the dams that we were going to attack. Now it was only 5ft from the top. When we had all got fully trained in our special form of attack we held a full-dress rehearsal which some few senior officers took an interest in. It was a complete failure. Aircraft went astray, some nearly collided, others went home browned off. The trouble was intercommunication. On attacks of this sort there must be no allowance for anything to go wrong, and things had gone wrong here. The radio-telephone sets which we were using were just not good enough. We would have to use fighter sets. When we got back I told the AOC that unless we

465

were equipped with VHF[1] the whole mission would be a failure. I told him that I had been asking for it for some time. He said, "I'll fix it." He was as good as his word. Within a few hours a party of men landed on the aerodrome and went to work. Next day the whole squadron was equipped with the very best and most efficient radio-telephonic sets in the whole of the Royal Air Force. And not only this, but my aircraft and the deputy-leaders had two sets on board, so that if one should go wrong we would have the other.

Next night we carried out another dress rehearsal, and it was a complete success. Everything ran smoothly and there was no hitch: that is, no hitch except that six out of the twelve aircraft were very seriously damaged by the great columns of water sent up when their mines splashed in. They had been flying slightly too low. Most of the damage was around the tails of the aircraft; elevators were smashed like plywood, turrets were knocked in, fins were bent. It was a miracle some of them got home. This was one of the many snags that the boys had to face while training. On the actual show it wouldn't matter so much because once the mines had dropped the job would be done and the next thing would be to get out of it, no matter how badly the aircraft were damaged by water or anything else. But the main thing was to get the mines into the right spot.

---

[1] Very High Frequency R/T

By now it was obvious that we would have to carry out the raid within the next few days — perhaps only two days, because the water level had been reported just right for the attack. The training was now complete. The crews were ready. In all we had done 2,000 hours of flying and had dropped 2,500 practice bombs, and all the boys were rather like a team of racehorses standing in the paddock, waiting for the big event. But the ground crews were working like slaves repairing the damage done to our aircraft.

Then there were visits to the Met Officer. Aircraft flew far out into the Atlantic, far out past Norway to see what was coming towards us in the way of "fronts". God was very kind to us; the weather was perfect. That was the last snag, and it seemed almost too good to be true that old man Met was behaving himself.

The AOC came over on May 15th and told me that we would take off the next night. As he left, a white aeroplane landed on our aerodrome and taxied up to our hangar. Out of it stepped Jeff and Mutt. They had come to see the end of all their work.

That night we stayed up late writing out the operation order. This was important because should the worst happen, and none of us got back, no one would know exactly what we had planned to do.

Hoppy was now told the target, so were Dinghy and Henry as well as Bob. And that night Hoppy saved our lives. The route that SASO and I had

467

planned between us had taken us over Huls, a vast well-defended rubber factory on the edge of the Ruhr which wasn't marked on the flak map. He happened to know all this, and suggested that we should go a little farther north. If Hoppy hadn't known, we would have gone over that factory, and it would have been just too bad. We went to bed at midnight. As we were leaving Charles came rushing up with a white face.

"Look here, Guy, I'm awfully sorry, Nigger's had it; he has just been run over by a car outside the camp. He was killed instantaneously."

And so I went back to my room on the eve of this adventure with my dog gone — the squadron mascot.

The Doc handed the boys some sleeping pills as they went to bed so that they should get a good night's sleep before they went off. Then I was alone in my room looking at the scratch-marks on the door Nigger used to make when he wanted to go out, and feeling very depressed.

Next day, on May 16th, reconnaissance aircraft reported that the defences on the dam had remained unchanged and that the water level was just right for the attack. It was a great moment when the public-address system on the station said, "All crews of No. 617 Squadron report to the briefing room immediately." The boys came in hushed, having waited two and a half months to hear what it was they were going to attack. There were about 133 young men in that room, rather tousled and a little scruffy, and perhaps a little old-looking in spite of their youth. But now they were experts, beautifully trained, and each one of them knew his job as well as any man had ever known any job he was to do.

I let the scientist tell them all about it. In his gentle, benign way he repeated almost exactly the things that he had told me a long time before. He told them how and why the dam had been made and of what it was built. He told them how thick it was and how difficult it would be to crack, and he told them of the principles upon which we were going to work. He told them that it was not going to be easy, and everyone understood what he was trying to say. At the same time they were relieved to know at last what they were going to attack. This was not going to be too bad, they thought. The strain had begun to tell on them, because it is not a very pleasant feeling when you know you are training for a dangerous job and do not know what the target is.

The rest of the day was a terrific flap. There was testing of aircraft and checking of instruments; there were tractors driving round the aerodrome carrying the mines which were to be fitted to our aircraft. There was Doc Watson rushing round on his motor-bike looking worried. There was the engineer staff putting finishing touches to the aircraft which had been damaged; a new turret here, a repaired fin there. They finished the last one at 5 that afternoon. There were Jeff and Mutt walking round inspecting each aircraft and satisfying themselves that everything was perfect. There was a lot to be done and very little time to do it in. And while I was going out to my aircraft to give it a bounce round I gave instructions to Chiefy Powell about Nigger. I realized that this was a very bad omen, and told him to keep it dark. I asked him to bury Nigger at midnight that night, when we would be crossing the enemy coast. And while he was being buried I hoped that we would be going over to give his friendly little soul an uplift with the job we were about to do.

There was no lunch that day. Jeff came running up at the last minute and said in a strange voice:

"We have got the wrong oil." He was nearly shouting. He said, "Stores here haven't got any. We shall have to find some from somewhere else. If we cannot they may not work."

I didn't understand what he was talking about, but an aeroplane was put at his disposal, and apparently the right stuff was found, because I heard nothing more about it.

It was a boiling hot day, but all air crews spent three hours of the afternoon studying the models of the dams. They studied and stared at them and drew them and photographed them on their minds until they knew exactly what they looked like. Then they asked each other questions from memory as to the position of the guns, the length of water and other vital points.

As the day cooled down we had our briefing. I will never forget that briefing. Two service policemen stood outside on guard. The doors were locked. No one was allowed in except the boys who were going to do the job and four other men. No one, not even Fighter Command or our own Group Headquarters, knew we were operating. They thought it was just a training operation.

I introduced Jeff to the boys, and he repeated more or less what he had said that morning, but this time he told them some of the difficulties he had had in developing the weapon. He was very worried, I knew, because he felt responsible for sending these boys off to this target and personally responsible for each and every one of their lives. He said to me, "I hope they all come back." I said, "It won't be your fault if they don't." He said, "You know, I hardly look upon this as an operational mission. My job has just been to develop something which will break down a dam wall. I look upon this raid as my last great experiment to see if it can be done on the actual thing."

While we were talking, the AOC was giving the boys a pep talk. He spoke well, but one remark I shall always remember.

"Now you are off on a raid which will do a tremendous amount of damage. It will become historic. Everyone will want to know how you did it, and it will be very difficult not to tell them. You must not do so because we have other uses for the

471

weapon. I am giving you this warning now because, having watched your training from the beginning, I know that the attack will succeed."

Then I got up and explained the type of attack which we were to use, although by now they knew it backwards because they had practised it so often. Nevertheless, I spoke for just over an hour and detailed the final plan. This was roughly as follows:

The Force was divided into three formations. The first consisted of:

> Myself,
> Hoppy,
> Mickey,
> Dinghy,
> Bill Astell,
> David Maitby,
> Henry,
> Les Knight,
> Dave Shannon,

and it was our job, being the best bomb crews in the squadron, to attack the Möhne Dam first and then carry on to the second dam, the Eder. When we had breached those, the attack would be over, but the big point was, we did not want a small breach; we wanted something really large; and so we were to carry on until we had used up all our mines. Our aim was to punch holes in them about 100 yards across.

The second formation consisted of:

> Joe McCarthy,
> F/Sgt Byers,
> F/L Barlow,
> P/O Rice,
> Les Munro.

This formation was really to act as a diversionary force and to attack the Sorpe. These boys were to fly out in formation and to cross the enemy coast far from where we were crossing it, so as to make a diversion and to split up enemy fighter forces. When they got to the Sorpe Dam they were to fire off Very lights and generally create a disturbance which would cause the fighters to go over there and draw them away from us. Their attack was a very special type which they had practised on their own for some time because the Sorpe was a different type of dam and required an entirely different technique.

The rest, consisting of:

> P/O Townsend,
> F/Sgt Anderson,
> P/O Brown,
> P/O Ottley,

were a rear formation which we would use to fill in gaps left in the first two. This would be easy because we would all be in radio touch. The other two crews which I have not mentioned had, unfortunately, fallen sick and couldn't fly. Nineteen of us were going to take the air.

So the briefing came to an end. Everyone knew exactly what to do; everyone knew the plan. We went up to the Mess and had some bacon and eggs.

Dinghy said to me, "Can I have your egg if you don't come back?"

This was the well-known Corney joke because each crew was allowed to have an egg after a successful operational mission, and eggs were considered delicacies because they were very scarce. I said "Sugar off," and told him to do something very difficult to himself. But there wasn't much time, and we went down to change.

Standing around for an hour and a half before the take-off, everyone was tense and no one said very much. The long practice and the waiting and the business of being kept in the dark had keyed them up to a point where one could feel that they would have been better if they had stood on their toes and danced and shouted out loud, or even screamed to get rid of it, but they stood there with their hands in their pockets, smoking cigarettes and saying little.

I said to Hoppy, "Hoppy, tonight's the night; tomorrow we will get drunk."

We always said this, Hoppy and I, before going off on a mission. Then he jumped into a van which carried him out to his aircraft.

I could never hope to describe a time like this, and will leave it to what Humphreys, the Adjutant, wrote in his squadron diary:

"This was Der Tag for 617 Squadron. Hardly a soul with the exception of the crews knew the target. Very few people outside the squadron knew we were operating — not even the Waafs. From 8 o'clock onwards the scenes outside the crew rooms were something to be remembered. It was not like an ordinary operational scene, all the crews on this occasion being aware of the terrific task confronting them. Most of them wore expressions varying from the "don't care a damn" to the grim and determined. On the whole I think it appeared rather reminiscent of a crusade.

"Dave was late, leaving the crew room quite a while after his own crew were in the plane and I anxiously wondered if our David, in his usual light-hearted manner, had forgotten all about it. The Wing-Commander turned up in his car prompt to time with crew. How they all got into that car beats me. He looked fit and well and quite unperturbed. [This was a complete lie. — G.G.] Our favourite Yank, F/L McCarthy, caused quite a disturbance. He arrived at his aircraft and after finding she had hydraulic trouble came dashing back to our only reserve aircraft. When inside he noticed he had no compass card and came rushing back to the Flights frantically screaming for one. He had also pulled his parachute by mistake and the white silk was streaming all over the ground, trailing behind him. With perspiration dropping off his face, good old Mac ran back to his aircraft with everyone behind him trying to fix him up with what he wanted. He got off just in time."

At exactly the right time Hutch fired a red Very light, and all the aircraft started up. There was to be RT silence until we crossed the enemy coast.

The AOC walked into my ship and wished me the best of luck, and I replied with a sickly grin. An RAF photographer came running up and asked to take a picture — these men certainly choose the queerest times. Then we ambled out on to the runway in our formation and stood there waiting to take off. Someone at the Control caravan waved a flag and I opened the throttles and we were off for Germany. The Adjutant wrote:

"The great machines, with their loads trundled off in formation and left the grass surface whilst onlookers held their breath. All went well, however, but they all seemed to get airborne after extremely long runs. After they had gone and Lincoln was silent once more and the evening mist began to settle on the aerodrome, the squadron personnel sat around talking in groups for a short time and then dispersed to their respective quarters with the object of returning when the machines were due to land. It all seemed very quiet and we wished the boys over there 'Good Luck' and a successful mission."

CHAPTER
EIGHTEEN

Some Were Unlucky

We had been flying for about an hour and ten minutes in complete silence, each one busy with his thoughts, while the waves were slopping by a few feet below with monotonous regularity. And the moon dancing in those waves had become almost a hypnotising crystal. As Terry spoke he jerked us into action. He said, "Five minutes to go to the Dutch coast, skip."

I said, "Good," and looked ahead. Pulford turned on the spotlights and told me to go down much lower; we were about 100ft off the water. Jim Deering, in the front turret, began to swing it from either way, ready to deal with any flak ships which might be watching for mine-layers off the coast. Hutch sat in his wireless cabin ready to send a flak warning to the rest of the boys who might run into trouble behind us. Trevor took off his Mae West and squeezed himself back into the rear turret. On either side the boys tucked their blunt-nose Lancs. in even closer than they were before, while the crews inside them were probably doing the same sort of things as my own. Someone began whistling nervously over the intercom. Someone else said, "Shut up."

Then Spam said, "There's the coast."

I said, "No, it's not; that's just low cloud and shadows on the sea from the moon."

But he was right and I was wrong, and soon we could see the Dutch islands approaching. They looked low and flat and evil in the full moon, squirting flak in many directions because their Radar would now know we were coming. But we knew all about their defences, and as we drew near this squat and unfriendly expanse we began to look for the necessary landmarks which would indicate how to get through that barrage. We began to behave like a ship threading its way through a minefield, in danger of destruction on either side, but safe if we were lucky and on the right track. Terry came up beside me to check up on Spam. He opened the side windows and looked out to scan the coast with his night glasses. "Can't see much," he said. "We're too low, but I reckon we must be on track because there's so little wind."

"Hope so."

"Stand by, front gunner; we're going over."

"OK. All lights off. No talking. Here we go."

With a roar we hurtled over the Western Wall, skirting the defences and turning this way and that to keep to our thin line of safety; for a moment we held our breath. Then I gave a sigh of relief; no one had fired a shot. We had taken them by surprise.

"Good effort, Terry. Next course."

"105 degrees magnetic."

We had not been on the new course for more than two minutes before we came to more sea again; we had obviously just passed over a small island, and this was wrong. Our proper track should have taken us between the two islands, as both were fairly heavily defended, but by the grace of God the gunners on the one we had just passed over were apparently asleep. We pulled up high to about 300ft to have a look and find out where we were, then scrammed down on the deck again as Terry said, "OK — there's the windmill and those wireless masts. We must have drifted to starboard. Steer new course — 095 degrees magnetic, and be careful of a little town that is coming up straight ahead."

"OK, Terry, I'll go around it."

We were turning to the left now, and as we turned I noticed with satisfaction that Hoppy and Mickey were still flying there in perfect formation.

We were flying low. We were flying so low that more than once Spam yelled at me to pull up quickly to avoid high-tension wires and tall trees. Away on the right we could see the small town, its chimneys outlined against the night sky; we thought we saw someone flash us a "V", but it may have been an innkeeper poking his head out of his bedroom window. The noise must have been terrific.

Our new course should have followed a very straight canal, which led to a T-shaped junction, and beyond that was the Dutch frontier and Germany. All eyes began looking out to see if we were right,

479

because we could not afford to be wrong. Sure enough, the canal came up slowly from underneath the starboard wing and we began to follow it carefully, straight above it, for now we were mighty close to Eindhoven, which had the reputation of being very well defended. Then, after a few minutes, that too had passed behind and we saw a glint of silvery light straight ahead. This was the canal junction, the second turning point.

It did not take Spam long to see where we were; now we were right on track, and Terry again gave the new course for the River Rhine. A few minutes later we crossed the German frontier, and Terry said, in his matter-of-fact way: "We'll be at the target in an hour and a half. The next thing to see is the Rhine."

But we did not all get through. One aircraft, P/O Rice, had already hit the sea, bounced up, lost both its outboard engines and its weapon, and had flown back on the inboard two. Les Munro had been hit by light flak a little later on, and his aircraft was so badly damaged that he was forced to return to base. I imagined the feelings of the crews of these aircraft who, after many weeks of intense practice and expectation, at the last moment could only hobble home and land with nothing accomplished. I felt very sorry for them. This left sixteen aircraft going on; 112 men.

The journey into the Ruhr Valley was not without excitement. They did not like our coming. And they knew we were coming. We were the only aircraft operating that night; it was too bright for the main forces. And so, deep down in their underground plotting-rooms, the Hun controllers stayed awake to watch us as we moved steadily on. We had a rough idea how they worked these controllers, moving fighter squadrons to orbit points in front of us, sounding air-raid sirens here and there, tipping off the gun positions along our route and generally trying to make it pretty uncomfortable for the men who were bound for "Happy Valley". As yet they would not know where we were going, because our route was planned to make feint attacks and fox their control. Only the warning sirens would have sounded in all the cities from Bremen southwards. As yet, the fighters would be unable to get good plots on us because we were flying so low, but once we were there the job would have to take quite a time and they would have their chance.

We flew on. Germany seemed dead. Not a sign of movement, of light or a moving creature stirred the ground. There was no flak, there was nothing. Just us.

And so we came to the Rhine. This is virtually the entrance to the Ruhr Valley; the barrier our armies must cross before they march into the big towns of Essen and Dortmund. It looked white and calm and sinister in the moonlight. But it presented no difficulties to us. As it came up, Spam said, "We are 6 miles south. Better turn right, skip. Duisburg is not far away."

As soon as he mentioned Duisburg my hands acted before my brain, for they were more used to this sort of thing, and the Lanc banked steeply to follow the Rhine up to our crossing point. For Duisburg is not a healthy place to fly over at 100ft. There are hundreds of guns there, both light and heavy, apart from all those searchlights, and the defences have had plenty of experience . . .

As we flew up — "How did that happen?"

"Don't know, skip. Compass u/s?"

"Couldn't be."

"Hold on, I will just check my figures."

Later — "I'm afraid I mis-read my writing, skip. The course I gave you should have been another 10 degrees to port."

"OK, Terry. That might have been an expensive mistake."

During our steep turn the boys had lost contact, but now they were just beginning to form up again; it was my fault the turn had been too steep, but the name Duisburg or Essen, or any of the rest of them, always does that to me. As we flew along the Rhine there were barges on the river equipped with quick-firing guns and they shot at us as we flew over, but our gunners gave back as good as they got; then we found what we wanted, a sort of small inland harbour, and we turned slowly towards the east. Terry said monotonously, "Thirty minutes to go and we are there."

As we passed on into the Ruhr Valley we came to more and more trouble, for now we were in the outer light-flak defences, and these were very active, but by weaving and jinking we were able to escape most of them. Time and again searchlights would pick us up, but we were flying very low and, although it may sound foolish and untrue when I say so, we avoided a great number of them by dodging behind the trees. Once we went over a brand-new aerodrome which was very heavily defended and which had not been marked on our combat charts. Immediately all three of us in front were picked up by the searchlights and held. Suddenly Trevor, in the rear turret, began firing away trying to scare them enough to turn out their lights, then he shouted that they had gone behind some tall trees. At the same time Spam was yelling that he would soon be shaving himself by the tops of some corn in a field. Hutch immediately sent out a flak warning to all the boys behind so that they could avoid this unattractive area. On either side of me, Mickey and Hoppy, who were a little higher, were flying along brightly illuminated; I could see their letters quite clearly, "T.A.J.", and "M.A.J.", standing out like Broadway signs. Then a long string of tracer came from Hoppy's rear turret and I lost him in the momentary darkness as the searchlights popped out. One of the pilots, a grand Englishman from Derbyshire, was not so lucky. He was flying well out to the left. He got blinded in the searchlights and, for a second, lost control. His aircraft reared up like a stricken horse, plunged on to the deck and burst into flames; five seconds later

483

his mine blew up with a tremendous explosion. Bill Astell had gone.

The minutes passed slowly as we all sweated on this summer's night, sweated at working the controls and sweated with fear as we flew on. Every railway train, every hamlet and every bridge we passed was a potential danger, for our Lancasters were sitting targets at that height and speed. We fought our way past Dortmund, past Hamm — the well-known Hamm which has been bombed so many times; we could see it quite clearly now, its tall chimneys, factories and balloons capped by its umbrella of flak like a Christmas tree about 5 miles to our right; then we began turning to the right in between Hamm and the little town of Soest, where I nearly got shot down in 1940. Soest was sleepy now and did not open up, and out of the haze ahead appeared the Ruhr hills.

"We're there," said Spam.

"Thank God," said I, feelingly.

As we came over the hill, we saw the Möhne Lake. Then we saw the dam itself. In that light it looked squat and heavy and unconquerable; it looked grey and solid in the moonlight, as though it were part of the countryside itself and just as immovable. A structure like a battleship was showering out flak all along its length, but some came from the powerhouse house below it and nearby. There were no searchlights. It was light flak, mostly green, yellow and red, and the colours of the tracer reflected upon the face of the water in the lake. The reflections on the dead calm of the black water made it seem there was twice as much as there really was.

"Did you say these gunners were out of practice?" asked Spam, sarcastically.

"They certainly seem awake now," said Terry.

They were awake all right. No matter what people say, the Germans certainly have a good warning system. I scowled to myself as I remembered telling the boys an hour or so ago that they would probably only be the German equivalent of the Home Guard and in bed by the time we arrived.

It was hard to say exactly how many guns there were, but tracers seemed to be coming from about five positions, probably making twelve guns in all. It was hard at first to tell the calibre of the shells, but after one of the boys had been hit, we were informed over the RT that they were either 20mm type or 37mm, which, as everyone knows, are nasty little things.

We circled around stealthily, picking up the various landmarks upon which we had planned our method of attack, making use of some and avoiding others; every time we came within range of those bloody-minded flak-gunners they let us have it.

"Bit aggressive, aren't they?" said Trevor.

"Too right they are."

I said to Terry, "God, this light flak gives me the creeps."

"Me too," someone answered.

For a time there was a general bind on the subject of light flak, and the only man who didn't say anything was Hutch, because he could not see it and because he never said anything about flak, anyway. But this was not the time for talking. I called up each member of our formation and found, to my relief, that they had all arrived, except, of course, Bill Astell. Away to the south, Joe McCarthy had just begun his diversionary attack on the Sorpe. But not all of them had been able to get there; both Byers and Barlow had been shot down by light flak after crossing the coast; these had been replaced by other aircraft of the rear formation. Bad luck, this being shot down after crossing the coast, because it could have happened to anybody; they must have been a mile or so off track and had got the hammer. This is the way things are in flying; you are either lucky or you aren't. We, too, had crossed the coast at the wrong place and had got away with it. We were lucky.

Down below, the Möhne Lake was silent and black and deep, and I spoke to my crew.

"Well, boys, I suppose we had better start the ball rolling." This with no enthusiasm whatsoever. "Hello, all Cooler aircraft. I am going to attack. Stand by to come in to attack in your order when I tell you."

Then to Hoppy: "Hello, 'M Mother'. Stand by to take over if anything happens."

Hoppy's clear and casual voice came back. "OK, Leader. Good luck."

Then the boys dispersed to the pre-arranged hiding-spots in the hills, so that they should not be seen either from the ground or from the air, and we began to get into position for our approach. We circled wide and came around down moon, over the high hills at the eastern end of the lake. On straightening up we began to dive towards the flat, ominous water two miles away. Over the front turret was the dam silhouetted against the haze of the Ruhr Valley. We could see the towers. We could see the sluices. We could see everything. Spam, the bomb-aimer, said, "Good show. This is wizard." He had been a bit worried, as all bomb-aimers are, in case they cannot see their aiming points, but as we came in over the tall fir trees his voice came up again rather quickly. "You're going to hit them. You're going to hit those trees."

"That's all right, Spam. I'm just getting my height."

To Terry: "Check height, Terry."

To Pulford: "Speed control, Flight-Engineer."

To Trevor: "All guns ready, gunners."

To Spam: "Coming up, Spam."

Terry turned on the spotlights and began giving directions — "Down — down — down. Steady — steady." We were then exactly 60ft.

Pulford began working the speed; first he put on a little flap to slow us down, then he opened the throttles to get the air-speed indicator exactly against the red mark. Spam began lining up his

487

sights against the towers. He had turned the fusing switch to the "ON" position. I began flying.

The gunners had seen us coming. They could see us coming with our spotlights on for over 2 miles away. Now they opened up and their tracers began swirling towards us; some were even bouncing off the smooth surface of the lake. This was a horrible moment: we were being dragged along at four miles a minute, almost against our will, towards the things we were going to destroy. I think at that moment the boys did not want to go. I know I did not want to go. I thought to myself, "In another minute we shall all be dead — so what?" I thought again, "This is terrible — this feeling of fear — if it is fear." By now we were a few hundred yards away, and I said quickly to Pulford, under my breath, "Better leave the throttles open now and stand by to pull me out of the seat if I get hit." As I glanced at him I thought he looked a little glum on hearing this.

The Lancaster was really moving and I began looking through the special sight on my windscreen. Spam had his eyes glued to the bomb-sight in front, his hand on his button; a special mechanism on board had already begun to work so that the mine would drop (we hoped) in the right spot. Terry was still checking the height. Joe and Trev began to raise their guns. The flak could see us quite clearly now. It was not exactly inferno. I have been through far worse flak fire than that; but we were very low. There was something sinister and slightly unnerving about the whole operation. My aircraft was so small and the dam was so large; it was thick and solid, and now it was angry. My aircraft was very small. We skimmed along the surface of the lake, and as we went my gunner was firing into the defences, and the defences were firing back with vigour, their shells whistling past us. For some reason, we were not being hit.

Spam said, "Left — little more left — steady — steady — steady — coming up." Of the next few seconds I remember only a series of kaleidoscopic incidents.

The chatter from Joe's front guns pushing out tracers which bounced off the left-hand flak tower.

Pulford crouching beside me.

The smell of burnt cordite.

The cold sweat underneath my oxygen mask.

The tracers flashing past the windows — they all seemed the same colour now — and the inaccuracy of the gun positions near the power-station; they were firing in the wrong direction.

The closeness of the dam wall.

Spam's exultant, "Mine gone."

Hutch's red Very lights to blind the flak-gunners.

The speed of the whole thing.

Someone saying over the RT, "Good show, leader. Nice work."

Then it was all over, and at last we were out of range, and there came over us all, I think, an immense feeling of relief and confidence.

Trevor said, "I will get those bastards," and he began to spray the dam with bullets until at last he, too, was out of range. As we circled round we could see a great 1,000ft column of whiteness still hanging in the air where our mine had exploded. We could see with satisfaction that Spam had been good, and it had gone off in the right position. Then, as we came closer, we could see that the explosion of the mine had caused a great disturbance upon the surface of the lake and the water had become broken and furious, as though it were being lashed by a gale. At first we thought that the dam itself had broken, because great sheets of water were slopping over the top of the wall like a gigantic basin. This caused some delay, because our mines could only be dropped in calm water, and we would have to wait until all became still again.

We waited.

We waited about ten minutes, but it seemed hours to us. It must have seemed even longer to Hoppy, who was the next to attack. Meanwhile, all the fighters had now collected over our target. They knew our game by now, but we were flying too low for them; they could not see us and there were no attacks.

At last — "Hello, 'M Mother'. You may attack now. Good luck."

"OK. Attacking."

Hoppy, the Englishman, casual, but very efficient, keen now on only one thing, which was war. He began his attack.

He began going down over the trees where I had come from a few moments before. We could see his

490

spotlights quite clearly, slowly closing together as he ran across the water. We saw him approach. The flak, by now, had got an idea from which direction the attack was coming, and they let him have it. When he was about 100 yards away someone said, hoarsely, over the RT: "Hell! he has been hit."

"M Mother" was on fire; an unlucky shot had got him in one of the inboard petrol tanks and a long jet of flame was beginning to stream out. I saw him drop his mine, but his bomb-aimer must have been wounded, because it fell straight on to the power-house on the other side of the dam. But Hoppy staggered on, trying to gain altitude so that his crew could bale out. When he had got up to about 500ft there was a livid flash in the sky and one wing fell off; his aircraft disintegrated and fell to the ground in cascading, flaming fragments. There it began to burn quite gently and rather sinisterly in a field some 3 miles beyond the dam.

Someone said, "Poor old Hoppy!"

Another said, "We'll get those bastards for this."

A furious rage surged up inside my own crew, and Trevor said, "Let's go in and murder those gunners." As he spoke, Hoppy's mine went up. It went up behind the power-house with a tremendous yellow explosion and left in the air a great ball of black smoke; again there was a long wait while we watched for this to clear. There was so little wind that it took a long time.

Many minutes later I told Mickey to attack; he seemed quite confident, and we ran in beside him and a little in front; as we turned, Trevor did his best to get those gunners as he had promised.

Bob Hay, Mickey's bomb-aimer, did a good job, and his mine dropped in exactly the right place. There was again a gigantic explosion as the whole surface of the lake shook, then spewed forth its cascade of white water. Mickey was all right; he got through.

But he had been hit several times and one wing-tank lost all its petrol. I could see the vicious tracer from his rear-gunner giving one gun position a hail of bullets as he swept over. Then he called up, "OK. Attack completed." It was then that I thought that the dam wall had moved. Of course we could not see anything, but if Jeff's theory had been correct, it should have cracked by now. If only we could go on pushing it by dropping more successful mines, it would surely move back on its axis and collapse.

Once again we watched for the water to calm down. Then in came Melvyn Young in "D Dog". I yelled to him, "Be careful of the flak. It's pretty hot."

He said, "OK."

I yelled again, "Trevor's going to beat them up on the other side. He'll take most of it off you."

Melvyn's voice again. "OK. Thanks." And so as "D Dog" ran in we stayed at a fairly safe distance on the other side, firing with all guns at the defences, and the defences, like the stooges they were, firing back at us. We were both out of range of each other, but the ruse seemed to work, and we flicked on our identification lights to let them see us even more clearly. Melvyn's mine went in, again in exactly the right spot, and this time a colossal wall of water swept right over the dam and kept on going. Melvyn said, "I think I've done it. I've broken it." But we were in a better position to see than he, and it had not rolled down yet. We were all getting pretty excited by now, and I screamed like a schoolboy over the RT: "Wizard show, Melvyn. I think it'll go on the next one."

Now we had been over the Möhne for quite a long time, and all the while I had been in contact with Scampton Base. We were in close contact with the Air Officer Commanding and the Commander-in-Chief of Bomber Command, and with the scientist, observing his own greatest scientific experiment in Damology. He was sitting in the operations room, his head in his hands, listening to the reports as one after another the aircraft attacked. On the other side of the room the Commander-in-Chief paced up and down. In a way their job of waiting was worse than mine. The only difference was that they did not know that the structure was shifting as I knew, even though I could not see anything clearly.

When at last the water had all subsided I called up No. 5 — David Maltby — and told him to attack. He came in fast, and I saw his mine fall within feet of the right spot; once again the flak, the explosion and the wall of water. But this time we were on the wrong side of the wall and could not see what had happened. We watched for about five minutes, and it was rather hard to see anything, for by now the air was full of spray from these explosions, which had settled like mist on our windscreens. Time was getting short, so I called up Dave Shannon and told him to come in.

As he turned I got close to the dam wall and then saw what had happened. It had rolled over, but I could not believe my eyes. I heard someone shout, "I think she has gone! I think she has gone!" Other voices took up the cry and quickly I said, "Stand by until I make a recco." I remembered that Dave was going into attack and told him to turn away and not to approach the target. We had a closer look. Now there was no doubt about it; there was a great breach 100 yards across, and the water, looking like stirred porridge in the moonlight, was gushing out and rolling into the Ruhr Valley towards the industrial centres of Germany's Third Reich.

Nearly all the flak had now stopped, and the other boys came down from the hills to have a closer look to see what had been done. There was no doubt about it at all — the Möhne Dam had been breached and the gunners on top of the dam, except for one man, had all run for their lives towards the safety of solid ground; this remaining gunner was a brave man, but one of the boys quickly extinguished his flak with a burst of well-aimed tracer. Now it was all quiet, except for the roar of the water which steamed and hissed its way from its 150ft head. Then we began to shout and scream and act like madmen over the RT, for this was a tremendous sight, a sight which probably no man will ever see again.

Quickly I told Hutch to tap out the message, "Nigger", to my station, and when this was handed to the Air Officer Commanding there was (I heard afterwards) great excitement in the operations room. The scientist jumped up and danced round the room.

Then I looked again at the dam and at the water, while all around me the boys were doing the same. It was the most amazing sight. The whole valley was beginning to fill with fog from the steam of the gushing water, and down in the foggy valley we saw cars speeding along the roads in front of this great wave of water, which was chasing them and going faster than they could ever hope to go. I saw their headlights burning and I saw water overtake them, wave by wave, and then the colour of the headlights underneath the water changing from light blue to green, from green to dark purple, until there was no longer anything except the water bouncing down in great waves. The floods raced on, carrying with them as they went — viaducts, railways, bridges and everything that stood in their path. Three miles beyond the dam the remains of Hoppy's aircraft were still burning gently, a dull red glow on the ground. Hoppy had been avenged.

Then I felt a little remote and unreal sitting up there in the warm cockpit of my Lancaster, watching this mighty power which we had unleashed; then glad, because I knew that this was the heart of Germany, and the heart of her industries, the place which itself had unleashed so much misery upon the whole world.

We knew, as we watched, that this flood-water would not win the war; it would not do anything like that, but it was a catastrophe for Germany.

I circled round for about three minutes, then called up all aircraft and told Mickey and David Maltby to go home and the rest to follow me to Eder, where we would try to repeat the performance.

We set our course from the southern tip of the Möhne Lake, which was already fast emptying itself — we could see that even now — and flew on in the clear light of the early morning towards the south-east. We flew on over little towns tucked away in the valleys underneath the Ruhr Mountains. Little places, these, the Exeters and Baths of Germany; they seemed quiet and undisturbed and picturesque as they lay sleeping there on the morning of May 17th. The thought crossed my mind of the amazing mentality of German airmen, who went out of their way to bomb such defenceless districts. At the same time a bomb or two on board would not have been out of place to wake them up as a reprisal.

At the Sorpe Dam, Joe McCarthy and Joe Brown had already finished their work. They had both made twelve dummy runs and had dropped their

mines along the lip of the concrete wall in the right
spot. But they had not been able to see anything
spectacular, for these earthen dams are difficult nuts
to crack and would require a lot of explosive to shift
them. It looked as if we would not have enough
aircraft to finish that job successfully because of our
losses on the way in. However, the Sorpe was not a
priority target, and only contributed a small amount
of water to the Ruhr Valley Catchment Area.

After flying low across the tree-tops, up and down
the valleys, we at last reached the Eder Lake and, by
flying down it for some five minutes, we arrived over
the Eder Dam. It took some finding because fog
was already beginning to form in the valleys, and it
was pretty hard to tell one part of the reservoir filled
with water, from another valley filled with fog. We
circled up for a few minutes waiting for Henry,
Dave and Les to catch up; we had lost them on the
way. Then I called up on the RT.

"Hello, Cooler aircraft — can you see the
target?"

Dave answered faintly, "I think I'm in the vicinity.
I can't see anything. I cannot find the dam."

"Stand by — I will fire a red Very light — right
over the dam." No sooner had Hutch fired his Very
pistol than Dave called up again. "OK — I was a bit
south. I'm coming up."

The other boys had seen the signal, too, and after
a few minutes we rendezvous'd in a left-hand orbit
over the target. But time was getting short now; the
glow in the north had begun to get brighter,

497

heralding the coming dawn. Soon it would be daylight, and we did not want this in our ill-armed and un-armoured Lancasters.

I said, "OK, Dave. You begin your attack."

It was very hilly all round. The dam was situated, beautifully, I thought, in a deep valley with high hills all around densely covered with fir trees. At the far end, overlooking it, was rather a fine Gothic castle with magnificent grounds. In order to make a successful approach, our aircraft would have to dive steeply over this castle, dropping down on to the water from 1,000ft to 60ft — level out — let go the mine — then do a steep climbing turn to starboard to avoid a rocky mountain about a mile on the other side of the dam. It was much more inaccessible than the Möhne Valley and called for a much higher degree of skill in flying. There did not seem to be any defences, though, probably because it was an out-of-the-way spot and the gunners would not have got the warning. Maybe they had just been warned and were now getting out of their beds in the nearby village before cycling up the steep hill to get to their gun emplacements. Dave circled wide and then turned to go in. He dived down rather too steeply and sparks came from his engine, as he had to pull out at full boost to avoid hitting the mountain on the north side. As he was doing so . . .

"Sorry, leader. I made a mess of that. I'll try again."

He tried again. He tried five times, but each time he was not satisfied and would not allow his bomb-aimer to drop his mine. He spoke again on the RT. "I think I had better circle round a bit and try and get used to this place."

"OK, Dave. You hang around for a bit, and I'll get another aircraft to have a crack — Hello, 'Z Zebra' " (this was Henry). "You can go in now."

Henry made two attempts. He said he found it very difficult, and gave the other boys some advice on the best way to go about it. Then he called up and told us that he was going in to make his final run. We could see him running in. Suddenly he pulled away; something seemed to be wrong, but he turned quickly, climbed up over the mountain and put his nose right down, literally flinging his machine into the valley. This time he was running straight and true for the middle of the wall. We saw his spotlights together, so he must have been at 60ft. We saw the red ball of his Very light shooting out behind his tail, and we knew he had dropped his weapon. A split second later we saw someone else; Henry Maudslay had dropped his mine too late. It had hit the top of the parapet and had exploded immediately on impact with a slow, yellow, vivid flame which lit up the whole valley like daylight for just a few seconds. We could see him quite clearly banking steeply a few feet above it. Perhaps the blast was doing that. It all seemed so sudden and vicious and the flame seemed so very cruel. Someone said, "He has blown himself up."

Trevor said, "Bomb-aimer must have been wounded."

499

It looked as though Henry had been unlucky enough to do the thing we all might have done.

I spoke to him quickly, "Henry — Henry. 'Z Zebra' — 'Z Zebra'. Are you OK?" No answer. I called again. Then we all thought we heard a very faint, tired voice say, "I think so — stand by." It seemed as though he was dazed, and his voice did not sound natural. But Henry had disappeared. There was no burning wreckage on the ground; there was no aircraft on fire in the air. There was nothing. Henry had disappeared. He never came back.

Once more the smoke from his explosion filled the valley, and we all had to wait for a few minutes. The glow in the north was much brighter, and we would have to hurry up if we wanted to get back.

We waited patiently for it to clear away.

At last to Dave — "OK. Attack now, David. Good luck."

Dave went in and, after a good dummy run, managed to put his mine up against the wall, more or less in the middle. He turned on his landing light as he pulled away, and we saw the spot of light climbing steeply over the mountain as he jerked his great Lancaster almost vertically over the top. Behind me there was that explosion which, by now, we had got used to, but the wall of the Eder Dam did not move.

Meanwhile, Les Knight had been circling very patiently, not saying a word. I told him to get ready, and when the water had calmed down he began his attack. Les, the Australian, had some difficulty, too, and after a while Dave began to give him some advice on how to do it. We all joined in on the RT, and there was a continuous back-chat going on.

"Come on, Les. Come in down the moon; dive towards the point and then turn left."

"OK, Digger. It's pretty difficult."

"Not that way, Dig. This way."

"Too right it's difficult. I'm climbing up to have another crack."

After a while I called up rather impatiently and told them that a joke was a joke and that we would have to be getting back. Then Les dived in to make his final attack. His was the last weapon left in the squadron. If he did not succeed in breaching the Eder now, then it would never be breached; at least, not tonight.

I saw him run in. I crossed my fingers. But Les was a good pilot and he made as perfect a run as any seen that night. We were flying above him, and about 400 yards to the right, and saw his mine hit the water. We saw where it sank. We saw the tremendous earthquake which shook the base of the dam, and then, as if a gigantic hand had punched a hole through cardboard, the whole thing collapsed. A great mass of water began running down the valley into Kassel. Les was very excited. He kept his radio transmitter on by mistake for quite some time. His crew's remarks were something to be heard, but they couldn't be put into print here. Dave was very excited and said, "Good show, Dig!" I called them up and told them to go home immediately. I would meet them in the Mess afterwards for the biggest party of all time.

The valley below the Eder was steeper than the Ruhr, and we followed the water down for some way. We watched it swirling and slopping in a 30ft wall as it tore round the steep bends of the countryside. We saw it crash down in six great waves, swiping off power-stations and roads as it went. We saw it extinguish all the lights in the neighbourhood as though a great black shadow had been drawn across the earth. It all reminded us of a vast moving train. But we knew that a few miles farther on lay some of the Luftwaffe's largest training bases. We knew that it was a modern field with every convenience, including underground hangars and underground sleeping quarters . . . We turned for home.

Dave and Les, still jabbering at each other on RT, had by now turned for home as well. Their voices died away in the distance as we set our course for the Möhne Lake to see how far it was empty. Hutch sent out a signal to Base using the code word, "Dinghy", telling them the good news and they asked us if we had any more aircraft available to prang the third target. "No, none," I said. "None," tapped Hutch.

Now we were out of RT range of our base and were relying on WT for communication. Gradually, by code words, we were told of the movements of the other aircraft. Peter Townsend and Anderson of the rear formation had been sent out to make one attack against the Sorpe. We heard Peter say that he had been successful, but heard nothing from Anderson.

"Let's tell Base we're coming home, and tell them to lay on a party," suggested Spam.

We told them we were coming home.

We had reached the Möhne by now and circled twice. We looked at the level of the lake. Already bridges were beginning to stick up out of the lowering water. Already mudbanks with pleasure-boats sitting on their sides could be seen. Below the dam the torpedo nets had been washed to one side of the valley. The power-station had disappeared. The map had completely changed as a new silver lake had formed, a lake of no strict dimensions; a lake slowly moving down towards the west.

Base would probably be panicking a bit, so Hutch sent out another message telling them that there was no doubt about it. Then we took one final look at what we had done and afterwards turned north to the Zuider Zee.

Trevor asked a question — Trevor, who had fired nearly 12,000 rounds of ammunition in the past two hours. "I am almost out of ammo," he called, "but I have got one or two incendiaries back here. Would you mind if Spam tells me when a village is coming up, so that I can drop one out? It might pay for Hoppy, Henry and Bill."

I answered, "Go ahead."

We flew north in the silence of the morning, hugging the ground and wanting to get home. It was quite light now, and we could see things that we could not see on the way in — cattle in the fields, chickens getting airborne as we rushed over them. On the left someone flew over Hamm at 500ft. He got the chop. No one knew who it was. Spam said he thought it was a German nightfighter which had been chasing us.

I suppose they were all after us. Now that we were being plotted on our retreat to the coast, the enemy fighter controllers would be working overtime. I could imagine the Füehrer himself giving orders to "stop those air pirates at all costs". After all, we had done something which no one else had ever done. Water when released can be one of the most powerful things in the world — similar to an earthquake and the Ruhr Valley had never had an earthquake.

Someone on board pointed out that Duisburg had been pranged the night before and that our water might put the fires out there.

Someone else said — rather callously, I thought — "If you can't burn 'em, drown 'em." But we had not tried to do this; we had merely destroyed a legitimate industrial objective so as to hinder the Ruhr Valley output of war munitions. The fact that people were in the way was incidental. The fact that they might drown had not occurred to us. But we hoped that the dam wardens would warn those living below in time, even if they were Germans. No one likes mass slaughter, and we did not like being the authors of it. Besides, it brought us in line with Himmler and his boys.

Terry looked up from his chart-board. "About an hour to the coast," he said.

I turned to Pulford. "Put her into maximum cruising. Don't worry about petrol consumption." Then to Terry — "I think we had better go the shortest way home, crossing the coast at Egmond — you know the gap there. We're the last one, and they'll probably try to get us if we lag behind."

Terry smiled and watched the air-speed needle creep round. We were now doing a smooth 2.40 indicated, and the exhaust stubs glowed red hot with the power she was throwing out. Trevor's warning light came on the panel, then his voice — "Unidentified enemy aircraft behind."

"OK. I'll sink to the west — it's dark there."

As we turned — "OK. You've lost it."

"Right. On course. Terry, we'd better fly really low."

These fighters meant business, but they were hampered by the conditions of light during the early morning. We could see them before they saw us.

Down went the Lanc until we were a few feet off the ground, for this was the only way to survive. And we wanted to survive. Two hours before we had wanted to burst dams. Now we wanted to get home — quickly. Then we could have a party.

Some minutes later Terry spoke. "Thirty minutes to the coast."

"OK. More revs."

The needle crept round. It got very noisy inside.

We were flying home — we knew that. We did not know whether we were safe. We did not know how the other boys had got on. Bill, Hoppy, Henry, Barlow, Byers and Ottley had all gone. They had all got the hammer. The light flak had given it to most of them, as it always will to low-flying aircraft — that is, the unlucky ones. They had all gone quickly, except perhaps for Henry. Henry, the born leader. A great loss, but he gave his life for a cause for which men should be proud. Boys like Henry are the cream of our youth. They die bravely and they die young.

And Burpee, the Canadian? His English wife about to have a baby. His father who kept a large store in Ottawa. He was not coming back because they had got him, too. They had got him somewhere between Hamm and the target. Burpee, slow of speech and slow of movement, but a good pilot. He was Terry's countryman, and so were his crew. I like their ways and manners, their free-and-easy outlook, their openness. I was going to miss them a lot — even when they chewed gum.

I called up Melvyn on the RT. He had been with me all the way round as deputy-leader when Mickey had gone home with his leaking petrol tank. He was quite all right at the Eder. Now there was no reply. We wondered what had happened.

Terry said, "Fifteen minutes to go."

Fifteen minutes. Quite a way yet. A long way, and we might not make it. We were in the black territory. They had closed the gates of their fortress and we were locked inside; but we knew the gap — the gap by those wireless masts at Egmond. If we could find that, we should get through safely.

Back at the base they would be waiting for us. We did not know that when they received the code word "Dinghy" there was a scene in the operations room such as the WAAF Ops Clerks had never seen before. The Air Officer Commanding had jumped up and had shaken Jeff by the hand, almost embracing him. The Commander-in-Chief had picked up the 'phone and asked for Washington. At Washington another US-Great Britain conference was in progress. Sir Charles Portal, the CAS, was giving a dinner-party. He was called away to the telephone. Back at Scampton, the C-in-C yelled, "Downwood successful — yes." At Washington, CAS was having difficulty in hearing. At last members of the dinner-party heard him say quietly, "Good show." From then on the dinner-party was a roaring success.

We did not know anything about the fuss, the Press, the publicity which would go round the world after this effort. Or of the honours to be given to the squadron or of trips to America and Canada, or of visits by important people. We did not care about anything like that. We only wanted to get home.

We did not know that we had started something new in the history of aviation, that our squadron was to become a by-word throughout the RAF as a precision-bombing unit — a unit which could pick off anything from viaducts to gun emplacements, from low level or high level, by day or by night. A squadron consisting of crack news using all the latest new equipment and the largest bombs, even earthquake bombs. A squadron flying new aeroplanes, and flying them as well as any in the world.

Terry was saying, "Rotterdam's 20 miles on the port bow. We will be getting to the gap in five minutes." Now they could see where we were going, the fighters would be streaking across Holland to close that gap. Then they could hack us down.

I called up Melvyn, but he never answered. I was not to know that Melvyn had crashed into the sea a few miles in front of me. He had come all the way from California to fight this war and had survived sixty trips at home and in the Middle East, including a double ditching. Now he had ditched for the last time. Melvyn had been responsible for a good deal of the training that made this raid possible. He had endeared himself to the boys, and now he had gone.

Of the sixteen aircraft which had crossed the coast to carry out this mission, eight had been shot down, including both Flight-Commanders. Only two men escaped to become prisoners of war. Only two out of fifty-six, for there is not much chance at 50ft.

They had gone. Had it been worth it? Or were their lives just thrown away on a spectacular mission? Militarily, it was cheap at the price. The damage done to the German war effort was substantial. But there is another side to the question. We would soon begin our fifth year of war — a war in which the casualties had been lighter than the last; nevertheless, in Bomber Command there have been some heavy losses. These fifty-five boys who had lost their lives were some of many. The scythe of war, and a very bloody one at that, had reaped a good harvest in Bomber Command. As we flew on over the low fields of Holland, past dykes and ditches, we could not help thinking, "Why must we make war every twenty-five years? Why must men fight? How can we stop it? Can we make countries live normal lives in a peaceful way?" But no one knows the answer to that one.

The answer may lie in being strong. A powerful, strategic bomber force based so that it would control the vital waterways of the world, could prevent and strangle the aggressor from the word "Go". But it rests with the people themselves; for it is the people who forget. After many years they will probably slip and ask for disarmament so that they can do away with taxes and raise their standard of living. If the people forget, they bring wars on themselves, and they can blame no one but themselves.

Yes, the decent people of this world would have to remember war. Movies and radio records should remind this and the future generations of what happened between 1936 and 1942. It should be possible to keep this danger in everyone's mind so that we can never be caught on the wrong foot again. So that our children will have a chance to live. After all, that is why we are born. We aren't born to die.

But we ourselves must learn. We must learn to know and respect our great Allies who have made the chance of victory possible. We must learn to understand them, their ways and their customs. We British are apt to consider ourselves the yardstick upon which everything else should be based. We must not delude ourselves. We have plenty to learn.

We must learn about politics. We must vote for the right things, and not necessarily the traditional things. We want to see our country remain as great as it is today — forever. It all depends on the people, their commonsense and their memory.

Can we hope for this? Can all this be done? Can we be certain that we can find the answer to a peaceful world for generations to come?

"North Sea ahead, boys," said Spam.

There it was. Beyond the gap, in the distance, lay the calm and silvery sea, and freedom. It looked beautiful to us then — perhaps the most wonderful thing in the world.

We climbed up a little to about 300ft.

Then — "Full revs and boost, Pulford."

As he opened her right up, I shoved the nose down to get up extra speed and we sat down on the deck at about 260 indicated.

"Keep to the left of this little lake," said Terry, map in hand.

This was flying.

"Now over this railway bridge."

More speed.

"Along this canal . . ." We flew along that canal as low as we had flown that day. Our belly nearly scraped the water, our wings would have knocked horses off the tow-path.

"See those radio masts?"

"Yeah."

"About 200 yards to the right."

The sea came closer. It came closer quickly as we tore towards it. There was a sudden tenseness on board.

"Keep going; you're OK now."

"Right. Stand by, front gunner."

"Guns ready."

Then we came to the Western Wall. We whistled over the antitank ditches and beach obstacles. We saw the yellow sand-dunes slide below us silently, yellow in the pale morning.

Then we were over the sea with the rollers breaking on the beaches and the moon casting its long reflection straight in front of us — and there was England.

We were free. We had got through the gap. It was a wonderful feeling of relief and safety. Now for the party. "Nice work," said Trevor from the back. "Course home?" I asked. Behind us lay the Dutch coast, squat, desolate and bleak, still squirting flak in many directions.

We would be coming back.